THE RIGHTS AND STATUS OF INDIGENOUS PEOPLES IN NIGERIA

BY

OLUGBENGA IFEDAYO ADEMODI

Bäuu Institute and Press

1 2 3 4 5 6 7 8 9 10

Library of Congress Cataloging-in-Publication Data

Ademodi, Olugbenga I.

The Rights and Status of Indigenous Peoples in Nigeria /
by Olugbenga I. Ademodi.
p. cm.
Includes bibliographic references and images.
ISBN 978-1-936955-06-0 (paperback : alk. paper)
1. Nigeria. 2. Indigenous People 3. Political Science

The paper in this book meets the guidelines for permanence and durability of the Committee on Production Guidelines for Book Longevity of the Council on Library Resources, Inc.

ACKNOWLEDGEMENTS

I am honored to be one of the first graduates of this groundbreaking academic program. This book reflects the updated version of my dissertation submitted to obtain the J.S.D. degree in Intercultural Human Rights at St. Thomas University School of Law in fulfillment of its publication requirement.

I would like to extend my deepest gratitude to Professor Siegfried Wiessner, Founder and Director of St. Thomas University's Graduate Program in Intercultural Human Rights Law, for his advice and guidance to help me reach my potential, while any errors are solely mine. His encouragement, support and challenges from the beginning to the completion enabled me to reach a previously unforeseen depth of understanding of the subject.

I extend my special appreciation to Professor Pierre-Michel Fontaine, Former Chief of the Office of the United Nations High Commissioner for Human Rights in the Democratic Republic of Congo, who reviewed my research at an early stage. I also thank Professor Federico Lenzerini of the University of Siena, Italy, who was my external examiner and also a member of my Rigorosum Committee. In addition, I thank Professor Alfred Light who chaired my Rigorosum Committee.

I would also like to express my appreciation to Professor Roza Pati and the staff of the Intercultural Human Rights department for their assistance during the course of this research and at all times.

My special thanks is reserved for all of my friends, including Mrs. Rash and her family, who have reviewed this manuscript several times, pointed out necessary corrections, and generally encouraged me.

I also thank Professor Bayonile Ademodi, my uncle and mentor over the years, and Barrister Bamidele Aturu for setting my feet on the path of Human Rights law and advocacy.

I am indebted to my family for their support and prayers towards successful completion of this book. My darling wife Olateju Obayomi-Ademodi was so patient with me during my late nights of work, and I want to thank her for her dedication, perseverance, cooperation and faithful support in writing this book.

Olugbenga Ademodi
Miami, Florida, USA
April, 2011

SHORT BIOGRAPHY

Dr. Olugbenga Ademodi is a barrister and solicitor of law from Nigeria. After completing his LL.B. and B.L., he practiced as an attorney with the law firm of Bamidele Aturu and Company where he was involved with some important human and civil rights cases. He rose to the position of Deputy Head of Chambers and managed the firm's law library. Dr. Ademodi then journeyed to the United States to earn his LL.M. in Intercultural Human Rights from St. Thomas University School of Law. While working as a law library researcher at St. Thomas, he finished his Master of Library Science. Afterwards, he was one of the first to achieve his doctoral degree in law from St. Thomas, a J.S.D. in Intercultural Human Rights. He is currently a Special Advisor on International Human Rights Research for the Global Guild for Human Survival, a non-governmental organization emphasizing the protection of human rights of the world's children.

DEDICATION

I dedicate this book to the GLORY OF GOD
and to the memories of my late father, Adegbule,
and my sisters, Omolabake and Bukola.

THE RIGHTS AND STATUS OF INDIGENOUS PEOPLES IN NIGERIA

BY

OLUGBENGA IFEDAYO ADEMODI[1]

---

1 LL.B, 1997, Obafemi Awolowo University; B.L, 1999, Nigerian Law School; LL.M., *cum laude,* 2004, Master of Laws in Intercultural Human Rights, St. Thomas University; M.L.S., 2009, Texas Woman's University; and J.S.D., *cum laude,* 2011, Doctor of Juridical Science in Intercultural Human Rights, St. Thomas University.

CONTENTS

INTRODUCTION

The plight of the indigenous peoples has generated enormous attention all over the world[2] and Nigeria is no exception.[3] The situation may be summed up in the words of Ledum Mitee, the President of the Movement for the Survival of the Ogoni People in Nigeria:

> The struggles of indigenous peoples the world over, whether expressed in terms of self determination, land rights, resource control or what ever, have as the central theme the desire by these peoples to be and express themselves as they were endowed by the Creator. It translates into the struggle against the dislocation of their societies, their cultural and spiritual values, the greedy exploitation of their resources and for the recovery of their independence over their affairs and territories.[4]

The indigenous peoples' demands and the responses by modern nation-states comprise so many different aspects. There are conflicting claims between peoples claiming to be indigenous and the various governments where they reside. There is controversy over whether some groups are indigenous or whether they are simply disenfranchised minorities. Specifically, this book will analyze whether "indigenous peoples" truly exist in my home country, Nigeria, and whether they are entitled to all of the rights enjoyed by their counterparts all over the world.

Chapter one will address the issue of the definition of "indigenous peoples," the various attempts made at definition, the working definition

---

2 Elazar Barkan, The Guilt of Nations: Restitution and Negotiating Historical Injustices 233 (Baltimore: Johns Hopkins University Press, 2001).

3 Ken Saro-Wiwa, *A Deadly Ecological War in Which No Blood is Spilled But People Die All the Time, in* Speaking of Earth: Environmental Speeches that Moved the World 186 (Alon Tal, ed., Rutgers University Press, 2006).

4 Ledum Mitee, *The Centrality of Self-Identity in Indigenous Peoples' Struggles: the Struggle of the Ogoni People* (paper submitted at Indigenous Rights in the Commonwealth Project Africa Regional Expert Meeting, Cape Town, South Africa, October 16-18, 2002).

propounded, and the way indigenous ancestry should be determined. After an analysis of these definitions, the author will formulate a working definition for the purpose of this subject.

In chapter two, the rights of indigenous peoples will be analyzed in the international and regional conventions, customary international law, and other sources of law. This chapter will also examine some past trends in case law where the principles dealing with the indigenous peoples' question have been discussed. The indigenous peoples' question from the perspective of the African governments will be reviewed in chapter three.

Chapter four will consider the underlying Nigerian historical context, including the Atlantic slave trade, British colonization, administration under colonial rule, Nigerian social groups, and Nigerian prehistory. Additionally, this chapter will review the relations between the ethnic groups and the Nigerian state, the socioeconomic relationships among the Nigerian ethnic communities, and the religions of the Nigerian ethnic groups.

Nigerian laws and rules related to indigenous peoples from statutes to customs will be discussed in chapter five, while chapter six will examine the applicability of the indigenous peoples' rights to the Nigerian situation. Finally, a conclusion addressing all the issues addressed with recommendations for the road forward for indigenous peoples will conclude this subject.

At the outset, there are several arguments as to who are "indigenous peoples." "Indigenous" means born or produced in a particular land or region; it also means native or belonging naturally to a region, a soil, and so forth.[5] The designation applies generally to peoples that have been invaded and their land was possessed by the invaders. The situations with the American Indians and the aboriginals of Australia provide insight into this point. One argument is that to be considered "indigenous," the peoples must have been under imperialistic rule by another dominant society. This criterion cannot be strictly applied to the African indigenous peoples because it may be difficult for them to qualify for this status. Second, these peoples must have been adversely affected by the imperialistic dominant society. The situation in Africa, however, is different because the majority of peoples claiming to be "indigenous" have not been put in this position.

---

5   The Oxford English Dictionary (2nd ed. 1989), s.v. "indigenous;" *see also* James R. Fox, Dictionary of International and Comparative Law (Oceana 2003).

They have suffered discrimination from the dominant group in their own society, not from invaders. This dominant society discriminating against the minority ethnic groups has made them vulnerable. The discrimination/vulnerability criterion cannot solely qualify any group for indigenous status, but it complements other factors.[6]

Further, determining who the earliest natives of particular lands were in Africa is very difficult. This is not always the case. In America, for instance, the colonists were met by the indigenous peoples, the American Indians (or Native Americans), and the Indians are still considered the indigenous peoples of America today. Since time began in Africa the indigenous peoples' have often been herders following the necessary vegetation thereby making the migratory nature of these peoples a distinction of the African populace. In Nigeria for instance, the members of the Fulani tribe are predominantly herdsmen or cattle rearers and are always on the move depending on the adequateness of the grass or vegetation for their cattle. It will, therefore, be almost impossible for the Fulanis of Nigeria to demonstrate that they belong to the group of original natives necessary to being considered "indigenous" because they do not remain in a particular place for long periods.

A major area of controversy has been whether the concept of "indigenousness" and specific "indigenous" rights are applicable in the African context. Most African governments have until now maintained that all their citizens are indigenous or alternatively argued that there is no such thing as an indigenous group in their country. There has also been a considerable debate as to whether indigenous peoples really exist and if they do, whether they are entitled to any rights.

In short, enormous research has been done with respect to this issue in America, Europe, Asia and parts of Africa while extensive research work has not been accomplished in this respect concerning Nigeria. The author will examine whether there truly are indigenous peoples in Nigeria and if they are whether the status is appurtenant to any rights. Consequently, the book will look into the definition of "indigenous peoples" to determine what conditions have to be met before a group could qualify as "indigenous." In this context, the book will further examine the position of various

---

6   Gunnvor Berge, *Reflections on the Concept of Indigenous Peoples in Africa*, in HANNE VEBER, JENS DAHL, FIONA WILSON, ESPEN WAEHLE: "... NEVER DRINK FROM THE SAME CUP." Proceedings of the conference on Indigenous Peoples in Africa. Tune, Denmark, 235,237-38 (1993) (IWGIA Doc. No.74, Copenhagen, 1993).

international instruments dealing with the issues of the indigenous peoples. The inquiry will also extend to Nigerian social groups and their inter-relations in reference to their religions, economy and cultures. The author will then apply the elements of the definition of an "indigenous people" to the Nigerian situation.

CHAPTER ONE

THE DEFINITION OF INDIGENOUS PEOPLES

1.1 INDIGENOUS PEOPLES: THE ISSUE OF DEFINITION

The first thing that one encounters whenever a discussion about "indigenous peoples" is raised is the issue of definition. For this inquiry to have any meaning at all, the problem needs to be fully addressed, as this will be the foundation on which the study rests.

The issue of the indigenous peoples' definition has been debated over the years. The need for a definition cannot be overlooked. Eminent scholars have pointed out the need for a concise delimitation of the concept. Stressing the need for a definition, Professor Wiessner has pointed out that the holders of those rights and the persons entitled to the rights need to be defined with specificity.[7] Also, in situations where rights may involve claims made in the political sphere, the definition will be determined by the groups concerned which may lead to chaos; and, since some of these rights have been recognized as part of international law, treaty or the customary variety, the need for a definition has become necessary.[8] The International Law Association (ILA) interim report of 2010 reiterates the need for a common understanding of the meaning of the term "indigenous peoples" so as to assess the proper scope of application of the United Nations Declaration of Rights of Indigenous Peoples (UNDRIP) and to prevent nation states from being the sole determinant of who are and who are not indigenous peoples.[9]

---

7   Siegfried Wiessner, *The United Nations Declaration on the Rights of Indigenous Peoples: Essays in Honor of Professor Koufa,* in THE DIVERSITY OF INTERNATIONAL LAW: ESSAYS IN HONOUR OF PROFESSOR KALLIOPI K. KOUFA 350 (Martinus Nijhoff Publishers, 2010).

8   *Id.*

9   International Law Association, "Rights of Indigenous Peoples," The Hague Conference, Interim Report (2010) 7.

If nation states are empowered to determine indigenous peoples' status, groups desirous of indigenous peoples' status will be at the mercy of nation states which may very well result in unfairness and exclusion of justified claims.

It is true that there is no single, agreed-upon definition of the term "indigenous peoples." It is, however, reassuring to find that various research efforts have been undertaken to provide proper definition. To that end, attempts have been made at definition by the United Nations, the World Bank, the International Labor Organization, notable scholars, and certain interest groups, starting with a working definition proffered by Jose Martinez Cobo. Some of the efforts made towards establishing a precise definition for "indigenous peoples" and how it applies on the peoples of Nigeria and Africa in particular will be examined in the course of this book.

1.1(A) Distinction Between Indigenous Peoples and Minority Groups

At this juncture, the author will differentiate indigenous peoples from minority peoples. This becomes necessary because of the age long misconception that the terms "minority people" and "indigenous people" mean the same thing. Professor Siegfried Wiessner in his paper explained the definition by Francesco Capotorti, UN special rapporteur on this issue which states that:

> A minority is a group which is numerically inferior to the rest of the population of a state and in a non-dominant position, whose members possess ethnic, religions or linguistic characteristic which differs from those of the rest of the population and who, if only implicitly, maintain a sense of solidarity directed towards preserving their culture, traditions, religion or language.[10]

Professor Wiessner listed the four elements embedded in the definition and they are as follows:

(a) Their number is few when compared with other groups in the

---

10   Siegfried Wiessner, *Demographic Change and the Protection of Minorities* in GLOBALER DEMOGRAPHISCHER WANDEL UND SCHUTZ DER MENSCHENRECHTE 155-85 (Eckart Klein ed., 2005)

society.

(b) Minority groups are less dominant when compared with others in the society.

(c) They have common characteristics of ethnicity, religion and or languages.

(d) They always show solidarity to one another, and practice self-identification.

While all the elements listed in the above definition are peculiar to indigenous peoples, minority people can still not be referred to as indigenous peoples because of two distinct factors which are the backbone of the indigenous peoples' argument and this is that:

(a) The people are regarded as the first settler or first in time at a place;

(b) The people must have age-long means of survival which must be strongly tied to the land.

It could be deduced from the above stated factors that as close as the definition of minority people and indigenous people are to each other, they denote often two different types of communities that cannot be classified as the same.

Professor Erica Daes submitted in her book[11] that a minority can be created by the actions of the state, its citizens, or by the group itself.[12] This could be through the determination of a group to maintain their cultural distinctiveness and also through the refusal of the assimilation of a group into national life by the state institution.

1.1.1 United Nations: Attempt at Capturing the Meaning of the Term "Indigenous Peoples"

The United Nations, an international organization established to facilitate peace, cooperation in international law, international security, economic development, human rights issues and social progress is central to global efforts to solve global problems. It has made valuable efforts to find a solution to the indigenous peoples' definition issue and is responsible for

---

11   Erica-Irene A. Daes, Indigenous Peoples: Keepers of Our Past-Custodians of Our Future 25 (Copenhagen, 2008).

12   Id.

the working definition presented by Mr. Jose R. Martinez Cobo.

1.1.2 Working Definition by Mr. Jose Martinez Cobo

As earlier stated, many debates have been dedicated to the question of finding a definition for "indigenous peoples" but to no avail. Finally, Jose R. Martinez Cobo, the Special Rapporteur of the Sub-Commission on Prevention of Discrimination and Protection of Minorities, provided a working definition that has been widely quoted.[13]

Mr. Cobo's working definition was born in the course of his study on the problem of discrimination against indigenous populations. In tackling this problem, it was deemed fit that the study should start with a "working definition" of the indigenous peoples.[14] The working definition by Mr. Jose Martinez Cobo is as follows:

> Indigenous communities, peoples and nations are those which, having a historical continuity with pre-invasion and pre-colonial societies that developed on their territories, consider themselves distinct from other sectors of the societies now prevailing on those territories, or part of them. They form at present non-dominant sectors of society and are determined to preserve, develop and transmit to future generations their ancestral territories, and their ethnic identity, as the basis of their continued existence as peoples, in accordance with their own cultural patterns, social institutions and legal system.[15]

Cobo identified a number of criteria as relevant including "consideration of both objective and subjective elements such as ancestry, cultural aspects including religion, tribal organization, community membership, dress and livelihood, language, group consciousness, residence in certain parts of the

---

13   LUNDE TRINE, ESCAPING POVERTY: PERCEPTIONS FROM TWELVE INDIGENOUS COMMUNITIES IN SOUTHERN MEXICO 108 (The Johns Hopkins Univ. Press, 2009); Dorothy Hodgson, *Becoming Indigenous in Africa,* 52.3 AFR. STUD. REV. 1, 9 (2009); *see also* Michael Davis, *Establishing a Workable Autonomy in Tibet,* 30.2 HUM. RTS. Q. 227, 250 (2008).

14   Recommendation of Sub-Commission on Human Rights, Resolution 4B (XXIII) of 26 August 1970.

15   Study of the Problem of Discrimination Against Indigenous Populations, U.N. Doc. E/CN.4/Sub.2/1986/ 7/Add.4, U.N. Sales No. E.86.XIV.3 (1986).

country and acceptance by the indigenous community."[16] This working definition to an extent was able to point out the factors and conditions which any group desiring indigenous peoples status must meet or comply with.

It could be deduced from Martinez Cobo's working definition that a people or a group desiring indigenous people status must fulfill the condition of self-identification. As good as this criterion is, however, it is susceptible to abuse. Therefore, for any group to consider itself as being distinct, its claim must be corroborated with other evidence or facts which could be oral history from the oldest living member of the community or burial sites of claimants ancestors.

The criteria of "non-dominancy" by Cobo is also open to abuse, but the criteria could add weight to a group's claim if the vulnerability of such group could be proved and it could be shown that they are defenseless against the dominant society.

Cultural distinctiveness of a group is another vital criterion listed by Cobo. These are objective factors which could be supported by the groups' cultures and their language.

As good as Martinez Cobo's working definition is, this author is concerned about the element of "historical continuity with pre-invasion and pre-colonial societies." This factor tends to make it mandatory for a group to experience invasion and colonization before they could be entitled to indigenous status. This factor is too strict and has the tendency to eliminate potential indigenous peoples from ever attaining that status, particularly in the context of Africa.

1.1.3 Position of Professor Erica-Irene Daes, WGIP

Professor Erica-Irene Daes, the former Chairperson-Rapporteur of the United Nations Working Group on Indigenous Populations, through the Working Group was commissioned to research a definition of indigenous peoples with the aim of providing the factors to identify them. Information provided by governments, intergovernmental organizations, and indigenous

---

16   *Standard-Setting Activities: Evolution of Standards Concerning the Rights of Indigenous People*, U.N.ESCOR, Commission on Human Rights, Sub-Commission on Prevention of Discrimination and Protection of Minorities, 13th sess., at 5, U.N. Doc. E/CN.$/Sub.2/AC.4/1995/3 (June 21, 1995).

peoples' organizations was the basis for this research. Although Professor Erica-Irene Daes advised against a formal definition for the indigenous peoples, she proffered some factors which she felt might lead to better understanding of the "indigenous" term. Indigenousness in the words of Professor Daes amounts to the following:

> The factors which modern international organizations and legal experts have considered relevant to the understanding of the concept of "indigenous" include:
> (a)   Priority in time, with respect to the occupation and use of a specific territory;
> (b)   The voluntary perpetuation of cultural distinctiveness, which may include the aspects of language, social organization, religion and spiritual values, modes of production, laws and institutions;
> (c)   Self-identification, as well as recognition by other groups, or by state authorities, as a distinct collectivity; and
> (d)   An experience of subjugation, marginalization, dispossession, exclusion or discrimination, whether or not these conditions persist.[17]

Professor Daes's factors emphasize the need for the people claiming to be indigenous to be first in time to occupy the respective territory. While this is a thoughtful condition, it might be difficult to fulfill it because the fact of "first in time" will be difficult to prove. The only thing that can be proven as far as this condition is concerned is that a group of people can claim that they are "traditionally regarded" as the first settler of a territory. The reason for this is that while a group of people may claim in all honesty that they are the first settlers of a territory, some other group of people may have actually inhabited the territory long before the claimant came; as a result, it is not unusual to see archaeologists making surprising discoveries or findings that reveal that a particular territory was formerly occupied by some other people over a centuries ago.

The second condition required for the people claiming to be indigenous is to have culture that is distinct from that of any other group. This is an objective and factual condition which careful and impartial analysis will reveal.

17   Chairperson-Rapporteur Mrs. Erica-Irene A. Daes, "On the Concept of "Indigenous People," (working paper for Working Group on Indigenous Populations) U.N.ESCO, Commission on Human Rights, Sub-Commission on Prevention of Discrimination and Protection of Minorities, 14th sess., at 22, U.N. Doc. E/CN.4/sub.2/AC.4/Sub.2AC.4/1996/2 (1996).

The self-identification condition as stated by Professor Daes is another objective condition which the author believes will assist in classifying the indigenous peoples although self-identification alone might not be recognized by nation-state as conclusive. A country like Nigeria, for example, does not, at least not fully support the cause of indigenous peoples' rights. This was made manifest during the process of adoption of the 2007 UN Declaration on the Rights of Indigenous Peoples when Nigeria abstained from voting. If the Nigerian government truly admits that it has indigenous peoples in its domain or would care about their welfare, the country's representative during the adoption process would have voted in support of its adoption. While the country has not come to say this openly, its true intention can be inferred from their attitude and action during the vote for adoption of the indigenous peoples' declaration. The attitude of a majority of African nation states during the process of adoption of the Declaration is enough to reveal their stand, where they voted against the declaration of indigenous peoples' rights at the initial stage before the declaration was eventually adopted in 2007.[18] Consequently, any insistence on the identification of indigenous peoples by their African nation states as a factor to determine indigenousness might be misplaced.

As to the condition that subjugation or marginalization must be proven, this condition tends to be somewhat subjective. It is the view of the author that this group of people claiming to be indigenous must in addition to other factors be vulnerable; for example, they must be at the mercy of other more dominant groups.

1.1.4 The International Labor Organization

The International Labor Organization (ILO), a specialized agency of the United Nations system, has also made its contribution to finding a solution to the indigenous peoples' definitional imbroglio. It was the first international body to address indigenous issues in a comprehensive manner.[19] The ILO is responsible for the only two international instruments relating exclusively to indigenous and tribal peoples: the Indigenous and Tribal Populations Convention, 1957 (No.107) and the Indigenous and

---

18   General Assembly GA/10612, Sixty-first General Assembly Plenary 107th & 108th Meetings (AM & PM).

19   *The ILO and Indigenous and Tribal Peoples*, U.N., International Labour Organization, Leaflet no. 8, http://www.unhchr.ch/html/racism/indileaflet8.doc.

Tribal Peoples Convention 1989 (No.169).[20]

The ILO Conventions played a leading role by making available provisions that addressed the indigenous peoples' cause. While the ILO Convention No.107 supported the protection of indigenous peoples, it advocated for the integration of indigenous peoples into the life of their respective countries.[21] The ILO Convention No. 169, on the other hand, rejected this assimilationist theory and advocated for the recognition and protection of the social, cultural and spiritual values and practices of indigenous peoples.[22] These conventions extensively address the indigenous peoples' problem by their inclusion of provisions that will place the indigenous peoples in a situation that allows them to control and maintain their institutions, their ways of life, and their identities. They also made provision for their economic development by agitating for the need to close the socioeconomic gap between the indigenous peoples and the dominant groups of society. The ILO conventions of 1957 and 1989 highlighted the rights of indigenous and tribal populations and the duties of the nation states that ratified the convention, especially to the indigenous peoples.[23] The ILO Convention of 1957 was the pioneer international provision. It illuminated the world as to the rights of indigenous peoples and tribal populations and the duties of the nation states that gave formal sanction to the convention, especially their duties to the indigenous peoples.[24] The ILO Convention of 1989 maintained that the customs and ways of life of the indigenous peoples should be given due recognition and their existence must not be threatened in any way within the nation state.[25]

Moreover, the ILO Convention of 1989 adopted an approach based on both objective and subjective criteria. Under its objective criterion, a specific indigenous or tribal group or people must meet the requirement of the provision in Article 1 of the 169 convention which states that the convention pertains to the following type of group:

---

20   Id.
21   Convention Concerning the Protection and Integration of Indigenous and Other Tribal and Semi-Tribal Populations in Independent Countries, June 26, 1957, International Labour Organisation Convention No. 107, Art. 2(1).
22   Convention Concerning Indigenous and Tribal Peoples in Independent Countries, adopted June 27, 1989, 169 I.L.O. 1989, Art. 5(a).
23   Id.
24   Id.
25   Id.

(a)   tribal people in independent countries whose social, cultural and economic conditions distinguish them from other sections of the national community, and whose status is regulated wholly or partially by their own customs or traditions or by special laws or regulations;

(b)   peoples in independent countries who are regarded as indigenous on account of their descent from the populations which inhabited the country, or a geographical region to which the country belongs, at the time of conquest or colonization or the establishment of present state boundaries and who, irrespective of their legal status, retain some or all of their own social, economic, cultural and political institutions.[26]

The ILO's definition emphasized the conditions of cultural distinctiveness and "being regarded as first settler or occupant" of the territory in question as the two major factors that any group of people must be in accordance with if they desire indigenous peoples' status. This definition is in agreement with Professor Daes's suggested elements.

It is the ILO's contention that under the subjective criterion, the people or group of people who lay claim to indigenous people's status based on their personal belief or conviction that they are indeed indigenous must meet the criteria to qualify for indigenous peoples' status.[27] This author, however, feels that the "self-identification" criterion should be used with caution. This is because this criterion is subject to abuse and manipulation in the absence of a concrete factor or evidence to prove that such a person or a group of people are indigenous. The criterion should be corroborated with other items of evidence such as burial sites of the claimant's ancestors or oral history before much weight could be attached to it.

A careful look at the above provision of the 1989 ILO Convention[28] reveals it to be a statement of coverage rather than a definition. The provision indicates that self-identification as tribal is a fundamental criterion for determining whether a group or person qualifies as indigenous. While self-identification can be a factor, it should not be the sole element, but should only complement other factors.

---

26   *Id*
27   *Id.*
28   *Id.*

1.1.5 The World Bank

The World Bank, a multilateral financial institution, in its effort to embrace the indigenous peoples' issue, established in 1982 a safeguard policy for indigenous peoples. This was designed initially to consider the needs of neglected tribal groups affected by development projects.

The World Bank pointed out in its policy that there is "no single definition that could capture indigenous peoples' diversity."[29] This necessitated the use of various terms such as "indigenous peoples," "indigenous ethnic minorities," "tribal groups" and "scheduled tribes"[30] to define social groups whose socio-cultural image differs from that of the ruling group in the society and minority status makes them susceptible to the other ruling group. This minority status makes them disadvantaged both politically and economically, and less developed when compared to the other dominant groups. The World Bank policy further revealed that indigenous peoples are always poor and at the bottom of the economic scale of the population and primarily practice the agricultural and pastoral occupations such as farming and herding, as well as small-scale trading.[31]

Further, the World Bank listed numerous characteristics by which the status of indigenous peoples can be ascertained:

(a) a close attachment to ancestral territories and to the natural resources in these areas;
(b) self-identification and identification by others as members of a distinct cultural group;
(c) an indigenous language, often different from the national language;
(d) presence of customary social and political institutions; and
(e) primarily subsistence-oriented production.[32]

The World Bank's operational policy of 2005 recognizes the fact

---

29   "*Indigenous Peoples,*" Operational Directive OD 4.20, THE WORLD BANK OPERATIONAL MANUAL, (September 1991) http://www.worldbank.org/html/fpd/em/power/wbpolicy/420OD.stm.

30   *Id.*

31   *Id.*

32   *Id.*

that identities and cultures of indigenous peoples are inseparable from their lands and its appurtenant resources because it is from this land that they get their means of sustenance.[33] The 2005 policy of the World Bank in expanding upon its 1991 policy went further to add the condition that indigenous peoples must have "customary cultural, economic, social, or political institutions that are separate from those of the dominant society and culture."[34] This additional condition confirms that indigenous peoples must always have cultural, economic, social or political institutions that differ from those of the dominant group.

1.1.6 Contribution of the African Commission's Working Group on Indigenous Populations / Communities

The African Commission on Human and Peoples' Rights which was established by the African Charter on Human and Peoples' Rights (also known as Banjul Charter) after its adoption in Kenya in 1981 by the Assembly of Heads of State and Governments of the Organization of African Unity (OAU) and which has the obligation of ensuring the promotion and protection of Human and peoples' rights throughout the African Continent[35] lent its support to the indigenous peoples' cause and outlined characteristics which it believes should qualify any group for indigenous peoples' status. The characteristics included for such groups are as follows:

(a) they must maintain an age-long subsistence economy such as hunter-gathering, pastoral pursuits, and farming;
(b) they must adhere to distinctive cultural backgrounds and utilize their own social institutions; and
(c) they must conform to their own religious practices.[36]

The Commission listed models of the hunting-gathering communities in Africa who perceive themselves as indigenous peoples such

---

33   *Id.*

34   "*Indigenous Peoples,*" Operational Policies OP 4.10, THE WORLD BANK OPERATIONAL MANUAL (July 2005) http://wbln0018.worldbank.org/Institutional/Manuals/OpManual.nsf./B52929624EB2A3538525672E00775F66/0F7D6F3F04DD70398525672C0 07D08ED?OpenDocument.

35   African Commission on Human and Peoples' Rights History, *available at* http://www.achpr.org/ english/_info/history_en.html.

36   INDIGENOUS PEOPLES IN AFRICA: THE FORGOTTEN PEOPLES?, THE AFRICAN COMMISSION'S WORK ON INDIGENOUS PEOPLES IN AFRICA 9, 9-10 (Transaction Publishers 2006).

as the Batwa Pygmies of the Great Lakes Region, the San of Southern Africa, the Hadzabe of Tanzania and the Ogiek, Sengwer and Yakuu of Kenya. The Pokot of Kenya and Uganda, Barabaig of Tanzania, Maasai of Kenya and Tanzania, Karamojong of Uganda, Himba of Namibia and the Tuareg, Fulani and Toubou of Mali, Burkina Faso and Niger are all comprised of rustic communities of herders who also envision themselves as indigenous peoples.[37]

The Commission reiterated "the principle of self-identification" as a chief element in distinguishing indigenous peoples; this involves presenting themselves as distinctly different from the other groups.[38] Further, the Commission stated that the cultures of the indigenous peoples must not only be dissimilar from the governing population but their manner of living must also be unique. The indigenous peoples' survival generally depends upon their attainability of and the rights to their ancestral lands and the land's natural resources. Additionally, it must be shown that indigenous peoples are subjected to domination and exploitation within national political and economic structures of the nation state.[39] After the independence of Africa, the governing populations have been in the habit of stifling the marginalized groups causing the activation of various indigenous peoples' movements pursuing reforms of the situations.[40]

This author supports the characteristics listed by the African working group on indigenous peoples which include evidence of age-long subsistence economy, cultural distinctiveness and willingness to maintain their own religious practices. This author, however, wishes to state that the characteristics are incomplete as they do not mention characteristics such "being regarded as the first inhabitant of a territory" and as being vulnerable to the dominant society. This author agrees with the African working group that self-identification could be used to show the distinctiveness of indigenous people from other groups.

1.1.7 The Understanding of the Term "Indigenous Peoples" by the United Nations Permanent Forum on Indigenous Issues (UNPFII)

The United Nations Permanent Forum on Indigenous Issues has

---

37   *Id.* at 10.
38   *Id.* at 11.
39   *Id.* at 10.
40   *Id.*

not adopted any official definition of the term "indigenous peoples" but developed some characteristics for the purpose of identifying indigenous peoples. The characteristics are as follows:

(1) Self-identification as indigenous peoples at the individual level and accepted by the community as their members.
(2) Historical continuity with pre-colonial and /or pre-settler societies.
(3) Strong link to territories and surrounding natural resources.
(4) Distinct social economic or political systems.
(5) Distinct language, culture and beliefs.
(6) Resolves to maintain and reproduce their ancestral environments and system as distinctive peoples and communities.[41]

In examining the characteristics developed by the United Nations Permanent Forum on Indigenous Issues (UNPFII), this author agrees with the condition that anyone desirous of indigenous peoples' status must be self-identified as such, both at the individual level and by the community as a member. The corroboration by the community is a strong factor that could help prove status as indigenous peoples.

The condition of historical continuity with the pre-colonial or pre-settler societies is similar to "being regarded as first in time." Any group desirous of indigenous peoples status must be able to prove historical continuity with pre-settler societies; however, "pre-colonial" experience should not be made a factor because a group does not necessarily need to be colonized before it can qualify for the status.

Strong links to territories and surrounding natural resources is another characteristic that the author agrees could prove indigenous peoples' status. Such strong links could be indigenous peoples' age long subsistence economy, or it could be spiritual worship centers or burial sites or cemeteries of their forefathers.

Distinct economic, social and political systems as well as distinct language cultures and beliefs are dependable characteristics that could be relied upon to prove indigenous peoples status. It must be shown that the

41   United Nations Permanent Forum on Indigenous Issues, Fact Sheet, *available at* http://www.un.org/esa/socdev/unpfii/documents/5session_factsheet1.pdf.

ways of life of "groups desirous of indigenous peoples' status are different from that of the dominating communities.

Any group desirous of indigenous peoples' status must be willing to maintain its distinctiveness and its ancestral environment. This is a strong factor that shows that groups desirous of indigenous peoples' status are not only distinct, but that they intend to preserve this heritage for the coming generations. As good as these characteristics are, the vulnerability factor is missing; in other words, groups desiring indigenous peoples' status must be vulnerable within the larger society in which they reside.

1.2 SCHOLARSHIP

Noteworthy scholarship has been conducted with the aim of finding a lasting solution to the indigenous peoples' definition. The authors that should be discussed in this context are Siegfried Wiessner, Martin Scheinin and Benedict Kingsbury.

1.2.1 Definitional Commentary by Professor Siegfried Wiessner

Professor Siegfried Wiessner, while justifying the importance of a definition for the indigenous peoples, made it clear that formal definitions might help to protect indigenous peoples against governments who deny their existence. In his work on the definition of indigenous people, he pointed out that any attempt to make "historic continuity with pre-invasion and pre-colonial societies" part of the conditions to be met before a group of people could qualify as indigenous will not work. This might establish a "mandatory link to the era of European colonization and invasion a prerequisite which might lead to the limitation of the concept of indigenous communities to peoples in the Americas and Oceania and thus leaving out indigenous people of Africa, Asia and other places that are oppressed by equally original inhabitants of neighboring lands that are now dominant."[42]

Professor Wiessner also pointed out that the condition of the groups of indigenous peoples' resolve to maintain their "ancestral territories" could possibly cause them to be compelled or pressured from their land even though they live in urban areas against their wishes while still maintaining

---

42   Siegfried Wiessner, *Rights and Status of Indigenous Peoples: A Global Comprehensive and International Legal Analysis,* 12 Harv. Hum. Rts. J. 57, 111 (1999).

their indigenous identity.[43] It must be noted that indigenous people do not necessarily have to be a numerical minority in a state. Examples of indigenous peoples who are the majority sector of the society are the Fijians and the Bolivians. While it is a fact that most indigenous people are "non-dominant" in the society, this condition cannot be the sole factor to determine indigenous peoples' status either. At best, it can act as an additional element to the other factors.

According to Professor Wiessner, a definition should not be aspired to for the sake of mere formality. It ought to have a purpose. The professor pointed out that a definition might be sought in order to exclude certain communities from benefiting from the protection offered by international instruments, while it might also be used to protect indigenous peoples against governments who deny their existence.[44]

While examining the "priority in time" factor by Professor Erica-Irene Daes, Professor Wiessner pointed out that in order to avoid the problems associated with the narrow definition, it will be better to refer to those intended beneficiaries of the definition as "peoples that have traditionally been regarded as the original inhabitants of a particular territory."[45] Since it will be difficult to prove exactly who the original inhabitants of a particular territory are, it is Professor Wiessner's contention that a "longtime identification" of a group of people will meet the condition of original inhabitant as long as such a group maintains continuous residency. It is, therefore, safer and more realistic to rephrase the condition as "regarded as original inhabitant" instead of "original inhabitant" because of the difficulty of proving the original inhabitant factor.[46]

Additionally, Professor Wiessner advocated that indigenous peoples' strong ties to their ancestral lands should be made one of the factors in determining whether a person or a group is indigenous or not. It is the view of this author that there are several ties to the land which could support this factor; for instance, cemeteries or burial grounds of the indigenous peoples' ancestors could serve as a strong tie to the land. The traditional religion of some people may also serve as their strong tie to their land because some of the traditional religions have a permanent place of worship called the shrine

---

43   *Id.*

44   *Id.* at 113.

45   *Id.* at 114-115.

46   *Id.* at 115.

where the people commune with the spirit of their ancestors which they strongly believe in. That the indigenous peoples do not presently reside in their territory should not deprive them of indigenous people status because most of them have been involuntarily deprived of the land through war or conquest while some have left voluntarily in search of better pastures of land necessary for their survival outside their original lands.

Professor Wiessner is, therefore, of the opinion that indigenous peoples/communities are peoples traditionally regarded and self-defined as descendants of first inhabitants of lands with which they share spiritual ties. According to the professor, these peoples are also culturally, socially and or economically different from the dominant groups in the society who have marginalized, discriminated and excluded them.

1.2.2 Contribution by Professor Martin Scheinin

Martin Scheinin, while supporting the need for a definition for the indigenous peoples, pointed out that the lack of a definition for indigenous peoples "will not grant far reaching rights to indigenous people unless the scope of application of the legal concept of indigenous peoples is at least reasonably precise."[47] He listed some characteristics that are required to be met in order to qualify for indigenous peoples' status and these are as follows:

(1) Distinctiveness and the desire to remain different,
(2) Dispossession of land through colonization,
(3) Located in a specific geographical area and their economic activity must depend on the land,
(4) Being first in time, and
(5) Lack of political control.[48]

In examining the characteristics listed by Scheinin, the distinctiveness of indigenous peoples is an objective factor which could be proved with facts while the desire to remain different could be subjective. It could also be corroborated since this is similar to and supports the self-identification condition.

---

47   Martin Scheinin, *What are Indigenous Peoples?* in Nazila Ghanea, Nazila Ghanea-Hercock, Alexandra Xanthaki and Patrick Thornberry, Minorities, Peoples, and Self-Determination: Essays in Honour of Patrick Thornberry 13 (Martinus Nijhoff Publishers/Brill Academic, 2004).
48   *Id.* at 3-4.

While the dispossession of land is a vital condition and there is an avalanche of several cases buttressing the fact that the majority of indigenous peoples were removed from their land, such dispossession does not necessarily have to be through colonization. The condition of being located in a specific geographical area with their economy depending on the land will satisfy the condition of having an age-old means of sustenance with a special tie to the land.

The condition of being first in time corresponds to "being regarded as first occupant of a territory." The condition of a "lack of political control" is good, but it is debatable. While it is a fact that most indigenous peoples lack political control, there could be exceptions. For example, the present president of Bolivia is from indigenous Aymara descent.

This author supports all the factors listed by Scheinin except the condition of dispossession of land through colonization on the ground that it is possible for people to be dispossessed of their land without being colonized; therefore, colonization should not be made a factor. Also, the lack of political control as a factor should be used with caution; otherwise indigenous people that now have political power such as President Evo Morales may be made to lose their indigenous status.

1.2.3 Contribution by Professor Benedict Kingsbury

Benedict Kingsbury has been sympathetic to the extension of the "indigenous peoples' category beyond the Americas and Australasia. He did not want the strict historical test to be the key in a definition and suggested a "flexible" "constructivist" approach.[49] He enumerated the essential requirements as follows:

(a) Self-identification as a distinct ethnic group;
(b) Historical experience of, or contingent vulnerability to, severe disruption, dislocation or exploitation;
(c) Long connection with the region;
(d) The wish to retain a distinct identity.[50]

---

49   Benedict Kingsbury, *"Indigenous Peoples" in International Law: A Constructivist Approach to the Asian Controversy*, 92. Am. J. Int'l 420, 420-21 (1998).
50   *Id.* at 421.

A thorough examination of Kingsbury's contribution on this subject indicates that he is in alliance with the earlier discussed positions on this subject. While this author agrees with Kingsbury that self-identification could serve as a factor for identifying any group of people laying claim to indigenous peoples' status, the author humbly submits that such identification must be well corroborated by other evidence showing the claimant as a distinct ethnic group from others, vulnerable to the other dominant groups of the society, and able to meet the long connection factor of Kingsbury which is similar to "being regarded as the original inhabitants." The preference of such a group to retain their distinct identity is also similar to the desire of the group to preserve their culture, as this is their heritage which they intend to bequeath to their coming generations. In sum, this author generally approves of Kingsbury's position. The only factor missing in Kingsbury's analysis is the need of the peoples claiming indigenous peoples' status to show proof of an age old means of sustenance, which could also be referred to as subsistence economy, this factor is very vital because it is one which any group claiming to be indigenous could use to substantiate their argument that they have been around since time immemorial and that they have a dependable economy that has been sustaining them.

1.3 THE ROLE OF NON-GOVERNMENTAL ORGANIZATIONS (NGOs)

Efforts have also been made by Non-Governmental Organizations (NGOs) to proffer solutions to the indigenous people's definitional issue. Despite the fact that these organizations lack any authority to make or enact law; they serve as pressure groups whose views may be persuasive. One such organization is the Independent Commission on International Humanitarian Issues.

The Independent Commission on International Humanitarian Issues (hereinafter referred to as ICIHI) propounded four elements that should be included in the definition of "indigenous peoples". According to ICIHI, the term "indigenous persons" is usually used in reference to those individuals and groups who are descendants of the original populations residing in a country.[51] The commission went on to point out that in the majority of cases they are numerical minorities, and as a group they do not control the governments of the countries where they live. Most, but not all,

---

51   INDEPENDENT COMMISSION ON INTERNATIONAL HUMANITARIAN ISSUES, INDIGENOUS PEOPLES: A GLOBAL QUEST FOR JUSTICE 6 (London: Zed Press, 1987).

indigenous groups are ethnic minorities who tend to lack power, feel that they are marginalized from the political process, and are disenfranchised.

ICIHI also stated that "indigenous peoples" generally possess ethnic, religious, or linguistic characteristics that are different from the dominant or numerically superior groups in the societies of which they are a part. They tend to have a sense of cultural identity or social solidarity that many members of indigenous groups attempt to maintain. In some cases members of indigenous communities attempt to hide their identities in order not to suffer racial prejudice or poor treatment at the hands of others. In a number of cases they proclaim their ethnic affiliation proudly and openly. Indeed, an important criterion for "indigenousness" is the identification of their distinct cultural identity by the peoples themselves.[52]

Most self-proclaimed "indigenous peoples" could not meet these criteria. This is because most of them have been dispossessed and this makes it impossible for them to still be in their traditional ancestral territories. Even though some people claim to be indigenous, the countries where they live also may not recognize them as indigenous.

Those peoples considered to be the progeny of the first settlers in the given territory are designated as "indigenous." The term is also used to refer to those individuals and groups who are descendants of the population that is regarded as the first settler in the given territory. In the case of Africa, this raises particular problems because Africa is noted for having the longest record of early human residency and includes numerous variations of cultural diversity; for instance, although Nigeria is just one country in Africa, it has over three hundred and fifty ethnic groups with diverse cultures and languages.[53] It is almost impossible in some cases to prove the history of most of the ethnic groups because of the mobility of some of the groups who are in the habit of short-term residency because of either their occupation or the search for needed pasture land.[54] Robert Hitchcock pointed out that the absence of a clearly delineated definition has not in any way helped the indigenous peoples' situation, but it has culminated in confrontations between the people regarded as the early settlers and those regarded as the

---

52   *Id.* at 8-10.

53   Robert K. Hitchcock and Diana Vinding: Indigenous Peoples' Rights in Southern Africa : An Introduction 8 (2004).

54   *Id.* at 8-9.

late comers.[55]

The acknowledgment by Finland, Norway and Sweden of the Saami living in their countries as indigenous people "established a precedent for the recognition of a group as indigenous even where the majority population in the state as a whole was indigenous or very old."[56] This is an example of self-identification of indigenous peoples by nation-states and governments; however, as valuable as this element is, it seems to be applicable more in the Western and developed countries than in the Third World and developing countries.

Professor Douglas Sanders in his research, stated that in "some of the World Bank's regions," especially in Africa, borrower countries are generally unwilling to the "use of the term 'indigenous peoples' because of the general belief that all members of the respective national populations are 'indigenous.'"[57] He further observed that the various regional and national usages of the term "indigenous peoples" have not made it easy to have a universal definition to cover all the groups encompassed by the World Bank's policy.[58] It is because of the confusion caused by the various terminologies offered that the term "indigenous peoples" was recommended by the United Nations.[59]

The World Council of Indigenous Peoples in its first meeting held in Georgetown, Guyana, in 1974 developed this definition of "indigenous people" for delegate status:

> The term indigenous people refers to people living in countries which have a population composed of differing ethnic or racial groups who are descendants of the earliest populations living in the area and who do not as a group control the national government of the countries within which they live.[60]

---

55   *Id.* at 8.

56   Douglas E. Sanders, *Indigenous Peoples: Issues of Definition*, 8.1 JOURNAL OF CULTURAL PROPERTY 4, 7 (1999).

57   *Id.* at 4-5.

58   *Id.*

59   *Id.* at 5.

60   Douglas Sanders, *The Formation of the World Council of Indigenous Peoples* 12 (IWGIA Document, 1977).

1.4 ANALYSIS OF THE WORKING DEFINITION AND THE VARIOUS ATTEMPTS AT DEFINITIONS

A critical examination of the various definitions propounded revealed the "historical continuity" condition or requirement as one of the objective elements. All of the other elements, such as "consider themselves distinct from other factors of the societies" and "form at present non-dominant sectors of society" are subjective and debatable. In proving continuity, the relationship to their ancestors of the community or the place in question has to be determined. This is necessary because it could be argued that the fact that a group of people are living on a particular land does not automatically mean that they have any relationship with the ancestors of the place.

The author agrees with the various attempts at definition made by eminent scholars and institutions which include the working definition of Jose R. Martinez Cobo and the additional element of the indigenous people's strong ties to their ancestral land pointed out by Professor Wiessner. Also, worthy of note is the World Bank Operational Directive of 2005,[61] which has similar elements or conditions. For the purpose of this subject, the author would like to assert that the determination of "common ancestry with the original occupants of the land" in question is very vital to effect any progress in classifying any group of people as indigenous.

1.4.1 Determination of Ancestry

Since it will be difficult to request that a group of people undergo a DNA test to confirm whether they have common ancestry with the original occupants of a land, a person's ancestry can simply be determined by asking the person what ancestry does he or she most closely identify with. Whatever the answer given however is, it must be corroborated with convincing evidence. For instance, the members of a group to which they are claiming ancestry must be able to identify themselves as part of the group. Since there may be difficulty in obtaining a written history of such groups, oral history and circumstantial facts may have to be relied upon. The descendants of such a group may have to be verified through oral interviews with the oldest living people in the community. Such interviews will shed more light on the parentage or line of descent of such groups claiming to be indigenae of a place. Circumstantial facts will also assist in the verification of the relationship and long connection with a region. Such circumstantial

61 World Bank Operational Manual, *supra* note 34.

facts could include shrines from time immemorial where people worship according to their beliefs, burial grounds of their fore-fathers, and age-old professions.

According to John Alan Cohan in his article, many of these elements are difficult for indigenous peoples to satisfy even though the "indigenous peoples generally have ethnic, religious and linguistic traits that are different from the dominant peoples in their countries."[62]

The case of *Mason v. Tritton and Anor*[63] established that membership of the indigenous people depends on the biological descent from the indigenous people and on the mutual recognition of a particular person's membership by that person and by the elders or other persons enjoying traditional authority among those people.

Professor Rebbeca Tsosie in her article[64] listed four intertwined strands that are necessary for any group to claim indigenous status. The first strand relates to the association of a people "with a particular place or locality."[65] This implies a connection of a people with an "ancestral territory."[66] The second factor has to do with "prior habitation." Any group claiming indigenous status within a territory must be able to prove that they were inhabitants of the territory prior to now. Many indigenous people have had to leave their land either voluntarily or involuntarily due to war, coercion, or necessitated due to the nature of their occupation. For instance, the movement of cattle breeders in Northern Nigeria was always determined by the availability of fresh vegetables for their cattle. Thus, as soon as they consumed the green vegetables in a particular place, they had to move to another location to prevent the cattle from starving. Professor Thornberry opined that it is this "priority claim that gives 'indigenous' groups their unique status."[67] The indigenous peoples must be able to demonstrate this "prior habitation" or their indigenous status will be in jeopardy.

---

62   John Alan Cohan, *Environmental Rights of Indigenous Peoples Under the Alien Tort Claims Act, the Public Trust Doctrine and Corporate Ethics, and Environmental Dispute Resolution*, 20 UCLA J. ENVTL. L. & POL'Y 133, 137 (2001-2002).

63   1994 NSW LEXIS 13901; BC 9404979.

64   Rebecca Tsosie, *The New Challenge to Native Identity: An Essay to "Indigeneity" and "Whiteness*, 18 WASH. U. J. L. & POL'Y 55 (2005).

65   *Id.* at 66 [citing PATRICK THORNBERRY, INDIGENOUS PEOPLES AND HUMAN RIGHTS 37 (2002)].

66   *Id.*

67   *Id.*

Professor Tsosie's third factor is that any group claiming indigenous status must be "original or first inhabitants" of the territory in question. This puts the burden on such a group to prove not only "prior habitation" in a historical sense, but that they are the "first human beings to inhabit a territory."[68] It is, however, the view of this author that the element of "original or first inhabitant" will be very difficult to prove. Professor Thornberry and Professor Wiessner also share this view. Professor Wiessner while articulating his view on this element pointed out that no one can with definiteness lay claim to being the original or first settler of a place; thus a group can only be "traditionally regarded" as a first settler of a place.[69] This author agrees that archaeologists are making new discoveries every once in a while, and it is possible for them to come up with findings that show that a particular territory had been inhabited by some group of people centuries ago before the coming of any present group laying claim to being the original settlers of the given territory.[70]

The fourth element provided by Professor Tsosie is that the indigenous peoples must be distinct. This concerns the nature of indigenous groups as "whole societies exhibiting cultural patterns which differ from those of the dominant society."[71] Thus, indigenous people must not only be distinct from the dominant society but "must be seen" to be distinct; this means that the distinction must be glaring and visible. This author submits that the issue of people marrying outside their ancestral group should not affect their right to be classified as members of groups claiming to be indigenous; this is because marriage cannot extinguish one's ancestral status.

Further, a person or group's ancestry could be determined by asking what ancestry they most closely identify with.[72] This confirmation could be done by making recourse to history which could be oral or written and by reliance on circumstantial evidence.

---

68   *Id.* at 67.

69   Wiessner, *supra* note 42, at 114-115.

70   Sidsel Saugestad, The Inconvenient Indigenous: Remote Area Development in Botswana, Donor Assistance, and the First People of the Kalahari 23 (Uppsala, Sweden: Nordic Africa Institute, 2001).

71   Tsosie, *supra* note 64, at 67.

72   Australian Census Analytic Program: Australians' Ancestries: 2001, 4 (Australian Bureau of Statistics, Cat. No 2054.0).

The author further submits that the "pre-invasion and pre-colonial" condition in the working definition by Cobo is too strict and most potential indigenous peoples might not be able to meet this condition. Objectively, it will be unfair to insist that unless a group had experienced invasion and colonization, they would not be seen as indigenous. In the post-conquest indigenous society of the Nahuas of central Mexico, it was stated that while "the majority of the indigenous population continued to live in their traditional units across the countryside, their lives were nonetheless profoundly affected by the conquest and its aftermath."[73] It could be deduced from the above phrase that the Nahuas of central Mexico were seen as an indigenous society before the Spanish conquest. In view of this fact, the pre-invasion and pre-colonial condition proffered by Cobo cannot be a determinative factor in deciding who indigenous peoples are and who are not. At best, this condition will just be an additional requirement to which much weight cannot be attached.

It is possible for groups within a society that have never been invaded or colonized to still be non-dominant and oppressed by other groups within the same society. There are several groups today, especially in Nigeria, who were dominated by other groups, not because of any invasion or colonialism, but as a result of their attitude towards development, especially education. It is, therefore, the submission of the author that before any group of people may claim "indigenous status" the following conditions must be met:

(1) There must be proof that the group was "traditionally regarded" as the first inhabitants of the said territory, and they must have a special relationship or tie with the land;
(2) There must be proof of age-old subsistence economy by the group;
(3) The group must be vulnerable; in other words they must be defenseless against the dominant group of society; and
(4) The group must be seen to be culturally distinct from the dominant society.

It is the author's view that the above four vital conditions should be the yardstick for determining whether any group qualifies for "indigenous peoples' status." As earlier stated, a group must be traditionally regarded as the first inhabitants of any territory in question and they must show that they have a special relationship or tie with the land or territory this could be

---

73   Rebecca Horn, Postconquest Coyoacan 19-30 (1997).

substantiated by evidence of their age long land-based religion or worship centers, burial grounds or graves of their fore-fathers. The fact of being descendants of the first inhabitants has to be proven by the group of people claiming to be indigenous. This is where the World Bank characteristic stressing self-identification and identification by others as members of a distinct cultural group comes into play. Such a group must be self-identified and identified by others as members of a distinct cultural group. While it is easier for a group of indigenous peoples to be identified by others, it is always difficult for governments or nation states to identify indigenous people in their territory as indigenous peoples. This problem is rampant in Africa. It also came to the forefront during the adoption of the United Nations Declaration of Indigenous Peoples' Rights where most nations refused to vote because of their claim that they have no indigenous peoples in their territory. Further, the condition stated by Professor Erica-Irene Daes in her attempt at definition that indigenous peoples must be recognized by nation states will not work in Africa because many nation states there do not recognize any of their people as being indigenous or they recognize all of their people as indigenous.[74] In other words, the nation-states often recognize no separate group of indigenous peoples. If this condition is made one of the determinative factors for obtaining "indigenous peoples' status," potential indigenous peoples on the continent of Africa will be unjustly deprived of their proper status and associated rights.

The other important condition to be proven is that the people have a subsistence economy. This means that such people must prove that they have a reliable economy since time immemorial that provides them with a means of livelihood. Such ancient occupations could involve hunting and gathering, and cultivation and pastoralism. This condition is employed to demonstrate that they are not only first settlers in a territory, but that there is an age-old occupation that they have engaged in to provide for their needs in order for them to survive.

The vulnerability condition is another important factor that must be proven by groups desiring "indigenous status." It must be clearly shown that the group is defenseless against the dominant society and as a result, they are suffering all forms of injustices. Professor Wiessner adds that the discrimination against the indigenous group could be "past or present,"

---

74   Gumisai Mutume, "*Indigenous' People Fight for Inclusion*, 21.1 AFRICA RENEWAL 1, 2 (January 2007) (United Nations Department of Public Information) *available at* http://www.unep.org/indigenous/pdfs/Newsletter-Africa-indigenous-struggle-Eng.pdf.

thus including now dominant groups such as the ethnic Fijians or for that matter, Bolivians whose majority is indigenous and who now are having a president of their own in the person of Evo Morales. It must be noted that groups discriminated against in the past still need protection just as those presently being discriminated against are in urgent need of human rights protection. While groups discriminated in the past may not be in "urgent need" of human rights protection, they are still entitled to certain specific rights because of their cultural specificity. They need these rights to preserve their cultural identity to be able to transmit it to the coming generations.

The "culturally distinct" condition is another vital factor which must be proven by a group desiring "indigenous peoples" status. It is, however, not enough for a group to claim to be culturally distinct; the distinctiveness must be objectively seen to be so. This is where the factor of "self-identification" that is corroborated with evidence comes in. Self-identification could be used to prove cultural distinctiveness of a group and the willingness to remain different.

In laying a foundation for this subject, the author will use the above four elements as the yardstick of determining whether any group in Nigeria deserves or qualifies for "indigenous peoples' status," and if they do whether they are entitled to any rights. In the next chapter, the author will examine the rights of indigenous peoples.

CHAPTER TWO

RIGHTS OF INDIGENOUS PEOPLES

2.1 WHAT ARE RIGHTS

In discussing the rights of indigenous people, the author will discuss what a right actually is. This is to make this topic meaningful.

In the words of Professor Wiessner, human rights are collectively enforced stop signs against the violation of the weak, the vulnerable, the few, the hated, the powerless and the oppressed.[75]

Peter Jones has also defined right to be a term used to cover four different forms of entitlements. These entitlements are claim-rights, liberty-rights, powers and immunities.[76]

A claim-right is recognized by legal systems in modern societies, constitutions, and such. It is a claim that one party has over another and it always exists in conjunction with duties.[77] A liberty-right is an entitlement to make a choice that one desires.[78] In exercising this right, a person is not under any obligation. For example, everybody is entitled to dress according to their taste. Power is the entitlement which is due to one and the state is under an obligation to provide legal facilities for its actualization. For example, one has the right to vote and the state is obliged to provide necessary machineries to exercise it.[79] Immunity is another form of right

---

75   Siegfried Wiessner, *Dedication,* 1 Intercultural Hum. Rts. L. Rev. 1 (2006).

76   Peter Jones, Rights 7 (St. Martin's Press, 1994).

77   *Id.* at 12.

78   *Id.*

79   *Id.*

which entitles a person not to be subjected to another person's power.[80] For example, the President and State Governors in Nigeria have immunity rights which protect them from being sued while in office.

A right is, therefore, an entitlement for all individuals which they may claim regardless of societal opinion or view. Rights will be deemed to have been breached if there is a failure to perform the correlative duty.

There are situations where infringements may be justified or unjustified. For example, if the infringement of a right is morally justified, then the right will be deemed not violated. It is a fact that all violations are infringements, but not all infringements are violations. An infringement of a right may also occur where a possessor forfeits his or her rights.

2. 2 INDIVIDUAL AND COLLECTIVE RIGHTS

The discussion on rights will not be complete without drawing a distinction between individual rights and collective rights. Robert Clinton in his article[81] referred to collective rights as a group or societal rights. Professor Wiessner shed light on this in his article[82] where he clarified that individual rights are ascribed to an individual human being, while collective rights are ascribed to groups of people and thus, can only be claimed by the collective entity and its authorized agents. The professor went further to explain that one's clan, kinship and family identities are integral parts of one's personal identity and therefore, rights and responsibilities exist within this community. There are also structures of authority that exist among groups of people where there is a formation of common will. It is this process of decision making and its cultural, geographical, social and economic environment that the assembly of collective rights of indigenous peoples is designed to protect. It could be seen from the provisions of the United Nations Declaration on Indigenous People's Rights that it acknowledged certain collective rights.[83] The provisions of collective rights in the instrument protect culture, internal decision making and the control and use of land.[84]

80   *Id.* at 13.

81   Robert Clinton, *The Rights of Indigenous Peoples as Collective Group Rights,* 32 ARIZ. L. REV. 739, 742 (1990).

82   Wiessner, *Rights, supra* note 42, at 121.

83   UN Declaration on the Rights of Indigenous Peoples, UN General Assembly, Arts. 6, 7, 8, 34 & 39 (2007), *available at* http://www.un.org/esa/socdev/unpfii/documents/DRIPS_en.pdf.

84   *Id. at* Art. 32.

This instrument, in other words, encompasses cultural right, the right to self-government and right to land. These provisions of the United Nations Declaration contain collective rights. Other such right include the right to enjoy all human rights and fundamental freedoms collectively; the rights to live in freedom, peace and security as distinct people; the right to maintain their institutional structures and distinctive customs and traditions; and the right to access and receive prompt decisions through just and fair procedures for conflict resolution and remedies for all infringements of individuals and collective rights of indigenous peoples.[85]

Individual rights alone will not be able to serve the purpose for which the rights were meant. For example, culture is a group phenomenon which will need the collective rights to be effective. Since culture includes the tribal ways of life and the natural and spiritual environment in which these traditions are maintained and developed, it is most appropriate to provide a right that will accommodate the whole group or community.

According to Professor Wiessner, group rights in the context of indigenous peoples also complement the individual rights of their members. Robert Clinton shared this same view in his article.[86] Opining on the relationship between individual and collective rights, he pointed out that collective and individual rights are not contrary concepts, but are complementary notions, because they complement each another. There is usually a fear that the collective rights demanded by ethnic and national groups are by definition, contrary to individual rights, but this is not necessarily so. According to Will Kymlicka,[87] there are two types of collective rights. The first involves the claim of a group against its own members, while the second involves the claim of a group against the larger society. Both claims, however, are seen as protecting the stability of national or ethnic communities.

The first type of a collective right is intended to protect the group from the destabilizing impact of internal dissent. For instance, the decision of individual members not to follow traditional practices or customs might be limited and sanctioned by the collective right to autonomy. The second type, on the other hand, is intended to protect the group from the

---

85   *Id.* at Arts. 1, 7, 34 & 40.

86   ·   Clinton, *supra* note 81, at 741.

87   WILL KYMLICKA, MULTICULTURAL CITIZENSHIP: A LIBERAL THEORY OF MINORITY RIGHTS 37-9 (Oxford: Clarendon Press, 1995).

impact of external decisions. This could be protection against decisions of the dominant group of the society; these dominant groups are usually groups in government who do not involve the indigenous peoples in the act of governance. The first type of collective right that deals with internal restrictions involves intra-group relations, which means that the ethnic or national group may seek the use of state power to restrict the liberty of its own members in the name of group solidarity. Internal protections involve intra-group relations, which mean that the ethnic or national groups may seek to protect its distinct existence and identity by limiting the impact of the decisions of the larger society. According to Kymlicka, this is seen as putting the various groups on a more equal footing. This reduces the extent to which the smaller groups would be vulnerable to the dominant or larger group. The collective rights become necessary to ensure that the larger society does not deprive groups of the conditions necessary for their survival. Additionally, collective rights will come into play on the issue of indigenous land rights. It is a fact that the survival of indigenous cultures throughout the world is heavily dependent on protection of their land base which they have fought tenaciously to maintain.[88]

Robert Clinton in his essay[89] pointed out that the UN declaration of indigenous rights mostly consists of collective or group rights. A cursory study of the declaration shows that most of the provisions indeed provided for collective or group rights. One of the provisions which deals with collective or group rights expresses that "indigenous peoples have the right to maintain and strengthen their distinct political, economic, social and cultural characteristics, as well as their legal systems, while retaining their rights to participate fully, if they so choose, in the political, economic, social and cultural life of the state."[90]

One of the most important advantages of collective rights as far as indigenous peoples are concerned is to protect their land base which is so vulnerable to the greater economic and political power of the larger or dominant society. Kymlicka identified that history has shown that the most effective way to protect the indigenous community from this external power is to establish reserves where the land is held in common and or in

---

88   *Id.*

89   Clinton, *supra* note 81, at 742.

90   UN Draft Declaration on the Rights of Indigenous Peoples, UN General Assembly, Arts. 4 (2007), *available at* http://www.un.org/esa/socdev/unpfii/documents/DRIPS_en.pdf.

trust, and cannot be alienated without the consent of the community as a whole. Kymlicka observed that this practice is consistent with the traditional notions regarding land amongst indigenous peoples. One of the most common strategies that European settlers used for breaking open indigenous lands for settlements was to replace traditional communal ownership with individualized title, against the will of the indigenous peoples themselves. Thus, once the land is divided and alienable, it becomes possible for the wealthier members of the larger society to buy up the land and other resources on which the community depends. Kymlicka noted also that this individualized alienable land is more vulnerable to expropriation by the government.[91]

In discussing the rights of indigenous peoples, various laws and their inter-relations will be examined including international law, treaty law and customary law. This examination is necessary because the indigenous peoples' rights issue permeates through all these laws and this makes a thorough examination of these laws inevitable.

2.3 INTERNATIONAL LAW

International law designates those rules of law applicable to a state or international organization that cannot be modified unilaterally by it. The Restatement of Foreign Relations Law points out that international law has ceased to apply exclusively to states and international organizations, but it deals also with their relations with individuals and juridical persons.[92] International law is identical to the law of nations which is a legal term that embodies norms defined in judicial writings, national practices, international documents, regional agreements and treaties signed by majority of nations.[93]

The origins of the original international law on indigenous peoples are to be found largely in the domestic law of the former European colonies.[94] The international legal reasoning and the twentieth century international arbitration cases addressing the rights and status of indigenous peoples exhibit the prevailing Social Darwinist and statist ideological convictions

---

91   Kymlicka, *supra* note 87, at 43.

92   RESTATEMENT OF THE LAW THIRD, THE FOREIGN RELATIONS LAW OF THE UNITED STATES 25 (1987).

93   Siderman de Blake v. Republic of Argentina, 965 F. 2d. 699. (9th Cir. 1992).

94   BRADLEY REED HOWARD, INDIGENOUS PEOPLES AND THE STATE: THE STRUGGLE FOR NATIVE RIGHTS 99 (Northern Illinois Press, 2003).

that were the cornerstones of the pacification dispossession, domestication, and extermination of indigenous nations in the Americas, Oceania, Africa, the Middle East, and Asia. According to Anaya, in the late 1800 and early 1900, the international law metamorphosized from the natural law of nations to the positive laws of nations and this ensured that international law would become a legitimizing force for colonization and the empire rather than a liberating one for indigenous peoples.[95]

International law consists of rules and principles which govern the relations and dealings of nations with each other.[96] It includes the basic, classic concepts of law in national legal systems such as status, property, obligation, and tort. International law is rooted in acceptance by the nation states which constitute the system. Examples of the primary source of international law are customary law and conventional law. Customary international law results when states follow certain practices generally and consistently out of a sense of legal obligation. A very good example was the codification of customary law in the Vienna Convention on the Law of Treaties. International law does not restrict any nation from making laws governing its own territory. International law also imposes upon the nation certain duties with respect to individuals. For example, it is a violation of international law to treat an alien in a manner which does not satisfy the international standard of justice. While an individual's right under the international minimum standard of foreigners might be violated, only the state of which the individual is a national can complain to the allegedly violating state; the defending state, however, is not obligated to exercise this right as it has the discretion whether to grant diplomatic protection or not.[97]

2.3.1 Instruments Addressing the Issue of Indigenous Peoples Rights

There are various international instruments dealing with the issue of indigenous peoples. These instruments are in the form of a treaty and may be binding on the contracting states. Not all international instruments are legally binding treaties, however, as some of the most important ones are declarations which do not have any legal power to force compliance, but only rely on the moral weight they carry. Indigenous peoples' rights

95   James Anaya, Indigenous Peoples in International Law 26 (2d ed. Oxford University Press, 2004).

96   Statute of the International Court of Justice art. 38(1), June 26, 1945, 59 Stat. 1031, 33 U.N.T.S. 993 [hereinafter ICJ Statute].

97   W. Michael Reisman et al, International in Contemporary Perspective 111 (2004).

are largely not framed in specific indigenous peoples' rights treaties, but are part of more general treaties, like the International Covenant of Civil and Political Rights or the Convention on the Prevention and Punishment of the Crime of Genocide.

The author shall in the course of this subject discuss some of the instruments that address the Indigenous Peoples issues and rights.

2.3.1.1 Treaty Law

A treaty is an international agreement between states in written form and governed by international law.[98] It creates rights and duties and it is its obligatory nature that qualifies it as part of international law. It is to be interpreted in good faith in accordance with the ordinary meaning to be given to the term of the treaty in their context and in the light of its object and purpose.[99] The following are some of the agreements that directly address indigenous peoples' issues.

2.3.1.2 ILO Convention No. 107 (1957)

Convention 107 is the first international convention on the indigenous peoples' issue. It was adopted in 1957 by the International Labor Organization (ILO) with the backing of United Nations System. The convention protects indigenous peoples, particularly their rights to land. While Convention 107 had been superseded by Convention 169, it is still the foundation upon which Convention 169 was built because some of its provisions are identical to that of Convention 169 except for a few major differences. While it lasted, Convention 107 advocated for the integration of indigenous peoples into the national life of their respective countries.[100] This convention applies to populations regarded as indigenous on account of their descent from the populations which inhabited the country or a geographical region to which the country belongs and live more in conforming with their own social, economic and cultural institutions.[101]

---

98   Vienna Convention on the Law of Treaties, May 23, 1969, art. 1(a), 1155 U.N.T.S. 331, 333 [hereinafter Vienna Convention].

99   *Id.* at Art. 31(1).

100   Convention Concerning the Protection and Integration of Indigenous and Other Tribal and Semi-Tribal Populations in Independent Countries, June 26, 1957, International Labour Organisation Convention No. 107, Art. 2(1), 328 U.N.T.S. 247.

101   *Id.* at Art. 1(a).

The governments are obligated to ensure coordinated and systematic action for the protection of the indigenous peoples and progressive integration into the life of their respective countries.[102] Such an obligation includes enabling indigenous peoples to benefit on equal footing from the rights and opportunities granted by the national laws or regulations.[103]

In situations where social, economic and cultural conditions of the indigenous peoples prevent them from enjoying the benefits of the country general laws, the convention stipulated that special measures shall be adopted for the protection of the institutions, persons, properties and labor of the indigenous peoples.[104]

The convention stipulates that in the process of protecting indigenous peoples, the people or their representatives should be involved[105] and they should be given opportunities to fully develop their initiatives.[106] The convention states that in considering the rights and duties of the indigenous peoples, their customary laws should be put into consideration.[107]

In situations, however, where the customary laws are not compatible with the national legal system, the people should be allowed to retain their customs and institutions,[108] but this should not in any way deprive the indigenous peoples the rights granted to all citizens and the corresponding duties.[109]

Part II of the Convention dealt with land and stated that indigenous peoples' right of ownership, collective or individual, over the land which they traditionally occupy shall be recognized.[110] The convention protects the indigenous peoples against being removed from their land except if the land is needed for security reasons in accordance with national laws and regulations or for national economic development or for health of indigenous peoples. For whatever reason that the land is needed, the peoples' consent

---

102   *Id.* at Art. 2(1).
103   *Id.* at Art. 2(2)(a).
104   *Id.* at Art. 3(1).
105   *Id.* at Art. 5(a).
106   *Id.* at Art. 5(b).
107   *Id.* at Art. 7(1).
108   *Id.* at Art. 7(2).
109   *Id.* at Art. 7(3).
110   *Id.* at Art. 11.

must be sought before they are dislodged,[111] and their displacement shall be done in accordance with the indigenous peoples' custom.[112]

Under Part III of the Convention dealing with recruitment and conditions of employment, it was stated that indigenous peoples shall be protected and not be discriminated against in respect of employment and remuneration.[113] And they shall enjoy the same opportunities as other citizens concerning vocational training facilities.[114]

Part VI on education and the means of communication states that measures should be taken to extend education opportunities to indigenous peoples just like other citizens[115] and such education should be in modern tongue or in the language commonly used by the people.[116] Governments are obligated to make known to the indigenous peoples, their rights and duties in respect to labor and social welfare.[117]

Part VII dealing with administration states that the government is obligated to create agencies for planning, coordinating and executing appropriate measures for the social, economic and cultural development of indigenous peoples.

2.3.1.3 ILO Convention No. 169 (1989)

The convention is a legally binding international instrument and it deals specifically with the rights of indigenous peoples. While the convention does not define who indigenous peoples are, it listed the criteria which people claiming to be indigenous must have which includes:

...being descent from populations which inhabited the country, or a geographical region to which the country belongs, at the time of conquest or colonization or the establishment of present state boundaries and who despite their status still maintain all or some

---

111   *Id.* at Art. 12.
112   *Id.* at Art. 13.
113   *Id.* at Art. 15(2)(a)&(b).
114   *Id.* at Art. 16.
115   *Id.* at Art.21.
116   *Id.* at Art.23(1).
117   *Id.* at Art.26(1).

of their own social, economic, cultural and political institutions.[118]

The Convention is divided into ten parts. Part 1 formulates the general policy. Part of the positive side of the convention is that it enjoins governments to protect the rights of peoples regarded as indigenous peoples.[119] Such rights include amongst others, promotion of the social, economic and cultural rights of these peoples with emphasis on social, cultural identity, customs, traditions and their institutions.[120]

The convention also guarantees a full measure of human rights and fundamental freedom for the indigenous peoples without hindrance.[121] The convention states that indigenous peoples have the right to decide their own priorities for the purpose of developing their lives, beliefs, institutions and spiritual well-being; and to exercise control over their own economic, social and cultural development.[122] The convention guarantees indigenous peoples rights to their customs or customary law and institutions as long as such customs and laws are not in conflict with the fundamental rights defined by the national legal systems.[123]

Part II of the convention deals with the land. The convention advocates that the rights of ownership and possession of the peoples concern over the land which they traditionally occupy shall be recognized.[124] Governments have the obligation to guarantee effective protection of the indigenous peoples' right of ownership and possession.[125] The right shall also cover the natural resources pertaining to the lands[126] and the governments' need to consult these peoples before they can explore or exploit the said resources.[127]

---

118   Convention Concerning Indigenous and Tribal Peoples in Independent Countries, adopted June 27, 1989, 169 I.L.O. 1989, Art. 1(b), 28 I.L.M. 1382 (entered into force Sept. 5, 1991), *available at* http://www.unhchr.ch/html/menu3/b/62.htm. Now ratified by 22 countries, mostly from Latin America. For details see ILOLEX Database of International Labour Standards *available at* www.ilo.org/ilolex/english/newratframeE.htm.

119   *Id.* at Art. 2(1).

120   *Id.* at Art. 2(2)(b).

121   *Id.* at Art. 3(1).

122   *Id.* at Art. 7(1).

123   *Id.* at Art. 8(2).

124   *Id.* at Art. 14(1).

125   *Id.* at Art. 14(2).

126   *Id.* at Art. 15(1).

127   *Id.* at Art. 15(2).

While the peoples could be relocated on genuine grounds, the people have the right to return to their traditional lands as soon as the grounds for relocation cease to exist.[128]

Part III deals with recruitment and conditions of employment and states that the government should in its national laws and regulations make provisions for recruitment and conditions of employment of workers belonging to indigenous peoples just like other workers in general.[129]

Part IV of the convention deals with vocational training, handicrafts and rural industries and states that indigenous peoples shall enjoy opportunities in respect of vocational training measures just like other citizens[130] and whenever such training does not meet the special needs of the indigenous peoples, special training programs should be arranged for these peoples,[131] and in doing so, the economic environment, social and cultural conditions and practical needs of the indigenous peoples concerned should be put into consideration.[132]

Part V deals with social security and health and states that the government should provide adequate health services to the indigenous peoples and provide them with resources that will enable them to fashion a health service they can control.[133]

Part VI deals with education and means of communication and states that indigenous peoples should be given the opportunity to acquire education at all levels just like other citizens.[134] And such education shall incorporate their histories, their knowledge and technologies, their value systems and their further social, economic and cultural aspirations.[135] Thus, the government shall recognize the rights of indigenous peoples to establish their own educational institutions and facilities but such institutions must meet minimum standards.[136] The Convention further stressed that measures

---

128   *Id.* at Art. 16(3).
129   *Id.* at Art. 20(1).
130   *Id.* at Art. 21.
131   *Id.* at Art. 22(2).
132   *Id.* at Art. 22(3).
133   *Id.* at Art. 25.
134   *Id.* at Art. 26.
135   *Id.* at Art. 27(1).
136   *Id.* at Art 27(3).

should be taken to preserve and promote the development and practice of such indigenous peoples' languages.[137] Measures by the government shall be appropriate to the traditions and cultures of indigenous peoples.[138]

Part VIII deals with administration and states that the government should ensure that agencies or other appropriate mechanisms exist to administer the programs affecting indigenous peoples.[139]

Part IX deals with general provisions and states that the implementation of this convention shall be determined according to the characteristics of each country.[140] The convention recognizes the cultural and other specificities of indigenous peoples and also emphasizes that indigenous peoples are consulted and allowed to participate in issues that affect them. Indigenous peoples also have the right to decide their own priorities for the process of development as it affects their lives, beliefs, institutions and spiritual well-being and the lands they occupy or otherwise use, and to exercise control over their economic, social and cultural development.[141]

The provisions of Convention No. 169 are compatible with that of the United Nations Declaration on the Rights of Indigenous Peoples. Victor Montejo has pointed out that Convention 169 should be used as a negotiation tool for a peaceful solution to land problems and not to be used as a weapon for confrontation.[142]

ILO Convention No. 169 has a lot of significance among which it created treaty obligations among the states that ratified it. Anaya also pointed out that emergence of Convention No. 169 is a manifestation of the mobilization of social forces through the human rights frame of contemporary international system.[143]

---

137   *Id.* at Art. 28(3).

138   *Id.* at Art. 30.

139   *Id.* at Art. 33(1).

140   *Id.* at Art. 34.

141   *Id.* at Art. 7(1).

142   Victor Montejo, *Convention 169 and the Implementation of the Peace Accord in Guatemala,* 10.4 THE JOURNAL OF THE SOUTH AND MESO AMERICAN INDIAN RIGHTS CENTER (SAIIC) (Fall, 1997),   http://www.saiic.nativeweb.org/ayn/guatilo.html.

143   Anaya, *supra* note 95, at 72.

2.3.1.4 Comparative Analysis of Conventions No. 107 and No. 169

The International Labor Organization (ILO)[144] is concerned with protecting the rights of indigenous peoples and it incorporates the recommendations of indigenous organizations.[145] Although Convention No. 169 is a revision of Convention No. 107, Convention 169 makes a clear departure from the principle of integration advocated by Convention No. 107. It has been pointed out that the integration policy is a destructive concept as it is believed that it will extinguish the ways of life of the indigenous people which are different from those of the dominant society and the implication of this is that it will prevent the indigenous people from enjoying the strong protections embedded in some parts of the Convention.[146]

Anaya pointed out that Convention No.169 could be seen as a manifestation of the movement towards responsiveness to indigenous peoples' demands through international law.[147] Convention No. 169 is also different from the notion of Convention No.107 that the rights and obligations in the Convention are of a temporary nature which will diminish as the social, economic and political conditions of the indigenous people improve or when they are integrated into the dominant society.

While Convention No. 107 prohibits discrimination against indigenous peoples, Convention No. 169 advocates both against discrimination and for the peoples' right to determine their priorities as it affect their lives, beliefs, institutions and spiritual well-being and the land they occupy or otherwise use.[148] Convention No. 169 also removed from the Convention 107 condition that states that indigenous peoples must live more in conformity with the social, economic and cultural institutions "of that time". "Of that time" is the key phrase that was eliminated by Convention No.169. In a nutshell, Convention No. 107 supported assimilation and integration while Convention No. 169 supported self-determination.

---

144   ILO Convention 107, *supra* note 100.

145   ILO Convention No. 169, *supra* note 118.

146   Report of the Meeting of Experts, Para, 46 reprinted in: Partial Revision of the Indigenous and Tribal Population Convention, 1957 (No. 107); Report 6(1), International Labour Conference, 75th Sess. 1988, 100-118.

147   Anaya, *supra* note 95, at 59.

148   ILO Convention No. 169, *supra* note 118, at Art. 7.

2.3.1.5 Article 27: International Covenant on Civil and Political Rights (ICCPR) (1966)

The International Covenant on Civil and Political Rights (ICCPR) has only one specific provision on minority rights. It is Article 27 and it is a legally binding provision which confers on persons belonging to ethnic, religious or linguistic minorities the right to profess their own religion or to use their own language.[149] The Human Rights Committee (HRC) contends that Article 27 establishes and recognizes rights conferred on individuals belonging to minority groups which is distinct from and additional to all the rights to which all citizens can enjoy.[150] To douse the confusion of state about what their obligations are, Article 2(1) provides that states must "respect and ensure to all individuals within its territory and subject to its jurisdiction the rights recognized in the present Covenant, without distinction of any kind, such as race, color, sex, language, religion, political or other opinion, national or social origin, property, birth or other status." Thus, while Article 27 merely states that people must not be denied this right, it is the provisions of Article 2(1) that place the obligation on the state.

The HRC pointed out that self–determination is not a right recognized under the Optional Protocol, while rights under Article 27 of ICCPR are recognizable under Part III of the Covenant and also recognized under the Optional Protocol.[151] The HRC further pointed out that Article 27 cannot be enjoyed in a manner that is inconsistent with the provisions of the Covenant and concluded that the provision of Article 27 imposes specific obligations on the states parties. The article is aimed at ensuring survival and continued development of the cultural, religious and social identity of the minority concerned.

The significance on Article 27 of ICCPR, therefore, is that it gives minority religions protected status and it prohibits governments from imposing an official religion.

---

149   International Covenant on Civil and Political Rights Art. 27, adopted and opened for signature, ratification and accession by UN General Assembly Resolution 2200A(XXI) of 16 December 1996.

150   Human Rights Committee, General Comment 23, Article 27 (Fiftieth session, 1994), Compilation of General Comments and General Recommendations adopted by Human Rights Treaty Bodies, U.N. Doc. HRI/GEN/1/Rev.1 at 38 [hereinafter HRC General Comment on Art. 27].

151   *Id.*

It must also be noted that Article 1 of ICCPR grants all people the right to self-determination by virtue of which they can determine their political status and freely pursue their economic, social and cultural development. By implication, this right also covers indigenous peoples.

2.3.2 Other Instruments Supporting Indigenous Peoples' Rights

One of the other instruments on indigenous peoples' rights is the **Universal Declaration of Human Rights (UDHR)**[152] which proclaims that everybody is entitled to the rights in the declaration "without distinction of any kind, such as race, color, sex, language, religion, political or other opinion, national or social origin, property, birth or other status."[153] The **Convention on the Prevention and Punishment of the Crime of Genocide** is another instrument that protects the interest of indigenous peoples as evidenced in its provisions which states that the purpose of the convention is to prevent the destruction of racial, national, linguistic, religious or political groups.[154]

The **International Covenant on Economic, Social and Cultural Rights** not only describes the basic economic, social, and cultural rights of individuals, but has provisions for collective rights and protects the right of self-determination of all peoples.[155]

The **Convention on the Elimination of All Forms of Racial Discrimination** protects people of all races from any form of discrimination and by implication the indigenous peoples are inclusive.[156] The **Convention on the Rights of the Child**[157] is another instrument supporting the indigenous peoples' cause. It states that children of minorities or indigenous origin shall

---

152   Adopted and proclaimed by General Assembly Resolution 217 A (III) of 10 December 1948.

153   *Id.* at Art. 2.

154   Convention on the Prevention and Punishment of the Crime of Genocide, 78 U.N.T.S. 277, entered into force Jan. 12, 1951. Art.1.

155   International Covenant on Economic, Social and Cultural Rights, G.A. res. 2200A (XXI), 21 U.N.GAOR Supp. (No. 16) at 49, U.N. Doc. A/6316 (1966), 993 U.N.T.S. 3, Art. 1, entered into force Jan. 3, 1976, *available at* http://www1.umn.edu/humanrts/instree/b2esc. htm or http://www.unhchr.ch/ html/ menu3/b/a_cescr.htm.

156   Convention on the Elimination of All Forms of Racial Discrimination, art. 1, (1996).

157   Convention on the Rights of the Child, adopted and opened for signature, ratification and accession by General Assembly Resolution 44/25 of 20 November 1989, Art. 29(d), (1990) Art.30, *available at* http://www2.ohchr.org/english/law/crc.htm.

not be denied the right to their own culture, religion or language.[158]

Another instrument is the **Vienna Declaration and Programme of Action**[159] which recognizes the inherent dignity and the unique contribution of indigenous peoples to the development and plurality of society and strongly reaffirms the commitment of the international community to their economic, social and cultural well-being.[160]

The **Durban Declaration and Programme of Action**[161] is the first United Nations document that uses the phrase 'Indigenous Peoples" rather than "Indigenous People." This shows the enormous support for collective rights. The declaration also enjoins nation states to eradicate racial discrimination and other forms of intolerance towards indigenous peoples and individuals either directly or indirectly.[162]

The above instruments are part of the efforts made to show concern for the indigenous peoples' cause.

2.4 CUSTOMARY INTERNATIONAL LAW

The study of rights and status of indigenous peoples will not be thorough without an examination of customary international law.

Customary international law is an important part of international law. The Statute of the International Court of Justice[163] listed customary international law in Article 38(1)(b) as one of the sources of international law. In defining international custom, Ian Brownlie states the following: "Article 38 refers to 'international custom, as evidence of a general practice accepted as law,' and Brierly remarks that "what is sought for is a general recognition

---

158   *Id.*

159   Vienna Declaration and Program of Action, adopted by the World Conference on Human Rights in Vienna on 25 June 1993.

160   *Id.* at Art. 20.

161   Report of the World Conference Against Racism, Racial Discrimination, Xenophobia and Related Intolerance, General Assembly, Programme of Action, agenda item 9, adopted on September 8, 2001 in Durban, South Africa, U.N. Doc. A/CONF.189/5 (2001) *available at* http://www.unhchr.ch/huridocda/ huridoca.nsf/(Symbol)/A.Conf.189.12. En?Opendocument.

162   *Id.*, at para.19.

163   Statute of the International Court of Justice. Art. 38(1).

among states of a certain practice as obligatory."[164] Ingredients of customary international law are practice, repetition, *opinio juris sive neccessitatis* and international organizations practice.[165] State practice which is one of the most important ingredients of customary international law can be evidenced by many different types of documents, including domestic legislation, regulations, treaties, judicial decisions, diplomatic communications, and the practice of non-governmental organizations (NGOs). *Opinio juris*, another vital ingredient, can be evidenced by judicial decisions, executive communications and other documents.[166] Therefore, for a customary law rule to become an international customary law, such rule must have been continually or repeatedly practiced over a considerable period of time and it must be consistent with the prevailing international law and the practice must be generally recognized by other states.[167]

As stated above, the ICJ statutes have defined customary law as "international custom, evidencing general practice accepted as law."[168] The two major elements of customary international law are the consistent practice of a number of states consented to by others, and an understanding that the practice is required by or consistent with the prevailing law, *opinio juris*.[169] It had been reiterated by the International Court of Justice that for state practice to be in conformity with international law there are two conditions that must be fulfilled. The act concerned must be a settled practice and it must be carried out in such a way as to be evidence of a belief that this practice is rendered obligatory by the existence of law requiring it.[170] According to Siegfried Wiessner, [171] traditional international law permitted

---

164   IAN BROWNLIE, PRINCIPLES OF PUBLIC INTERNATIONAL LAW 4   (Oxford: Clarendon Press, 1998) citing JAMES L. BRIERLY, THE LAW OF NATIONS 61 (6th ed.,1963).

165   MICHAEL BYERS, CUSTOM, POWER AND THE POWER OF RULES: INTERNATIONAL RELATIONS AND CUSTOMARY INTERNATIONAL LAW 160 (Cambridge University Press, 1998).

166   ROSALYN HIGGINS & MAURICE FLORY, TERRORISM AND INTERNATIONAL LAW 58 (Routledge, 1997).

167   MARK VILLIGER. CUSTOMARY INTERNATIONAL LAW AND TREATIES 3 (Boston 1985).

168   ICJ Statute, *supra* note 96, at Art. 38.

169   PARRY AND GRANT ENCYCLOPAEDIC DICTIONARY OF INTERNATIONAL LAW 109 (2nd ed. 2003).

170   ICJ Statute, *supra* note 96; North Sea Continental Shelf (F.R.G. V Den./Neth.) 4, 41; MICHAEL REISMAN, MAHNOUSH ARSANJANI, SIEGFRIED WIESSNER, AND GAYL WESTERMAN. INTERNATIONAL LAW IN CONTEMPORARY PERSPECTIVE 15 (NY: Foundation Press 2004).

171   Wiessner, *supra* note 42, at 98.

only nation-states to act and hold legal rights and duties. Wiessner pointed out that there are several international instruments prohibiting all forms of racial discrimination, genocide and torture; treaties ensuring freedom and those that guarantee self-determination of peoples.[172] There are, however, questions as to whether these protections are sufficient to meet the needs of indigenous people. Wiessner's article showed that virtually all indigenous peoples share a common set of problems resulting from the tortured relationship between the conqueror and the conquered.

Oguamanan has also points out in his article[173] multi-juridical aspects of the developments leading to the emergence of customary international law and this includes, but is not limited to, efforts of the International Labor Organization (ILO) whereby it championed the institutional and international legal initiative that deals with every aspect of the indigenous peoples question. He also refers to the establishment of the United Nations Permanent Forum on Indigenous Issues (UNPFII) as another high point of international law on indigenous peoples.

It is a fact that most people purporting to be indigenous virtually always suffered the same treatment. An example of such is the Indians whose experience is not different from what other indigenous peoples have gone through. The indigenous peoples always have their land taken away most often by force. The conqueror's way of life is usually imposed on the conquered and this is evident in most of the colonized territories. This imposition which could be cultural or political usually continued even after the departure of the conquerors; and the political independence of the indigenous peoples is usually silenced by the dominant society. All the above stated factors always lead to extreme poverty, diseases and despair for the indigenous peoples.

The author strongly supports Wiessner's observation that as good as the international human rights instruments are, there are still some vital elements missing. In other words, there should be a specific protection of the distinctive cultural and group identity of indigenous peoples. For instance, the 1966 covenants do not make any provisions for property rights, and the protection of sacred objects was not specific as it was hidden under the right to free exercise

---

172   Convention on the Elimination of All Forms of Racial Discrimination, and Convention on the Prevention and Punishment of the Crime of Genocide, *available at* http://www.unhchr.ch/html/menu3/b/d_icerd.htm.

173   Chidi Oguamanan, *Indigenous Peoples and International Law: The Making of a Regime.* 30 QUEEN'S L.J 363 (2004).

of religion.[174] A major reason for such protection is the need for the indigenous peoples not to lose their lands because of their economic and spiritual ties to such lands. Such spiritual ties could be due to their age long religion, their ancestral burial grounds or cemetery, while the economic tie could be due to the occupation of the indigenous people. For instance, farmers and fishermen will value their land immensely because it is the source of their means of survival.

The frustration of the indigenous peoples could be deduced from the statement of Ailton Krenak where he stated that the:

> Government took our land … They wanted to give us another place for the (indigenous) people to live and to re-establish our existence, to speak to our Gods, to speak to our nature, to weave our lives, is where our God created us… It is useless for the government to put us in a very beautiful place, in a very good place with a lot of hunting and a lot of fish….We can continue dying and we dying insisting that there is possibility of life for us outside of where the origin of our life is. Respect our place of living, do not degrade our living condition, respect this life. We have no arms to cause pressure, the only thing we have is the right to cry for our dignity and the need to live in our land.[175]

The above statement clearly portrays the feeling and the grief that has been experienced by the indigenous peoples. It could be deduced that their lands, cultures, ways of life and religion has become part of them and that they are not ready to trade them for anything. Although one could see them as conservatives who are not ready for any change, their reasons for preferring their lands goes beyond the issue of being a conservative. The statement goes to show just a little of what indigenous peoples go through, and most times their voices are never heard unless the problem receives international attention.

In as much as the indigenous peoples' issue is a sensitive one, there is a dearth of decided cases or judicial authorities on this subject in Africa. For the purpose of this chapter, foreign judicial authorities shall be examined. This is to serve as working principles for African courts in their

---

174   International Covenant on Civil and Political Rights, *supra* note 149, at Article 49.

175   Ailton Krenak, World Commission on Environment and Development (WCED) public hearing, Sao Paulo (Oct. 28-29, 1985), quoted in Our Common Future: Report of the World Commission on Environment and Development, at A/42/427(1987).

adjudication of indigenous peoples' cases. Due to the dearth of decided cases on indigenous peoples study in Africa and particularly in Nigeria, the author will examine cases and court decisions from Australia, Canada, South-Africa and United States of America. For instance, Australia is home to the Koori in New South Wales and Victoria, the Murri in Queensland, and the Nunga in Southern South Australia; the Inuits inhabit Canada and the United States is the native home of the American Indians to mention a few. The issues of these peoples are very much the same.

The author will shed more light on customary international law by examining state practice, particularly judicial decisions, to see if there are those that establish indigenous peoples' rights. Legislations and executive decrees regarding indigenous rights will also be examined. Decided cases in Australia, Canada and South Africa will be inquired into by the author. The above countries were chosen because of their rich history with indigenous peoples. The assessments of the decided cases follow below.

2.4.1 Case Law in Australia

Professor Wiessner has pointed out in his article that the *Mabo* case marked a revolutionary departure from the *terra nullius* doctrine.[176]

The case of **Mabo v. Queensland**[177] is one of the leading *loci classici* on indigenous peoples' issues. It was the case that brought the plight of the indigenous peoples of Australia to the limelight. Before 1992, Australian law did not recognize traditional indigenous or Aboriginal rights to land.[178] It was through the *Mabo* case that Aboriginal rights were finally recognized by the Australian legal system. The *Mabo* case represents a landmark in the judicial treatment of native Australians. The decision paved the way for future litigation of native land claims by creating a binding legal precedent from the highest Australian authority.[179] According to Manwaring, this case has implications for non-Aboriginal Australians as well, therefore companies and individuals may now face native title claims against land in which they

---

176   Wiessner, *supra* note 42, at 72.

177   Mabo v. Queensland II (1992) 175 C.L.R. 1 (Austl.).

178   D. L. Ritter, *An Overview of the Recognition of Native Title in the Commonwealth of Australia,* 5 LEGAL ISSUES ON BURMA J. (April 2000), *available at* http://www.burmalibrary. org/docs/LIOB05-Ritter.htm.

179   Melissa Manwarring, *A Small Step or a Giant Leap? The Implications of Australia's First Judicial Recognition of Indigenous Land Rights: Mabo and Others v. State of Queensland,* 107 A.L.R. 177, 187 (1992).

already have or are considering acquiring an interest.[180]

The *Mabo* case established some cogent principles by stating the conditions to be met before a native title could exist. These conditions are that:

(1) There must be an indigenous group who held native title for the country in question at the time of sovereignty.
(2) That group must have had a continuing traditional connection to their country, and such connection must be unbroken to the present day; and
(3) The group's connection to the land must remain rooted in tradition.

The only unfavorable aspect of the court holding was the recognition by the court that native title could be extinguished by an act of government demonstrating a clear and plain intention to extinguish native title. The case of *Mabo v. Queensland* has reversed prior Australian jurisprudence and official policy and it now recognizes "native title" which is a right of property based on indigenous peoples customary land tenure.

The case of ***Members of the Yorta Aboriginal Community v. Victoria1 & Ors***[181] held that it is clear through available evidence that by 1881 the claimant group who seeks to establish native title is no longer in possession of its tribal lands and had, by force of the circumstances in which it found itself, ceased to observe those laws and customs based on traditions which might otherwise have provided a basis for the present native title claim; and the dispossession of the original inhabitants and their descendants has continued through to the present time. Although many members of the claimant group resides within the claimed area, many do not. The Australian High Court stated that no group or individual has been shown to occupy any part of the land in the sense that the original inhabitants can be said to have occupied it. The Court concluded by holding that the claimant group clearly fails *Toohey's* test of occupation by a traditional society now and at the time of annexation which states that modification of traditional society cannot extinguish traditional title. Traditional title arises from the fact of occupation, not the occupation of a particular kind of society or way of life. So long as occupation by a traditional society is established now and at

---

180   *Id.* at 189.
181   194 A.L.R. 538, [2002] HCA 58, (12 December 2002) – High Court Decision.

the time of annexation, traditional rights exist. Thus, an indigenous society cannot, as it were, surrender its rights by modifying its way of life. This case buttressed the role that 'first inhabitants" elements play in determining native title to land.

2.4.2 Case Law in Canada

Canada in its Charter of Rights and Freedom[182] pointed out that "every individual is equal before and under the law and has the right to the equal protection and equal benefit of the law without discrimination and, in particular, without discrimination based on race, national or ethnic origin, color, religion, sex, age or mental or physical disability.[183] This Charter is part of the Constitution of Canada and this makes it an important law in Canada; while the government may limit the rights provided by the Charter, such limitation must be and be seen to be reasonable and justified.[184] The Canadian Charter further stated that the guarantee of certain rights and freedoms shall not be interpreted to abrogate or derogate from any aboriginal, treaty or other rights and freedom that concerns the aboriginal peoples of Canada, and this includes:

(a) any rights or freedoms that have been recognized in the Royal proclamation of October 7, 1763; and
(b) any rights or freedoms that now exist by way of land claims agreements or may be so acquired.[185]

The Charter also recognized and affirmed the existing aboriginal and treaty rights of the aboriginal people of Canada.[186] The following are examples of Canadian decided cases on the issue of indigenous peoples' rights.

The case of *Cote et al. v. The Queen*[187] established that the accused in the case are not obliged to establish aboriginal title over the land in question whether at common law or under the Royal Proclamation, 1763, in order to establish an aboriginal right to fish under S. 35(1) of the Constitution

---

182   Canadian Charter of Rights and Freedoms, Part I of the Constitution Act, 1982, being Schedule B to the Canada Act 1982, ch. 11, §7 (U.K.).
183   *Id.* at Art. 15(1).
184   *Id.* at Art.1.
185   *Id.* at Art. 25.
186   *Id.* at Art. 35(1).
187   (1996) 3 S.C.R. 139.

Act, 1982. It was stated that the intervention of French sovereignty over the lands in question does not negate the existence of aboriginal rights. The court held that Section 35 would fail to achieve its purpose of preserving the integral and defining features of distinctive aboriginal societies if it only protected those which were legally recognized by European colonizers. In the case the aboriginal right claimed is the right to fish for food within the controlled zone. This right exists because it was part of a practice, custom or tradition, which prior to contact with the Europeans, was an integral part of the distinctive aboriginal society of the Algonquin people and there is continuity with a particular practice integral to the aboriginal community today. In view of this fact, the aboriginal right could not be negated by the act of French sovereignty over the land.

In the case of **Delgamuukw v. British Columbia**,[188] the court reiterated its existing tests for Aboriginal rights claims relating to activities on the land. The tests reiterated and established by the court[189] are as follows:

(1) The land must have been occupied prior to sovereignty; this becomes necessary because the Aboriginal title is a burden on the crown's title, which was gained only upon the crown's assertion of sovereignty.[190] Both the common law and the Aboriginal perspective on land are relevant for purposes of establishing occupancy. This condition pointed out that the fact of physical occupation proves legal possession of the land and also gives title to it.[191]

(2) There must be continuity between present and pre-sovereign occupation. The claiming group does not necessarily need to establish an unbroken chain of continuity, but rather "substantial maintenance of their connection with the land.[192]

(3) Occupation must have been exclusive at sovereignty. This is also proved by reference to both common law and Aboriginal perspectives. It was held that the test for exclusive occupation in Aboriginal title claims must consider the context of the Aboriginal

188   (1997) 153 DLR (4th) 193.

189   Mary C. Hurley, *Aboriginal Title: The Supreme Court of Canada Decision in Delgamuukw v. British Columbia*, (Parliamentary Research Branch, 1998, rev. February 2000).

190   *Id.* at par. 144-145.

191   *Id.* at par. 146-151.

192   *Id.* at par. 152-154.

society in question at sovereignty; such exclusivity requirement need not preclude the possibility of joint title shared between two or more Aboriginal nations.[193]

2.4.3 Case Law in South Africa

In the case of ***Alexkor Ltd. and Another v. Richtersveld Community and Others***[194] the land in question was inhabited by first respondent, the Richtersveld Community, whose members contended that they had a claim to the land and its natural resources. They had been dispossessed of this immovable property after June 19, 1913, as a result of racially discriminatory laws or practices. The Constitutional Court examined the nature of Richtersveld's title, and concluded that the real character of the title that the community possessed in the subject land was a right of communal ownership under indigenous law. It was held that the content of that right included the right to exclusive occupation and use of the subject land by members of the community. The content of that right also included the right to exclusive occupation and use of the subject land for grazing and hunting and to exploit its natural resources, above and beneath its surface. The court stated that prior to annexation the Richtersveld Community had a right of ownership in the subject land under indigenous law. The court further held that annexation did not extinguish the land rights of the Richtersveld Community. The court used the case to reiterate the fact that indigenous rights to private property in a conquered territory were recognized and protected.

2.4.4 Case Law in Botswana

In Botswana, Africa, the High Court on December 13, 2006, ruled that the indigenous peoples of the Kalahari Desert have been wrongfully deprived of their possessions, including the land where their ancestors may have hunted and gathered for more than 20,000 years.[195] The ruling not only opened the door for an unprecedented restoration of semi-nomads to their ancient practices, but also laid another brick in the legal framework of recognized indigenous rights that has spread from the United States in the

---

193   *Id.* at par. 155.
194   2003 SACLR LEXIS 79.
195   Mutume, *supra* note 74, at 2.

1950s to Australia, New Zealand, Canada and the world.[196]

All of the cases reviewed deal specifically with indigenous peoples' issues and establish some vital conditions that are needed to prove an aboriginal or native title. The cases were very particular about biological descent from the indigenous people and the recognition of such group's membership by the elders or persons enjoying traditional authority. The cases also established that groups agitating for indigenous people's status must acknowledge and continue to acknowledge the laws. The cases equally established that evidence of change in indigenous community's traditional laws and customs will not be fatal to a claim for native title. The cases established that native title arises from the fact of occupation, thus as long as occupation by a traditional society could be established now and at the time of annexation traditional rights existed.

2.4.5 Legislation and Executive Decrees Supporting Indigenous Peoples in Asia

The indigenous peoples of Asia include all or part of those groups that are officially distinguished from the society of the national majority and these include the aboriginal tribes of Taiwan, the aborigines of Malaysia, the Hill tribes of Thailand, the indigenous cultural communities of the Philippines, the isolated and alien peoples of Indonesia, the minority nationalities of China, the natives of Malaysia Borneo and the scheduled tribes of India.[197]

Indigenous peoples of Asia are diverse and range from small communities of hunters and gatherers to larger scale groups that engaged in struggles for autonomy and self-determination and they reside in countries such as Bangladesh, Burma, India and Thailand.[198]

The existence of legal vacuums in many Asian countries provisions which fail to recognize indigenous title derived from ancestral possession and use, or to recognize their traditional forms of cultivation and herding as

---

196   Jerry Reynold, *Africa's Indigenous San in Court, Now Face Regulations*, KNIGHT RIDDER/TRIBUNE BUSINESS NEWS (Washington, Jan 3, 2007), at 1.

197   FOREST AND INDIGENOUS PEOPLES OF ASIA 4 (Minority Rights Group International, ed. 98/4, 1999).

198   Robert K. Hitchcock, *Human Rights and Indigenous Peoples in Africa and Asia, in* HUMAN RIGHTS AND DIVERSITY: AREA STUDIES REVISITED, 205, 214 (David P. Forsythe & Patrice C. McMahon, eds., University of Nebraska Press, 2003).

sustainable forms of production, is another major reason for the violation of indigenous peoples' land and resource rights.

It must be noted that several efforts were made to address the legal vacuums and the results of these are the enactment of the Adivasis Forest Rights Act which was adopted by India in 2006. This Act mandates the state to ensure the rights of people of scheduled tribes over the forest lands provided that such tribes could prove that that they were living in the same forest prior to December 13, 2005; and in the case of other forest dwellers they must be able to prove that they were living in the same forest areas since before three generations or seventy-five years ago. Another effort made to address the legal vacuum is the coming into existence of the 1997 Indigenous Peoples Rights Act in the Philippines which was enacted to recognize, protect and promote the rights of indigenous cultural communities and indigenous peoples. The act affirmed that property rights within the ancestral domains already existing and or vested upon effectivity of the act shall be recognized and respected;[199] And the enactment of the Land Rights Act in Cambodia which made provisions for collective land ownership rights to indigenous communities[200] is another step taken to address the legal vacuum in respect of indigenous peoples' rights. However as specific as these legislations are, there are serious problems with their effective implementation.

In an effort to find a lasting solution to this raging problem, several recommendations have been proffered. Some of these are as follows. Arrangements should be made to provide for indigenous peoples' self-government in issues that affect them directly as well as various safeguards with relation to their cultures.

Also, peace accords between various insurgent groups and the governments of Bangladesh (in relation to the Chittagong Hill Tracts), India (in the case of Nagaland), or Indonesia (in the case of Western Papua) are constructive arrangements seeking to put an end to decades of conflicts through recognition of an autonomous status. These peace efforts as practicable as they look are being frustrated by lack of implementation of the peace agreement, or as a result of conflicting government policies which include militarization, internal migration and land dispossession.

James Anaya has pointed out that evidence of indigenous people

---

199   The Indigenous Peoples Rights Act of 1997, Republic Act No. 8371. Sec. 56.

200   DIANA VINDING. THE INDIGENOUS WORLD 337 (IWGIA 2005).

traditional and customary land tenure can be established by qualified experts and academic opinion as well as by objective facts that can be discerned from the oral accounts and documentation produced by the indigenous communities concerned.[201]

Anaya also stated that in most instances indigenous peoples' own knowledge provide the most reliable proof of the existence of property rights entitled to protection under a state's legal system.[202] He has also suggested that the indigenous groups claiming   property rights in land should not be denied by excluding or ignoring evidence derived from the culture and traditions of the indigenous group or community itself.

Violation of these indigenous peoples' rights will amount to the perpetuation of the long history of discrimination against indigenous peoples with regard to the use of their lands and natural resources.

The U.N. Committee on the Elimination of Discrimination (CERD) has pertinently pointed out that "in many regions of the world indigenous peoples have been, and are still being, discriminated against, deprived of their human rights and fundamental freedoms… and have lost their land and resources to colonists, commercial companies and state enterprises."[203]

2.4.6 Legislation and Executive Decrees in United States, Canada and Colombia

The United States Congress in 1988 authorized a project called "self-governance" which transferred programs and services hitherto handled by the Bureau of Indian Affairs to the tribes themselves. The Congress added Title III[204] to the Indian Self-Determination and Education Assistance Act (P.L 93-638); this stops federal domination of Indian programs.[205]

---

201   James Anaya and Robert A. Williams, Jr., *The Protection of Indigenous People's Right Over Lands and Natural Resources Under the Inter-American Human Rights System*. 14 Harv. Hum. Rts. J. 33 (2001).

202   *Id.* at 9.

203   Committee on the Elimination of Racial Discrimination, General Recommendation XXIII on Indigenous Peoples, adopted at the committee's 1234th meeting, 18 August 1997, CERD/C51/Misc.13/Rev., para.3 (1977).

204   Indian Self-Determination Act Amendments of 1988, P.L. 199-472, *available at* http://64.58.34.34/osg/Default.aspx?Info=BackGroundInformation.

205   *Id.*

In 1993, the government of Canada and the government of Yukon signed an umbrella final agreement which allows self-governing Yukon First Nations (SGFFNs) to make decisions governing their lands, resources, government and programs.[206] The Canadian Charter also recognized rights by way of land claim agreements. Canada on December 22, 1992, signed the agreement, amongst others, that provides negotiation of agreements on self-government.[207] The rights in the settlement include, amongst others, full ownership of certain lands in the area covered by the settlement, financial compensation, resource revenue sharing and specific measures for economic development.[208]

The Colombia Constitution also recognizes the communal land rights of ethnic groups and states that such land is unseizable.[209]

All the legislation and judicial decisions revealed that there are efforts made by nation states to come up with indigenous peoples' rights under customary international law. The most visible of these rights are rights to land and natural resources; and the right to self-determination. Federico Lenzerini pointed out that there is a tremendous number of significant international practices recognizing indigenous peoples' rights and this is accompanied and confirmed by state practices developed at domestic level by countries that have indigenous peoples in their territories.[210] Some of the key provisions in the United Nations Declaration of the Rights of Indigenous Peoples may be regarded as corresponding to established principles of general international law.[211] There has been evidence of state practice concerning indigenous peoples which are binding based on the law undergirding them; such state practice reveals indigenous peoples as a concern of customary international law.[212]

---

206   Building the Future: Yukon First Nation Self-Government, *available at* http://www.ayc.yk.ca/user/image/building_the_future_yukon_first_nation_self-government.pdf.

207   Gwich' in Comprehensive Land Claim Agreement (Annual Report of the Implementation Committee. April 11, 1999- March 31, 2000), *available at* http://www.ainc-inac.gc.ca/al/ldc/ccl/fagr/gwich/gwi/gwi-eng.pdf.

208   SHAUNNAGH DORSETT & LEE GODDEN, A GUIDE TO OVERSEAS PRECEDENTS OF RELEVANCE TO NATIVE TITLE 26 (Aboriginal Studies Press 1998).

209   Text of the Constitution of Colombia (1991). Art. 63, *available at* http://confinder.richmond.edu/admin/ docs/colombia_const2.pdf.

210   International Law Association, *supra* note 9, at 49.

211   *Id.* at 43.

212   *Id.* at 51.

2.5 BUILD-UP TO THE UNITED NATIONS DECLARATION ON THE RIGHTS OF INDIGENOUS PEOPLES

In 1945, the Charter of the United Nations affirmed fundamental human rights and the dignity and worth of the human person, including those of the inhabitants of non-self-governing territories. Also, in 1948 the Universal Declaration of Human Rights, a part of international customary law, gives recognition to equal rights and affirms the right of all peoples to participate in cultural and economic life. Trusteeships were set up to protect indigenous peoples in the overseas former territories of defeated powers, and the colonial states gave a commitment to promote the well-being of the colonized. The indigenous populations within sovereign member nations, however, are not specifically covered by these provisions.

In 1993-94, the United Nations (expert) Working Group on Indigenous Populations produced its revised draft Declaration on the Right of Indigenous Peoples, which was adopted by the UN Sub Commission on the Prevention of Discrimination and the Protection of Minorities. In 1995, the United Nations Human Rights Commission set up an inter-governmental working group to consider the revised draft declaration on the rights of indigenous peoples. Efforts of the United Nations, human rights organizations, governments and agencies also manifested themselves within the United Nations Permanent Forum on Indigenous Issues.[213]

Ambassador Louis D' Albert[214] who was in support of the draft declaration adoption stated in his address that part of the goals of the Human Right Council is to promote and protect the human rights and fundamental freedom of persons as stated in Resolution 62/51 and this fully includes the rights of the indigenous peoples. The council is guided by the principle of international dialogue and cooperation. The indigenous question is being discussed from different angles and different forums ranging from the question of mandate review to the agenda on the work of the council which proposed that the rights of indigenous peoples be included. There have been many propositions for the council to incorporate the rights of indigenous peoples in its work or agendas.

213   United Nations Permanent Forum on Indigenous Issues, Report on the Sixth Session, U.N. Doc. E/C.19/2007/12 (May 14-25, 2007).

214   President of the Human Right Council.

Ambassador D'Albert suggested that there is a need for complementary and cooperative work between the council and the forum. He believed the two should work jointly in an institutionalized way given our community of interest. He strongly believes this will help optimize the result achieved.

In June 2006 the United Nations Human Right Council adopted the draft declaration of the rights of indigenous peoples. The President of the Human Rights Council further appealed that the declaration be adopted and that the Permanent Forum should participate fully in the process.

Mr. José Ocampo,[215] also claimed that the indigenous peoples have now reached a stronger platform where they participate with a clear voice in United Nations and that it is through this dialogue by all concerned that success could be made. The Permanent Forum has been responding to global challenges of the kind that only the United Nations can confront and the forum stands at the center of the effort. In support of the indigenous peoples' agitation, the under-secretary claimed that no person would allow loss of its traditional knowledge. The agitation of the indigenous peoples is not about self-interest, it is about survival of humanity. He reiterates the determination of the Permanent Forum to implement the indigenous peoples' declaration.

The Forum focused on fundamental rights such as the right to land, territories and resources which are part of the essential rights in the declaration. Ocampo pointed out that indigenous people have a profound spiritual and material relationship attached to their lands on which they depend for spiritual and cultural survival. Indigenous sacred sites, indigenous traditional knowledge, indigenous religions, languages and ways of life are all tied to their land. He stated that most times indigenous peoples have been forcibly displaced from their traditional territories without any compensation or other means to sustain themselves and must join other migrants living fragile life in the cities or abroad. He reiterated the need for various governments in indigenous communities to address this issue. Contributions and reports of indigenous peoples' meetings, influential

---

215   Under-General Secretary for Economic and Social Affair and Coordinator of the Second International Decade of the World Indigenous People; *See* Statement by Mr. José Antonio Ocampo Under-Secretary-General for Economic and Social Affairs and Coordinator of the Second Decade of the World's Indigenous People to the Sixth Session of the United Nations Permanent Forum on Indigenous Issues, New York, May 14, 2007.

papers on land, territories and resources, the report of an extra meeting of the Convention on Biodiversity regime on benefit sharing and indigenous peoples' human rights, papers on the development and mono crop cultivation and its impact on indigenous peoples' territory and livelihoods were all evidence of the extensive studies and effort that had been made to resolve the indigenous peoples' issue. These documents pointed out the central importance of recognizing indigenous peoples' land rights including the establishing of benefit sharing regimes.

The efforts of agencies, indigenous organizations and various governments through incentives, implementation of norms and policy, which is a common challenge in public policies, were all tailored towards resolving the indigenous peoples' issues. He reiterated the problems faced in the effort to resolve the indigenous peoples' issues which include but are not limited to the financial and human resources problem, the lack of economic incentives, the incapacities in local communities and national institutions coupled with inappropriate laws and policies.

In its recommendation stated in the report on the sixth session for the economic and social development of the indigenous peoples, the Permanent Forum said the indigenous people should be allowed to participate in the development process. Reports from countries with indigenous peoples revealed that indigenous peoples are always excluded in the affairs of this type of things. Ocampo stated that it is a struggle for equality and equity that underlies the quest for human rights and development and he believes the issue of indigenous peoples is far from complete.

It was also reiterated at the session that the land, territories and related resources rights are of fundamental importance to indigenous peoples since they constitute the basis of their economic livelihood as well as the basis of their cultural, spiritual and social identity. It is the foundation of life and future of indigenous peoples all over the world. Acquisition of their land against their wishes, expropriation of their lands and extraction of their resources would have a devastating effect on the indigenous peoples' future, as this action may erode their future. The right to land and resources is a key demand of indigenous peoples all over the world, so they are, therefore, vehemently against laws that have no respect or regard for their land tenure systems.

While some indigenous peoples still live in rural areas, a large population is migrating to cities both voluntarily and involuntarily. One effort of the Permanent Forum resulted in the report on partnership for action and dignity. It was stated that the state should in accordance with international law take concerted positive steps to ensure respect of human rights and fundamental freedoms of indigenous people on the basis of equality and non-discrimination, and recognizing the value and diversity of their distinctive identities, cultures and social organizations.

Indigenous people were, however, shocked and disappointed at the General Assembly's decision to defer the adoption in November 2006. According to the chairperson, the declaration stands as one of the most extensively discussed and negotiated issues in the history of the United Nations with the full participation of indigenous peoples. The declaration represents the minimum standard for the survival, dignity and wellbeing of indigenous peoples. It is sad and pathetic that indigenous peoples lived in oppressive conditions and they are still the ones providing solutions to their devastated land, erosion and other problems. Concern was expressed that the only way the declaration could be adopted is if the Human Rights Council version is the one subjected to voting. The fate of the declaration was in the hands of the General Assembly and the governments that were represented at the session.

2.5.1 United Nations Declaration on the Rights of Indigenous Peoples

The draft declaration[216] served as a working document for several years until it was endorsed and adopted in 2007. On September 13, 2007, the United Nations General Assembly convincingly supported the protections for the human rights of indigenous peoples by adopting the United Nations Declaration on the Rights of Indigenous Peoples.[217] This action ended the contentious debate over the right to native peoples' lands and resources and their cultures and traditions. The United Nations Declaration on the Rights of Indigenous Peoples sets out the individual and collective rights of the world's 370 million native peoples.

The adoption of the Declaration on Rights of Indigenous Peoples was

---

216   Draft Declaration on the Rights of Indigenous Peoples, U.N. Doc. E/CN.4/Sub.2/1994/2/Add.1 (1994).

217   United Nations Declaration on the Rights of Indigenous Peoples, resolution adopted by the General Assembly,107th plenary meeting, 13 September 2007, *available at* http://www.un.org/esa/socdev/unpfii/ documents/DRIPS_en.pdf.

based on rights that had been approved by the United Nations system but which had somehow, over the years, been denied the indigenous peoples. The occasion brought to the forefront the reasons why some countries had been opposing the adoption of indigenous peoples' rights for twenty-five years.

The four countries that voted against the adoption of the declaration, the United States, New Zealand, Australia and Canada, and the eleven that abstained from voting stated that they could not support the declaration because of reservations they have about the provisions on self-determination, land and resources rights, and amongst others, certain language which gives indigenous peoples rights of veto over national legislation.

The Declaration on the Rights of Indigenous Peoples establishes collective rights in international human rights law, but only some of them it reflect customary international law. It establishes the rights of indigenous peoples to the protection of their cultural property and identity as well as the rights to education, employment, health, religion, language and more. It also protects the rights of indigenous peoples to own land collectively. It is divided into nine parts, namely fundamental rights; life and security; culture, religion, and language laws; education, media, and employment; participation and development; land and resources; self- government and indigenous; implementation; and minimum standards. James Anaya, the UN special rapporteur, pointed out that the declaration on the rights of indigenous peoples is a standard for evaluating state practices regarding indigenous peoples.[218] This view was also supported by Megan Davis that the Declaration on the Rights of Indigenous Peoples' only provides a framework that states adopt to establish and improve their relationship with indigenous peoples which will also guide the state in the development of their domestic law and policy.[219] Through the adoption of UNDRIP, the nation states recognized that indigenous peoples are different cultural groups.[220] Professor Wiessner observed that the adoption of UNDRIP showed that the indigenous peoples issue is of concern to international law,[221] and which

218   Report of the Special Rapporteur, S. James Anaya, on the Situation of Human Rights and Fundamental Freedoms of Indigenous People, Human Rights Council, 9th sess., agenda item 3, A/HRC/9/9 (August 11, 2008) *available at* http://www2.ohchr.org/english/bodies/hrcouncil/docs/9session/A-HRC-9-9AEV.doc.

219   Megan Davis, *Indigenous Struggles in Standard-setting: The United Nations Declaration on the Rights of Indigenous Peoples,* 9 MELB. J. INT'L L. 439, 465 (2008).

220   International Law Association, *supra* note 9, at 3.

221   *Id.* at 51.

translates into the existence of customary rules of binding force for all states notwithstanding whether they ratified the relevant treaties. The rules of customary international law that correspond to indigenous peoples' rights were listed by the ILA Committee on Indigenous Peoples' Rights in its 2010 Interim Report in the following manner: the right to self-determination, the right to self-government, the right to recognition and preservation of cultural identity, the right to traditional lands and natural resources, the rights to reparation, and so forth.[222] The UNDRIP preamble acknowledges that the situations of indigenous peoples vary from region to region and from country to country. Moreover, it outlines the significance of national and regional peculiarities as well as various historical and cultural backgrounds.

The Declaration comprises both the collective and individual rights of indigenous peoples. Self-determination is a key principle in the declaration, as is the right of indigenous peoples to full recognition of their own laws and customs, land tenure systems, and institutions for the management of land and natural resources. Its provisions on citizenship stated that: "Indigenous Peoples have the collective right to determine own citizenship according to their own customs and traditions including the structure membership of their institutions."[223] Additionally, the document highlighted the significance of indigenous peoples' land rights and ownership and control of natural resources.

The Declaration was faulted and objected to by several governments, including those in the West such as the United States and Canada, and those in Asia. The objection was due to several reasons. One of the reasons has to do with provisions on the rights of indigenous peoples to land, outlined in the declaration. Another one has to do with the rights of autonomy and self-determination, which many governments are reluctant to grant to groups inside their borders. A third issue relates to the rights of indigenous peoples to compensation and reparations for losses that they suffered as a result of colonization and post-colonial policies. All the above mentioned rights are provisions which the nations, that voted against or abstained from voting, are not comfortable with because they felt that if they agree with the terms of the Declaration, their authority over the indigenous peoples in their midst may be challenged.

222   *Id.* at 51–52.

223   United Nations Declaration on the Rights of Indigenous Peoples, resolution adopted by the General Assembly,107th plenary meeting, 13 September 2007, no. 61/295 Art.33 (1) & (2), *available at* http://www.un.org/esa/socdev/unpfii/documents/DRIPS_en.pdf.

2.5.1.1 Position of Various Nations on the Declaration of Indigenous Peoples' Rights

CANADA

Canada voted against the Declaration, particularly against the provisions on lands, territories and resources which it felt were unclear, too broad and capable of different interpretations and which it felt could cause confusion. On April 8, 2008, however, the House of Commons took some steps to reverse Canada's initial position by passing a resolution to endorse the Declaration as adopted by the UN and calling on the Canadian government and its parliament to fully implement the standards contained in the said declaration.[224] Contrary to the Canadian government's earlier opposition to the United Nations Declaration of the Rights of Indigenous Peoples, the government changed its position on November 12th, 2010, and formally endorsed the declaration to strengthen and reconcile the government's relationship with the aboriginal peoples in Canada.[225]

AUSTRALIA

Australia also voted against adoption of the declaration. It objected particularly against the self-determination provision in the text. It felt its support might encourage actions that may undermine the territorial and political integrity of the state. Part of the rights encouraged by the draft declaration is the right of indigenous peoples to their lands and resources, but Australia claimed that any right to traditional lands must be subject to national laws, or the provisions would be both arbitrary and impossible to implement. Australia also felt the Declaration on the Rights of Indigenous Peoples will inflict untold hardship on third parties who might acquire the lands innocently and legally under the national law. It felt the declaration was meaningless and not capable of being implemented and that the international community will not support the exercise. It is Australia's contention that customary law was not "law" in the sense that modern democracies use the

224   News Release, *UN Declaration on the Rights of Indigenous Peoples: Canadian Parliament Calls for Implementation* (April 11, 2008) *available at* http://www.indigenousportal.com/index2.php?option=com_content&task=view&id=3490&pop=1&page=0&Itemid=454.

225   *Canada Endorses the United Nations Declaration on the Rights of Indigenous Peoples,* WORLD NEWS REPORT, *available at* http://www.einnews.com/pr-news/227062-canada-endorses-the-united-nations-declaration-on-the-rights-of-indigenous-peoples.

term.[226]

In Australia, it is a fact that relations between federal and state or provincial governments have historically been a major source of friction in indigenous peoples' relationships with the state.[227] It is, however, important to note that recent history has shown that the Rudd Government would after all support the declaration and that the government had been looking for ways to reconcile support with its own approach to indigenous affairs. Joel Gibson, an indigenous affairs reporter with the *Sydney Morning Herald* reliably reported that the Australia could declare to abide with the United Nations Charter of Indigenous Peoples' Rights by as early as May 2009.[228] This is a clear departure from the policy of the Howard government who opposed the declaration based on the notion that the declaration would elevate customary international law above Western law and also conflict with aspects of government policy. On April 3rd, 2009, Australia's Indigenous Affairs Minister, Jenny Macklin, joined the international community to support the aspirations of all indigenous peoples by endorsing the United Nations Declaration on the Rights of Indigenous Peoples.[229]

NEW ZEALAND

New Zealand did not support the Declaration because it felt the declaration provisions, especially those dealing with the provision on lands and resources,[230] the provision on redress,[231] and the provision on the right of veto over the state[232] are incompatible with New Zealand's constitutional and legal arrangements. New Zealand felt that if it supports the declaration,

226   General Assembly Adopts Declaration on Rights of Indigenous Peoples, General Assembly, GA/10612, Sixty-first General Assembly, plenary 107th & 108th Meetings (AM & PM), *available at* http://www.un.org/News/Press/docs/2007/ga10612.doc.htm.

227   PAUL HAVEMAN, INDIGENOUS PEOPLES' RIGHTS IN AUSTRALIA, CANADA & NEW ZEALAND 910 (Oxford University Press, Auckland 1999).

228   Joel Gibson, *Australia Will Sign UN Charter on Indigenous Rights: Dodson*, THE SYDNEY MORNING HERALD (March 12, 2009), *available at* http://www.smh.com.au/national/australia-will-sign-un-charter-on-indigenous-rights-dodson-20090311-8vak.html.

229   Australia Government endorses UN Declaration on the Rights of Indigenous Peoples, *available at* http://www.indigenousportal.com/World/Australia-Government-endorses-UN-Declaration-on-the-Rights-of-Indigenous-Peoples.html (accessed on November 15th, 2010).

230   UN Declaration, *supra* note 83, at Art. 26.

231   *Id.* at Art. 28.

232   *Id.* at Art. 19 & 32.

it will work injustice especially against third parties who innocently acquired the lands in question lawfully. In April 2009, however, the New Zealand government changed its position on the Declaration by formally endorsing it. New Zealand Maori Affairs Minister Pita Sharple pointed out that the indigenous rights and indigenous culture are of profound importance to New Zealand and fundamental to its identity as a nation.[233]

UNITED STATES

The United States did not support the Declaration because it felt nations were not given the opportunity to discuss the Declaration together and contribute their input. The United States was also against the Declaration's adoption because states were not given opportunity to discuss it collectively. It felt that states should have been allowed to generate a consensus text and that the Declaration's terms should have been written in clear and transparent terms. The United States believes that the Declaration can never become customary international law because it does not describe current state practice or actions that the state might be obligated to take as matter of legal obligation. Despite the fact that the United States felt that terms of the Declaration are not capable of implementation, the country still recognized the Indian tribes as political entities with inherent power of self-government as first peoples and the government has a cordial relationship with their Indian tribes.[234] On December 16, 2010, however, the United States through its president, Barrack Obama, announced that the country is lending its support to the United Nations Declaration of the Rights of Indigenous Peoples.[235]

RUSSIA

Russia abstained from voting because it felt some states with large numbers of indigenous peoples were not represented in the discussion.

233   *Supporting UN Declaration Restores NZ's Mana,* statement by Hon. Dr. Pita Sharples, Minister of Maori Affairs, *available at* http://www.converge.org.nz/pma/NZ%20 UNDRIP%20statements.pdf (accessed on November 17th, 2010).

234   USUN Press Release, Robert Hagen, *Declaration on the Rights of Indigenous Peoples,* United States Mission to the United Nations, No. 204 (07) (September 13, 2007) *available at* http://www.shunpiking. com/ol0406/0406-IP-positionofUS.htm.

235   The White House, President Obama, *Remarks by the President at the White House Tribal Nations Conference,* Department of the Interior, Washington, D.C. (December 16, 2010)   *available   at*   http://www.whitehouse.gov/the-press-office/2010/12/16/remarks-president-white-house-tribal-nations-conference.

Additionally, it has concern about the provisions of lands and natural resources and the procedure for compensation or redress which it felt does not represent the opinion views of all concerned nations.

COLOMBIA

Colombia abstained from voting on the ground that it contradicts its internal legal system. The representative of Colombia at the sixty-first General Assembly Plenary in the person of Jairo Montoya pointed out that the provision of Article 19 which requires the state to consult and cooperate in good faith with indigenous peoples and obtain their free, prior and informed consent before adopting and implementing legislative or administrative decisions is what concerns them. Colombia is also against Article 30 which declares that the state cannot use the indigenous lands and territories for military activities unless it is justified by relevant public interest or the request is made by concerned indigenous peoples or they freely agreed. In addition, states are bound to effectively consult the indigenous peoples concerned through appropriate measures before their lands or territories could be used for military activities. Article 32 is another provision that Colombia is not happy with. The provision affirms that the state needed to consult and cooperate in good faith with the indigenous peoples through their representative institutions prior to approval of any project affecting their lands or territories and other resources. There has, however, been recent developments to the effect that Colombia has endorsed the Declaration.[236]

JAPAN

Japan supported the Declaration on the ground that the revised version of Article 46 correctly clarified the right of self-determination. The right to self-determination will not allow the indigenous peoples to be separate or be independent from their countries of residence and that the right will not be used to undermine the sovereignty of a state, its national and political unity or its territorial integrity.

---

236   Colombia Supports UN Indigenous Rights Declaration, *available at* http:// colombiareports.com/ colombia-news/news/3741-colombia-supports-indigenous-rights. html.

UNITED KINGDOM

The United Kingdom supported the Declaration, but was against the concept of collective human rights in international law.

JORDAN

Jordan supported the Declaration but stressed that the right to self-determination in the Declaration should be exercised in accordance with the framework of the United Nations Charter and that in exercising this right, the territorial integrity of states should be respected.

SWEDEN

Sweden voted in support of the Declaration, but is of the view that the individual human rights should prevail over the collective rights. It was of the opinion that self-determination rights should not be drafted in a way to undermine the territorial integrity or political unity of sovereign dependent states. It claimed that the article in the Declaration which dealt with the duty of the state to consult and cooperate with indigenous peoples[237] is enough to address self-determination rights.

BRAZIL

Brazil voted in support of the Declaration and admitted that indigenous peoples were crucial to the development of society at every level. In this opinion Brazil is not an exception.

INDIA

India supported the Declaration on the ground that self-determination rights will be interpreted to mean that it will only apply to peoples under foreign domination and will not apply to sovereign independent states or to a section of people or a nation.

NAMIBIA

Namibia supported the Declaration and justified its position by pointing out that the word "law" as used in Article 46(2) of the declaration

---

237   UN Declaration, *supra* note 83, at Art. 19.

referred to the national laws of states. This means that the exercise of the rights set out in the declaration will be subject to the constitutional framework and other national laws of states.

INDONESIA AND PAKISTAN

Indonesia and Pakistan, commenting on the Declaration, said that the absence of an indigenous peoples definition had prevented a clear understanding of the peoples to whom the declaration applied.

It could be deduced from the statement of states that they are all concerned about the possibility of the Declaration provision conflicting with the sovereignty or political unity of states.

SLOVAKIA

Slovakia supported the Declaration despite its disapproval of the distinction made between collective and individual human rights.

NIGERIA

Nigeria abstained from voting upon the Declaration because it felt some issues that are important to the country were not convincingly addressed such as the issue of self-determination and the control of lands, territories and resources. Because of these reasons, Nigeria abstained from voting on the declaration. Nigeria, however, promised to continue to promote the issue of indigenous peoples' rights, culture and dignity which is an indirect affirmation that indigenous peoples truly exist in the country.

SAMOA

The Samoan government has recently changed its abstention position on the UNDRIP and endorsed the UNDRIP [238]

---

238   *Samoa's UN Move Congratulated*, SUNDAY SAMOAN, *availability at* http://www. samoaobserver.ws/index.php?option=com_content&view=article&id=14481:samoas-un-move&catid=1:latest-news&Itemid=50.

2.5.1.2 Effect of the UN Declaration on the Rights of Indigenous Peoples

The Declaration on the Rights of Indigenous Peoples does not have legally binding effect because it is a mere declaration, soft law which cannot be legally enforced. Under domestic law, the declaration has no legal effect in most countries unless it becomes incorporated wholesale or in part, into domestic law as happened in Bolivia in 2007. However, those aspects of the provisions of the declaration which can be referred to as customary international law will still have their usual effect. Most importantly, particular rights in the Declaration which might have this effect need to be examined.

Professor Siegfried Wiessner while elaborating on the legal effect of the UN declaration pointed out that there is no difference between a declaration and a recommendation,[239] but stressed that a declaration may be considered to impact an international community to comply with it based on the organ adopting it. Thus, if an expectation is justified by state practice, a declaration may by custom become recognized as laying down rules binding nation states. A declaration may become binding if its provisions are binding and are backed by conforming state practice. James Anaya and Siegfried Wiessner have also pointed out that some of the indigenous peoples claims acknowledged as rights could be regarded as constituting part of customary international law.[240] UNDRIP demonstrates consensus among the nation states and this may be seen in various domestic laws and in some area of international law.[241]

The individual rights in the declaration that form evidence of customary international law would still be effective, since they have been in existence before the coming of the Declaration. Wiessner and Anaya pointed out that most states practice in states with indigenous peoples conform to most of UNDRIP's provisions directed at preservation of culture, language, religion and identity.[242]

---

239   Wiessner, *supra* note 7, at 345.

240   S. James Anaya and Siegfried Wiessner, *The UN Declaration on the Rights of Indigenous Peoples Peoples: Towards Re-empowerment,* JURIST, October 3, 2007.

241   International Law Association, *supra* note 9, at 3.

242   Anaya and Wiessner, *supra* note 240.

It was reiterated in the ILA interim report that UNDRIP is a declaration that deserves the utmost respect based on its preambular paragraph which goes thus: "Guided by the purposes and principles of the Charter of the United Nations, and good faith in the fulfillment of the obligations assumed by States in accordance with the Charter."[243]

The report states that important norms in the UNDRIP can be found in other traditional sources of international law such as customary international law; thus, a declaration may be or become binding if it is backed by conforming state practices and opinio juris.[244] Just like any declaration, UNDRIP cannot be considered as a binding legal instrument. Some of its major provisions could be regarded as being similar to established principles of international law, to which nation states are bound to comply.[245] Some of the indigenous peoples' rights which could be regarded as falling under customary international law are self-determination, self-government, cultural rights and identity, and land rights. These rights are interwoven and relate to one another and also reinforce one another.

Both Wiessner and Anaya pointed out that misunderstandings always arise when it comes to issues of definition and extent of the right to self-determination. These rights were always made subject to territorial integrity of nation states. The scholars pointed out that indigenous peoples are more interested in cultural and spiritual affirmation than political power. For example, the United States recognizes Indian tribes as political entities with the right of self-determination as first people, which means that they have tribal self-government over their internal and local affairs. Canada has also extended autonomy to its indigenous peoples through the aboriginal and treaty enshrined in the 1982 Canadian Charter of Rights and Freedoms. Colombia has also accorded internal autonomy to indigenous peoples within its territory.[246] Its Constitution recognized the peoples' right to self-determination.[247]

The Inter-American Commission on Human Rights has also referred to customary norm in deciding the case of *Awas Tingni v. Nicaragua*

---

243   International Law Association, *supra* note 9 at 5.

244   *Id.* at 6.

245   *Id.* at 43.

246   RACHEL SIEDER, MULTICULTURALISM IN LATIN AMERICA: INDIGENOUS RIGHTS, DIVERSITY AND DEMOCRACY 51 (Palgrave Macmillan (2002).

247   Colombia Constitution, *supra* note 208, at Art. 9.

government where determination of right to property was at issue. Anaya and Wiessner pointed out that once a rule has attained status of customary international law, only a new norm of customary international law could abrogate it. The Australian case of *Mabo* recognized indigenous peoples' right to their land while the Canadian government provided land claims and a self-government treaty. The United States, while showing their concern about indigenous peoples' welfare, pointed out that what is needed is a mechanism at the state level to implement the recognition of indigenous peoples' rights to lands, territories and resources.

The historical status of indigenous peoples as sovereign nations was affirmed by the International Court of Justice in the *Western Saharan Advisory Opinion* of 1975.[248] Specific indigenous peoples' rights could also be found in several international treaties ranging from those that deal specifically with indigenous peoples' rights, such as ILO Convention No. 169, to treaties dealing with human rights generally, such as The Convention on the Rights of the Child, and the UNESCO Convention on the protection and promotion of the diversity of cultural expressions, and so forth. The ICJ unanimously decided that the nation states must adopt in their domestic law "legislative, administrative and any other measures necessary to create an effective mechanism for delimitation, demarcation and titling of the property of indigenous communities."[249]

According to Wiessner, UNDRIP is a comprehensive and authoritative response of the international community of states to the claims of indigenous peoples.[250]

2.6 THE RIGHTS OF INDIGENOUS PEOPLES UNDER CUSTOMARY INTERNATIONAL LAW

There has been much debate about the entitlement of indigenous people to certain rights, but the question that would always comes to mind is: what right, and under what law? It is under international law through the

248   1975 I.C.J. Reports 18, para. 18.

249   THE CASE OF THE MAYAGNA (SUMO) AWAS TINGNI COMMUNITY V. NICARAGUA JUDGMENT OF AUGUST 31, 2001, 88, *available at* http://www.indianlaw.org/sites/indianlaw. org/files/AT%202001-08-31%20InterAmerican%20Court%20Judgment%20Official%20 English.pdf.

250   Siegfried Wiessner, United Nations Declaration on the Rights of Indigenous Peoples, General Assembly Resolution 61/295, New York (September 13, 2007), *available at* http://untreaty.un.org/cod/avl/ha/ga_61-295/ga_61-295.html.

efforts of the United Nations (UN), the International Labor Organization (ILO), the World Bank and a host of concerned human beings that the plight of indigenous peoples came into the limelight and was addressed legally.

Indigenous peoples traditionally had rules and customs that governed their daily activities before the arrival of the colonialists and, in some cases, before they were displaced by the dominant non-indigenous people. The coming of the "usurpers" silenced the voices of the indigenous peoples and the few or no rights that existed under the indigenous peoples' customary law were suppressed and in some cases were silenced outright. Their customary law was therefore replaced by the state or national law enacted by the usurpers. And since the state sees the customary law as an affront to its authority, the customary laws were relegated to the lowest level of authority, if any.

While the various state governments claim to allow the indigenous peoples the freedom to enjoy their fundamental rights, research has shown that the nation-states often only pay lip service to the implementation of the fundamental rights. They simply do not practice what they preach. Most of the nations do not even have provisions for the indigenous peoples' rights in their constitutions. Their excuse is always that they do not have indigenous peoples in their countries, with most African countries being guilty of this allegation. This was manifested by most of African nation states that were reluctant to support the United Nations Declaration on the Rights of Indigenous Peoples. They also often see the vital rights embedded in the declaration such as self-determination, land and resources rights, as a threat to their authority and sovereignty.

Research has shown that the global community through the generation of international law has been the primary impetus embracing the challenge to agitate for the rights of these groups of people, and a vivid example of this is the Declaration on the Rights of Indigenous Peoples,[251] a precedent-setting international instrument. It is the first United Nations (UN) instrument to develop standards on indigenous peoples' rights. It is, as well, the first UN instrument drafted with the direct participation by indigenous peoples in the process of its making.[252]

---

251   Kymlicka, *supra* note 87, at 35.

252   Sharon Helen Venne, Our Elders Understand Our Rights: Evolving International Law Regarding Indigenous Rights 137 (Penticton, British Columbia 1998).

Of all the rights that had been propounded for the indigenous peoples, the three that are most noticeable and controversial shall be examined and the reason for this is not far fetched. There is a need to shed more light on what these rights entail and what the issue is all about. With a critical analysis of the rights, an objective mind that is not conversant with the indigenous peoples plight will be able to draw a conclusion as to whether the rights are justified or not. The said rights are:

(1) Right to self-determination (self-government);
(2) Land rights; and
(3) Cultural rights.

2.6.1 Indigenous Peoples' Demands / Claims

In their international campaign since the 1970s, indigenous peoples across countries made various demands prompted by the various problems that they were facing. Professor Wiessner reiterated in his article that indigenous peoples face this common set of problems[253] :

(1) Indigenous peoples' land was taken away;
(2) The conqueror's way of life was imposed on Indigenous peoples;
(3) Indigenous peoples had limited political freedom ; and
(4) Indigenous peoples languish in abject poverty and despair.

Based on these problems; indigenous peoples made claims for rights that they believe would improve their condition. The indigenous peoples' demands are as follows:

(1) Need for state to respect and restore their traditional lands,
(2) Freedom to practice their traditions, cultures and religions (autonomy),
(3) Right to welfare, health, educational and social services,
(4) Need for conquering nations to comply with their treaty promises, and
(5) Right to self-determination.[254]

---

253   Wiessner, *supra* note 42, at 98.
254   *Id.*

2.6.2 Self-Determination

Self-determination is a wide topic as we have both the aspect of internal and external self-determination. It is a principle of the highest order within the contemporary international system. It is one of the rights repeatedly demanded for by the indigenous peoples.[255] Gudmundur Alfredsson has noted that the self-determination right is broad and can be given several interpretations.[256]

First, it could mean the right to establish a sovereign state, that is to determine its international status.[257] Second, self-determination could also be interpreted as the right of a population within a state to determine the form of government they want and to participate at all levels in the said government.[258] Third, self-determination can mean the right of the recognized nation-state to maintain its territorial integrity and to govern its international affairs devoid of any external interference.[259] Fourth, self-determination could also denote a minority within or across state boundaries entitled to special rights which may be active and declaratory in nature. Such rights could be of cultural, educational, social and economical autonomy for the purpose of preserving the group identity.[260] Claims of indigenous peoples to communal property rights and natural resources will fall into this category.[261]

According to James Anaya, self-determination is a human rights norm that already exists as part of international treaties and it is widely accepted as part of general or customary international law.[262] The content of self-determination is usually found in the relevant practice that extends

---

255   Anaya, *supra* note 95, at 97.

256   Gudmundur Alfredsson. *The Right to Self-determination and Its Many Manifestation* in THE RIGHT OF INDIGENOUS PEOPLES IN INTERNATIONAL LAW: SELECTED ESSAYS ON SELF-DETERMINATION 53, Ruth Thompson, ed. (Native Law Centre, University of Saskatchewan, 1987).

257   *Id.* at 53.

258   *Id.* at 54.

259   *Id.*

260   *Id.*

261   *Id.*

262   James S. Anaya, *The Right of All Peoples to Self-Determination in International Law* in OPERATIONALIZING THE RIGHTS OF INDIGENOUS PEOPLES TO SELF-DETERMINATION, 6 (Pekka Aikdo & Martin Scheinin, eds., Institute for Human Rights, ABO Akedemi University, 2000).

into the international arena. This practice includes the discourse and action by which claims are posited in the name of self-determination and by which authoritative responses to those claims are made. Anaya concluded that self-determination is a right that benefits all segments of humanity, by virtue of their humanity, and this could include the right of diverse groups to exist and develop freely according to their distinctive characteristics. Anaya opined that any individual or group should be permitted to petition for a change in the status quo as long as it is through peaceful means. But the entitlement goes only to those groups that have suffered violations of their rights to self-determination. These are for the purpose of ameliorating the situation and remedy the violation.

Countries such as Australia supported the idea of self-determination and indicated that the right should not be seen only as aiming at the attainment of national independence but should be considered broadly.[263] In the same vein, the Canadian government supports the indigenous peoples' right to self-determination which they felt respect the political, constitutional and territorial integrity of democratic states in the sense that it allows negotiations between states and the indigenous peoples existing in those states to determine political status of the said indigenous peoples.[264] The United States in its support of indigenous peoples' rights to self-determination prefers the use of the term "internal self-determination" which allows indigenous peoples to negotiate their political status within the framework of the existing nation state and also the freedom to pursue their economic, social and development.[265]

The general belief of the nation-states with respect to the self-determination right is that the right will never be exercised to the detriment of independence and territorial integrity of nation states and that the self-determination right does not imply the right to secede.[266] The success of the self-determination right is hinged on various elements and this includes, amongst others, the following: The need by the nation states and dominant groups of the society to eradicate discrimination against indigenous peoples.[267] Another element that could make the self-determination right successful is the need for the indigenous peoples to maintain and develop

---

263   *Id.* at 111.
264   *Id.* at 111.
265   *Id.* at 111.
266   *Id.* at 112.
267   *Id.* at 130.

their cultural identities and co-exist with other sectors of the community.[268] This element of respecting indigenous cultures has been supported by Convention on the Elimination of All Forms of Racial Discrimination[269] which, amongst others, recognizes and respects the indigenous peoples distinct culture, history, language and way of life. The provisions of the International Covenant on Civil and Political Rights[270] also supported the need for the indigenous peoples to enjoy their culture, to protect and practice their religion and to use their language.

Cultural rights can only be enjoyed collectively, thus culture is associated with collectivity and affirmation of a cultural practice is an affirmation of the associated group. [271]

One of the numerous rights to which indigenous peoples are entitled is the right to self-determination. The right to self-determination is one of the most controversial issues of the indigenous peoples' rights.[272] The first international attempt at recognizing indigenous rights addressed the plight of indigenous peoples,[273] within the context of the International Labor Organization (ILO).[274] Convention No. 107 did not support the cause of the indigenous peoples as it barely values the characteristics and traditions of the indigenous culture. The attitude was, however, reversed in 1986 with the coming of ILO's Convention No. 169[275] which placed greater emphasis on the right of indigenous communities to develop as culturally distinct entities.[276]

Numerous United Nations conventions and declarations which include the Universal Declaration of Human Rights (UDHR), the

---

268   *Id. at* 131.

269   CERD General Recommendation XXIII on the Rights of Indigenous Peoples, Par. 4(d), (51st session, 1997).

270   International Covenant on Civil and Political Rights, *supra* note 149, Art. 27.

271   Anaya, *supra* note 95, at 135; *see also* Siegfried Wiessner, *Cultural Rights of Indigenous People: Achievements and Continuing Challenges*, Eur. J. Int'l L. 124 (2011).

272   Raidza Torres Wick, *Revisiting the Emergency International Norm on Indigenous Rights: Autonomy as an Option*, 25 Yale J. Int'l L. 291, 296 (2000).

273   John A. Mills, *Legal Constructions of Cultural Identity In Latin America: An Argument Against Defining "Indigenous Peoples,"* 8 Tex. Hisp. J. L. & Pol'y 49 (2002).

274   ILO drafted its Convention No. 107 Concerning Indigenous and Tribal Populations, Leaflet 8, *available at* http://www.unhchr.ch/ html/racism/indileaflet8.doc.

275   ILO Convention No. 169, *supra* note 118.

276   *Id.*

International Covenant on Economic, Social and Cultural Rights, and the International Covenant on Civil and Political Rights recognize two fundamental principles from which all other inalienable rights and freedom flow. These are the principles of the dignity of the individual and that of the right of indigenous peoples to self-determination. The 1985 Indigenous NGO Draft Declaration of principles on indigenous rights lends credence to this when it states thus: "All indigenous nations and peoples have the right to self-determination, by virtue of which they have the right to whatever degree of autonomy or self-government they choose."[277]

This includes the right to freely determine their political status, freely pursue their own economic, social, religions and cultural development and determine their own membership and or citizenship without external interference. According to Douglas Sanders, the success of colonialism in Africa, Asia, and the Americas made indigenous peoples become the subject of colonial authorities and new states.[278] The situation in the Americas was that traditional rights only survived in hinterland areas or in the pockets of reserve lands. The various treaties were disregarded, which leads to denial of indigenous peoples of any international legal personality or access to international tribunals. The first two preambles of the Declaration state the following:

> Affirming that indigenous peoples are equal in dignity and rights to all other peoples, while recognizing the rights of all peoples to be difficult, to consider themselves different, and to be respected as such; and affirming also that all peoples contribute to the diversity and richness of civilizations and cultures, which constitute the common heritage of humankind.[279]

It could be deduced from the wordings of the two preambles to the Declaration that general human rights apply equally to indigenous peoples and indigenous individuals. A careful look at Article 19 and 20 of the Declarations shows that it grant rights of full participation in the institutions of the state within which the indigenous people find themselves.

277　The 1987 Declaration of Principles on the Rights of Indigenous Peoples, adopted by representatives of indigenous peoples and organizations in Geneva. Art. 2., UN Doc. E/CN.4/Sub.2/ 1987/22, Annex 5 (1987).

278　Douglas Sanders, *The Legacy of Deskaheh: Indigenous Peoples as International Actors*, Cynthia Price-Cohen, Human Rights of Indigenous Peoples 73 (NY: Transnational Pub., 1998).

279　1987 Declaration, *supra* note 277.

The right of indigenous peoples can never be conclusive without an examination of the Declaration on the Rights of Indigenous Peoples. Kofi Annan[280] also gave his view on the right to self-determination where he said:

> It is the product of many years of complex and at times contentious negotiations; the Declaration is an instrument of historic significance for the advancement of the rights and dignity of the world's indigenous peoples. Its expected adoption (this was before the declaration adoption) by the United Nation General Assembly before the end of the year will be a major achievement with potential to further mobilize indigenous people and their partners.[281]

Lots of efforts were put into realizing the dream of indigenous peoples' rights through a statement addressing the rights of indigenous peoples. The declaration, amongst others, emphasizes the rights of indigenous peoples to maintain and strengthen their own institutions, cultures and traditions.

Indigenous peoples' demands for political self-determination have been set back by the assumed implied right of secession with which many nation states are not comfortable. The lackadaisical attitude of most African states towards recognizing indigenous peoples' rights is due to the precaution to avoid any possible infringement of their national integrity. States are adhering to the principle of international law which does not allow violation of their territorial integrity and political independence. This is a major basis by the majority of the nation states for rejecting the right of indigenous peoples to political self-determination. However the true position is that most indigenous peoples are primarily striving for internal self-determination, not secession and national independence. The act of the various states is to prevent secession of indigenous peoples. The indigenous people, on the other hand, are threatened by the dissolution and extinction unless they have a guarantee of legal rights, political authority and sufficient financial means to maintain their identity in their homelands. This is because they need to protect the means of sustenance and legacy.

International law requires metropolitan and colonial powers to extend autonomy to their indigenous peoples, but the obligation is still

---

280   UN Secretary-General.
281   Statement made by UN Secretary-General Kofi Annan on International Day of the World's Indigenous People, August 2006.

subject to the principle of non-violation of state sovereignty. Fredrik Harhoff observed some issues[282] in order to substantiate the right of self-determination and these are as follows:

(1) Establishment of a local legislative body with power to regulate specific matters in its own name without state interference.
(2) Establishment of a local executive body with powers to carry out its executive functions.
(3) Establishment of a judiciary with exclusive authority to decide local judicial functions on validity and interpretation of local acts and orders. Non-local matters and cases which involve national legislation could be decided by national courts with appeal to Supreme Court.
(4) Certain areas of particular concern, such as foreign policy, security, citizenship, currency, customs functions should be exclusively reserved for the national authority without contravening the rights to self-determination.
(5) Area of natural resources which is of common interest to both the metropolitan and indigenous communities should be handled by both sides through their political organs.
(6) Title to land, including sub-surface resources, should be established wherever indigenous peoples have suffered loss of religious sites or traditional areas for game and hunting to industrial or military activities.

He concluded by stating that the right of self-determination for indigenous peoples must be embodied and shaped accordingly to local conditions. Both the metropolitan government and the indigenous people need to work together for self-determination practice to succeed.

Martinez Cobo's report[283] which was completed in 1983, stated that self-determination in its many forms must be recognized as the basic precondition for the enjoyment by indigenous peoples of their fundamental

---

282   Frederik Harhoff, *Self-Determination, Ethics and Law* in THE LIVING LAW OF NATIONS. ESSAYS ON REFUGEES, MINORITIES, INDIGENOUS PEOPLES AND THE HUMAN RIGHTS OF OTHER VULNERABLE GROUPS IN THE MEMORY OF ATLE GRAHL-MADSEN, 176 (Gudmundur Alfredsson & Peter Macalister-Smith, eds., 1996).
283   Special Rapporteur José R. Martínez Cobo, "Study of the Problem of Discrimination Against Indigenous Populations," Final Report (last part) UN Doc. Nº E/CN.4/Sub.2/1983/21/Add.8, 30th September, 1983, *available at* http://www.un.org/esa/socdev/unpfii/documents/MCS_xxi_xxii_e.pdf.

rights and the determination of their own future.

2.6.2.1 Distinction Between Internal Self-Determination and External Self-Determination

Self-determination can be divided into two forms. These are internal and external self-determination. While both are forms of self-determination, there is a major distinction between the two. External self-determination entails establishment of a sovereign and independent state, while internal self-determination refers to the right of internal autonomy which entails customary laws, oral traditions, leadership structures of past which may not necessarily be democratic and the right to participation in the public affairs of the state.[284] James Anaya has also distinguished internal self-determination as matters entirely internal to the people, such as the right of political participation in the community's decision-making process, while external self-determination deals exclusively with people's status such as freedom from alien rule.

While buttressing the distinction between the two types of self-determination, Howard Vogel defined external self-determination as the right of the people within a state to choose their form of government independent of any external interference or alien rule.[285] Internal self-determination, on the other hand, is the right of the people to choose their own form of government within the territory of an existing state.[286]

The Special Committee on European Affairs of the New York City Bar while corroborating the above facts[287] indicated that self-determination does not automatically amount to secession, but that self-determination could be either internal self-determination or external self-determination. While the former refers to the protection of group rights within a state, the latter refers to right of a group to secede from a state.

---

284   Alexandra Xanthaki, Indigenous Rights and United Nations Standards: Self-Determination, Culture and Land 159 (Cambridge University Press 2007).

285   Howard Vogel, *Reframing Rights from the Ground Up: The Contribution of the New UN Law of Self-Determination to Recovering the Principle of Sociability on the way to a Relational Theory of International Human Rights for the 21st Century*, 20 Temp. Int'l & Comp. L. J. 463 (2006).

286   *Id.*

287   Special Committee on European Affairs of the New York City Bar, *Executive Summary: Thawing a Frozen Conflict: Legal Aspects of the Separatist Crisis in Moldovia*, 14 ILSA J. Int'l & Comp. L. 379, 382.

2.6.2.2 Right to Self-Government / Internal Self-Determination/ Autonomy

As earlier stated, the right to self-government is a component of internal self-determination. Anaya noted that the component of self-government has become settled under customary international law, and it requires indigenous peoples to be consulted and their effective participation be ensured in all matters affecting them.[288] The major objective of self-government is to allow indigenous peoples to achieve meaningful self-determination through political institutions and consultative arrangements that allows them to partake in decisions affecting them.

In the "Reference *Re Secession of Quebec,*"[289] the Canadian Court stated that self-determination is fulfilled through internal self-determination which means peoples' pursuit of their political, economic, social and cultural development within the nation-state.[290] As earlier declared, external self-determination differs from internal self-determination. The internal self-determination right does not encourage threatening the territorial integrity of nation states or the stability of relations between sovereign states.[291]

John Hylton[292] has pointed out that aboriginal peoples have an inherent right to govern themselves and this can be traced to the common law. According to John W. Ekstedt,[293] self-government can be defined as the authority to create and maintain the organizational structures necessary to manage day to day affairs. It has been suggested that the success of self-government depends on the readiness of Aboriginal communities to support their own government financially. This self-financing will enhance the independence and autonomy of the aboriginal governments and enhance

---

288   Anaya, *supra* note 95, at 156.

289   [1998] 2 S.C.R. 217 *reprinted in* 23 Vt. L. Rev. 721, 760 (1998-1999).

290   *Id.*

291   *Id.*

292   John H. Hylton, *The Case for Aboriginal Self-Government: A Social Policy Perspective,* in John H. Hylton, Aboriginal Self-Government in Canada: Current Trends and Issues 34 (Canada: Purich Publishing, 1994).

293   John W. Ekstedt, *Aboriginal Self-Government: Implications of the Australian Experience,* in John H. Hylton, Aboriginal Self-Government in Canada: Current Trends and Issues 49 (Canada: Purich Publishing, 1994).

their legitimacy in the eyes of non-aboriginals.[294]

For self-government to be fully realized, it would have to deal with problems of people, place, resources and authority.[295] The issue of the right of aboriginal self-government against governments entails autonomy and the extent to which governments may interfere in the affairs of aboriginal self-government.[296] Self-government speaks of groups being in a position to determine the manner in which their social and economic development will follow.[297]

On the nature of the right to self-government, the government of Canada has expressed it to be "recognition of the inherent right based on the view that the Aboriginal people have the right to govern themselves in relations to matters that are internal to their communities, integral to their unique culture, identities, traditions, languages and institutions, and with respect to their special relationship to their land and their resources."[298] It appears that rights of self-government are claimed legitimately only by indigenous peoples.[299] It must also be noted that the term "self-determination" is more often used in the international legal context while self-government is used as an expression of the right of self-determination.[300]

Self-determination consists of five fundamental characteristics and these are freedom from discrimination, respect for cultural integrity, social

---

294   Allan Maslove, *The Financing of Aboriginal Self-Government*, in JOHN H. HYLTON, ABORIGINAL SELF-GOVERNMENT IN CANADA: CURRENT TRENDS AND ISSUES 159 (Canada: Purich Publishing, 1994).

295   Juan D. Lindau and Curtis Cook, *One Continent, Contrasting Styles: The Canadian Experience in North American Perspective*, in ABORIGINAL RIGHTS AND SELF-GOVERNMENT 3, 25, Juan D. Lindau and Curtis Cook, eds. (2000).

296   C. E. S. Franks, *Rights and Self-Government for Canada's Aboriginal Peoples*, in ABORIGINAL RIGHTS AND SELF-GOVERNMENT 101, 106, Juan D. Lindau and Curtis Cook, eds. (2002).

297   CBA's 2002 Aboriginal Self-government: What does it mean in practice?, CBA's 2002 Aboriginal Law Conference 9.

298   John Hunter, *Judicial Recognition of Aboriginal Self-government: Where do we stand?*, in Aboriginal Self-Government. What Does It Mean in Practice?, CBA's 2002 Aboriginal Law Conference.

299   Will Kymlicka, *The Internalization of Minority Rights*, 6 INT'L J. CONST. L. 1, 5 (2008).

300   Jennifer E. Dalton, *Aboriginal Self-determination in Canada : Protection Afforded by the Judiciary and Government*, 21.1 CAN. J. L. & SOC'Y 11, 12 (2006).

welfare and development, lands and natural resources and self-government.[301] The right to the self-government element strongly applies to the indigenous peoples. James Anaya pointed to the widely held convictions about the self-government concept which are based on the idea that the government is to function according to the will of the people being governed.[302]

Self-government is the opposite of the colonial institutions of government which subjected people to "alien subjugation, domination and exploitation.[303] Under the colonial institutions the people had no representation in government and could not contribute or influence the way they were being governed. A territory will be deemed self-governing upon fulfilling the conditions of (a) emerging as an independent state, ((b) free association with an independent state or (c) integration with an independent state on the basis of equality. Most indigenous communities have their autonomous governance and this is not limited to the Western world alone, but it applies to developing countries such as Nigeria where most groups used to be governed by the customary laws which are usually unwritten. States have been enjoined to uphold and encourage the existence and of the free development of indigenous institutions. Thus, the ILO in its Convention No. 169[304] upholds the right of indigenous institutions and peoples to "retain their own customs and institutions. The United Nations in its Declaration also states that "indigenous peoples have the right to promote, develop and maintain their institutional structures and their distinctive juridical customs, traditions, procedures and practices, in accordance with internationally recognized human rights standards."[305]

The norm of self-government encourages indigenous peoples' effective participation in the larger political order, too.[306] This was advocated for by the American Declaration on the Rights of Indigenous Peoples[307] and ILO Convention No. 169 which allows indigenous peoples to freely participate at all levels of decision making affecting them.[308] The

301   Anaya, *supra* note 95, at 97-98, 104-05, 109-10.

302   *Id.* at 150.

303   *Id.*

304   ILO Convention No. 169., *supra* note 118, at Art. 8(2).

305   International Law Association, *supra* note 9, at Art. 33.

306   Anaya, *supra* note 95, at 153.

307   Proposed American Declaration on the Rights of Indigenous Peoples, approved by the Inter-American Commission on Human Rights on February 26, 1997, at its 1333rd session, 95th Regular Session, OEA/Ser/L/V/.II.95 Doc.6 (1997). Article XV (1).

308   ILO Convention 169, *supra* note 118, at Art. 6.1 (b).

ILO Convention No. 169 also reiterates the duty of governments to consult the representative of the groups concerned,[309] and this consultation must be in good faith. Anaya remarked that the consultation must not be done as a mere formality, but must be done in such a way that it will allow the indigenous peoples the opportunity to genuinely influence and contribute to the decisions that affect their interest.[310] Anaya further affirmed that customary international law is positioned around the self-government component that requires consultation with indigenous peoples and their effective participation in all matters affecting them. The scholar additionally stated that the underlying objective of the self-government norm is to allow indigenous peoples to have a sense of belonging through political institutions and consultative arrangements that reflect their cultural patterns and allow them to be involved in decision making on issues that concerns them.

The right to self-determination is a fundamental principle and right under international law which is expected to be applied equally and universally.[311] The right not only means participating in a democracy,[312] but it also includes the people's right to be in control of their economic, social and cultural development. This right to self government is the first right among the rights being clamored for by the various indigenous peoples. This is because it is the foundation upon which the other rights will stand. Therefore, it could be submitted that if the indigenous peoples are still being denied this all important right, it will be very difficult, if not impossible, for the indigenous peoples to make any meaningful progress.

Internal self-determination could also be referred to as autonomy; it is conceived as a broad permission for ethnic groups to regulate their own affairs or to retain their customs.[313] Autonomy also implies the creation of a true collectivity within a national society, that is, it is a form of self-government for certain communities that desire to be authorities over themselves by administering their own affairs.[314] It must be noted that not everything that is called self-determination is autonomy.[315] Self-

309   *Id.* at Art. 69 (1)(a).

310   Anaya, *supra* note 95, at 154.

311   John Henriksen. *Implementation of the Right of Self-Determination of Indigenous Peoples,* INDIGENOUS AFFAIRS 7, 3/01, International Work Group for Indigenous Affairs (IWGIA), Marianne Jensen ed., (Copenhagen, 2001).

312   *Id.* at 10.

313   Anaya, *supra* note 95, at 95.

314   *Id.*

315   *Id.*

determination is often identified with the right to political independence and the establishment of a nation-state while the concept of autonomy is reserved for the assumption of certain special faculties such as self-government but without political independence.[316] Hector Diaz Polanco has indicated that autonomy is a resource that society can use at a given point in its development for the purpose of resolving ethnic-national conflicts.[317] An autonomous regime exists within the context of given nation states,[318] thus, an autonomous community or region is established as a component of the host nation-state.

Autonomy is not meant to cause conflicts within a nation state, but to keep interests from creating conflicts within a nation state. It must be noted that autonomy influences the nature of the state by limiting or modifying the state's territorial powers.[319]

In respect of autonomy and ethnic rights, autonomy is instituted so that certain groups with common historical traditions and characteristics such as customs, beliefs, language and ways of life can exercise their rights and conduct their own affairs. It must, however, be noted that social cultural differences is not the major reason for autonomy but the "identity" which it confers on the collectivities.[320]

Autonomy is a system through which socio-cultural groups exercise their right to self-determination; in other words, it is one way of exercising self-determination.[321] As earlier stated, autonomy in the case of indigenous peoples is often exercised through the observance of the customary laws, oral traditions and age long traditional leadership structures.

Customary law does not have a single definition agreed to by lawyers, jurists, social anthropologists and others who may be concerned with it.[322] This situation arises because of the fact that both "custom" and "law" may be used in a number of differing senses depending upon the motive of the user.

316   *Id.* at 99.
317   Hector Diaz Polanco, Indigenous Peoples in Latin America: The Quest for Self-Determination 94 (Westview, 1977).
318   *Id.* at 96.
319   *Id.* at 97.
320   *Id.* at 98.
321   *Id.*
322   C. M. N. White, *African Customary Law: The Problem of Concept and Definition.* 9 J. Afr. L. 86 (1965).

Alan Watson pointed out in his article that customs do not become law until institutionalized by the inclusion in an official court decision.[323] Customary law can, however, be explained as traditional common rule or practice that has become an essential part of the accepted and expected conduct in a community, profession, or trade and is treated as a legal requirement.

Alan Watson remarked that customary law flourishes where law is likely to be the least academic,[324] and for a law to be regarded as customary in Western private law, the law must be constantly practiced and must have flourished for a long time. In other words, for the customary law to be recognized, the said custom must have been in existence for a long time. Leon Sheleff in his book[325] made it clear that society life is dependent on the capacity of people to create rules to guide themselves in their everyday activities. Such rules represent a series of shared values and practices. Such customs are seen as the norms which not only guide social life, but also have influence over economic and political life. It is the duty of the state legislative and judicial organs to give concrete expressions and recognition to these rules. Such rules are rules of an obligatory or strongly persuasive nature, created without the formal procedures of parliament, courts, and other constituted bodies that characterize a state.

Custom has played a significant role in the formation of law, and this is evident in the common law legal system where the judicial approval of customary practices constitutes the bulk of the law in the early stages of its growth. Public international law is another field where customary practices were gradually accorded growing support from individual states, until they came to have a binding status.[326] The most striking example of the role of custom in rule making is in the prestate period, where society's way of life was governed by customary law, despite lacking the ability to inform members about what rights to which they are entitled.

Many indigenous communities have their own institution of autonomous governance which are usually based on customary or written law as well as systems of dispute resolution and adjudication which they

---

323   Alan Watson, *An Approach to Customary Law*, U. ILL. L. Rev. 561, 576 (1984).

324   *Id.* at 561.

325   LEON SHELEFF, THE FUTURE OF TRADITION: CUSTOMARY LAW, COMMON LAW AND LEGAL PLURALISM 3 (Frank Cass Publishers, 1999).

326   *Id.* at 4.

have practiced over the centuries.[327]

Anaya pointed out that autonomous governance for indigenous communities will be instrumental to their ability to control development of their distinct culture and use of land and resources.[328]

Indigenous peoples are economically disadvantaged and politically vulnerable, and thus need to have the right to autonomy or self-government in matters relating to internal and local affairs.[329] Anaya observed that many states have yielded to the demand of indigenous peoples in their states by granting them autonomous governance and recognizing their culturally specific institutions of social and political control. A good example of this is the Nicaraguan government who granted autonomy to its indigenous peoples as a way of advancing their self-determination.[330] According to Marc Weller, most autonomy settlements that have been achieved contain strong references to the guarantee of continued territorial unity and integrity.[331]

Erica Daes opined that for a group to enjoy the right to self-government, such a group must not be widely dispersed and must not lack a principal centre of population and activity.[332] Professor Erica Daes pointed out that if the indigenous peoples are granted the right to autonomy, there will surely be a conflict between the national authority and the indigenous peoples' local authority, but this conflict can be minimized if the indigenous peoples are allowed to participate at both levels of law-making,[333] which, in other words, will lead to partnership in decision-making on the national issues.

2.6.3 The Right of Indigenous Peoples to Their Land and Territories

Another entitlement of indigenous peoples is their right to their land and territories. The issue of indigenous rights over land, territories and natural resources is difficult and sensitive. It is, however, at the core

---

327   Anaya, *supra* note 95, at 152.

328   *Id.*

329   UN Declaration, *supra* note 83, at Arts. 4 & 33.

330   Anaya, *supra* note 95, at 111.

331   Marc Weller, *Settling Self-Determination Conflicts: Recent Development,* 20 Eur. J. Int'l L. 159 (2009).

332   Daes, *supra* note 11, at 28.

333   *Id.* at 61.

of the demands of indigenous people over the years. Henriksen denoted that the issue of land and resources rights is closely related to the right of self-determination[334] and this is one right that various indigenous peoples all over the world had been agitating for. The Niger-Delta area people of Nigeria are not left out in this agitation for land and resources rights.

There have been many competing claims on land rights issues. A very good example is the case of Enxet-Lamenxay and Kayleyphapopyet[335] where the Paraguay government in 1885 began selling the indigenous peoples traditional land to third parties. Land was everything to the communities as the means of their sustenance comes from hunting, fishing and faming; they also breed domestic animals. The community got an injunction restraining the third parties from making any modifications to the said land, but the legal injunction was ignored by the third parties. At a settlement meeting held at the initiative of the Inter-American Commission on Human Rights, the Paraguay government recognized the existence of the indigenous communities' right to their land at the local and international level.

The case of Maya indigenous communities[336] is another case where the government of Belize competed with the indigenous peoples over their land. The government regarded the land as "public land" against the claims of the indigenous people. The Inter-American Commission on Human Rights decided that the state violated the Maya peoples' property rights to their land and also violated Maya's right to judicial protection by frustrating judicial proceedings brought by the community. The Commission mandated Belize to adopt in its domestic law legislative, administrative and protection of territories in which the Mayan peoples have communal property rights.

The above cases in addition to the Australian case of *Mabo* show that there are always competing claims to indigenous peoples' rights to their communal lands.

The Declaration[337] states that indigenous peoples have the right to <u>maintain and st</u>rengthen their distinctive spiritual and material relationship

334   Henriksen, *supra* note 311, at 10.

335   Report No. 90/99, Case 11.713, *available at* http://www.cidh.org/annualrep/99eng/Friendly/ Paraguay11.713.htm

336   *Maya Indigenous Community of the Toledo District v. Belize*, Case 12.053, Report No. 40/04, Inter-Am. C.H.R., OEA/Ser.L/V/II.122 Doc. 5 rev. 1 at 727 (2004) *available* at http://www1.umn.edu/humanrts/ cases/40-04.html.

337   UN Declaration, *supra* note 83, at Arts. 25.

with the land, territories, waters and coastal seas and other resources which they have traditionally owned or otherwise occupied or used, and to uphold their responsibilities to future generations in this regard. Moreover, the Declaration gives indigenous peoples the ownership and control over the land and resources.[338]

It is noteworthy that Erica Daes[339] has conducted a tremendous study of the rights of indigenous peoples to their land in her study titled "Indigenous Peoples and Their Relationship to Land" where she concluded that indigenous peoples have a distinctive and profound spiritual and material relationship with their lands and with the air, waters, coastal service, floral, fauna, and other resources and that the relationship has various social, cultural, spiritual, economic and political dimensions and responsibility.[340] This statement means that land is part of the indigenous peoples' life and it is what they rely on for economic survival. The ILO Convention No. 169 indicated that the right of ownership and possession of indigenous peoples over lands which they traditionally occupy shall be recognized.[341] It further required states to safeguard indigenous peoples' rights to natural resources throughout their territories, including, amongst others, the right to participate in the use, management and conservation of resources.[342]

Martinez Cobo's report[343] also states that "indigenous people have a natural and inalienable right to keep the territories they possess and claim the lands which have been taken from them." The indigenous right to land is natural and inalienable because it is a hereditary possession that is not transferable, since land is inherited from generation to generation by families and groups according to their customs, and the groups or families are obliged to keep the territories they possess.

In 1921 in the Privy Council, Lord Haldane in *Amodu Tijani v. Secretary, Southern Nigeria* states that the original title of peoples in ceded

---

338   *Id.*

339   Special Rapporteur of the former Sub-Commission for the promotion and protection of human rights.

340   Chairperson-Rapporteur Mrs. Erica-Irene A. Daes, "Indigenous Peoples and Their Relationship to Land," (working paper for Working Group on Indigenous Populations) U.N.ESCO, Commission on Human Rights, Sub-Commission on Prevention of Discrimination and Protection of Minorities, 53rd sess., E/CN.4/Sub.2/2001/21 (11 June 2001).

341   Convention No. 169, *supra* note 118, Arts. 14(1).

342   *Id.* at Art. 15.

343   Cobo, *supra* note 283.

or conquered territory ought to be recognized even if it did not conform to the concepts of ownership known in English. This decision established the fact that native title to land should be recognized even if colonialism was in existence.

2.6.3.1 Land-Related Cases Under the Inter-American Court of Human Rights

(Λ) *Mayagna Awas Tigni & Community v. Nicaragua*[344]

The *Mayagna Awas Tigni & Community v. Nicaragua* is a case where the Nicaraguan government granted logging concessions to a third party without consulting the *Awas Tingni*. The Court ruled that the state had violated Articles 1, 2, 21 and 25 of the American Convention on Human Rights which deals with the obligations to respected rights, domestic legal effects, right to property and right to judicial protection respectively. The Court held that the Nicaraguan government violated the property rights of the indigenous peoples by the act of granting a foreign company the concession to log on the traditional land of the community and by its failure to recognize and protect the community's traditional land tenure.

The Court was of the opinion that the property right stipulated in the Convention[345] also covered the communal property of the indigenous peoples. The Court further held that the possession of the land should suffice for indigenous communities lacking real title to property to the land to obtain official recognition of that property.[346] The Commission held that in view of the emergent international consensus on indigenous peoples' rights to their traditional land, the right has become a matter of customary international law.

---

344   Awas Tingni, Judgment of 31 August, 2001, Inter-Am. Ct. H.R. (Ser.C) No. 79 (2001); *see also* Anaya, *supra* note 95, at 149.

345   American Convention on Human Rights, O.A.S.Treaty Series No. 36, 1144 U.N.T.S. 123, entered into force July 18, 1978, reprinted in Basic Documents Pertaining to Human Rights in the Inter-American System, OEA/Ser.L.V/II.82 doc.6 rev.1 (1992) Art 21 at 25.

346   Awas Tingni, *supra* note 344, at Para. 151.

(B) *Mary and Carrie Dann v. United States*

Moreover, in the case of ***Mary and Carrie Dann v. United States***,[347] at trial the U.S. Federal Court held that the individual aboriginal land title of Mary and Carrie Dann was restricted to the land that they or their linear ancestors who preceded them in interest actually occupied prior to November 26, 1934. Their individual aboriginal grazing right was also restricted to the number of and type of animals grazed by them or by their lineal ancestors who preceded them.[348] The Inter-American Commission, however, held that the manner in which the Western Shoshone land rights proceeding was handled did not give the Western Shoshone group a fair hearing because they were denied the normal procedural and substantive protections which property holders are entitled to under the U.S. law;[349] such protection includes, but is not limited to the just compensation standard.

(C) *Indigenous Community Yakye Axa v. Paraguay*[350]

This is a case where Paraguay refused to acknowledge *Yakye Axa Community's* right to property over their ancestral land. The Inter-American Court of Human Rights concluded that Paraguay violated the indigenous community's right to property by depriving them from their traditional means of livelihood. The state also failed to adopt in its domestic laws measures to enable the community to make effective use of and enjoy their traditional land.

(D) *Coulter v. Brazil (Yanomami) Case*[351] (Brazil)

This is a case where it was alleged that the government violated the human rights of the Yanomami Indians by its various acts and omissions which include the granting of permission in 1973 to construct highways and mining activities on Yanomami land without demarcating the indigenous peoples' land, and with no domestic remedy available to the Yanomami

---

347 U.S. v. Dann, 873. F. 2d 1189 (9th Cir. 1989), Mary and Carrie Dann, Case 11. 140 (United States), Inter-Am. C.H.R. Report No. 75/02.

348 *Id.*

349 Anaya, *supra* note 95, at 147.

350 Yakye Axa Indigenous Community of the Enxet-Lengua People v. Paraguau, Case 12.313, Report No. 2/02, Inter-Am. C.H.R., Doc. 5 rev. 1 (2002), Inter-American Court of Human Rights, June 17, 2005.

351 Coulter v. Brazil (Yanonami), Case 7615, Inter-Am. C.H.R.

people.[352] The Inter-American Commission on Human Rights held that despite the fact that there is no visible violation of right to property of the Yonomami by the Brazilian government, there is a violation of the Yanomami right to life, liberty, personal security, residence and movement.

(E) Moiwana Community v. Suriname [353]

This is a case where state agents attacked a Moiwana Village, massacred several men, women and children, and razed the village to the ground. This led to internal displacement of the inhabitants and the driving of survivors into exile. Thus, the villagers were displaced from their lands and from their traditional way of life.

The Inter-American Court of Human Rights declared that the state violated the right to property enshrined in Article 21 of the Convention to the detriment of the Moiwana Community members. The court decided that the state should adopt such legislative, administrative and other measures as are necessary to ensure that the Moiwana community members enjoy their property rights and the traditional territories from which they were expelled, and to create avenues for community members to enjoy their territories.[354]

2.6.3.2 Land-Related Cases Under the African Commission on Human and Peoples' Rights

(A) The Social and Economic Rights Action Center and the Center for Economic and Social Rights v Nigeria (Ogoni case)[355]

This is a case where the African Commission on Human and Peoples' Rights found that the Nigerian government violated the Ogoni peoples' economic, social, cultural and collective rights through their act

---

352   ANNA MEIJKNECHT, TOWARDS INTERNATIONAL PERSONALITY: THE POSITION OF MINORITIES AND INDIGENOUS PEOPLES IN INTERNATIONAL LAW 197 (2001).

353   Case of the Moiwana Community v. Suriname, Inter-American Court of Human Rights (IACrtHR), 15 June 2005, available at: http://www.unhcr.org/refworld/docid/4721bb292.htm.

354   Moiwana Village v. Suriname, Judgment of June 15, 2005, Inter-Am Ct. H.R., (Ser. C) No. 145 (2005), *available at* http://www1.umn.edu/humanrts/iachr/C/145-ing.html.

355   *The Social and Economic Rights Action Center and the Center for Economic and Social Rights v. Nigeria* (known as the Ogoni case), Decision Regarding Communication 155/96 (2001) Case No. ACHPR/COMM/A044/1, *available at* http://www.umn.edu/humanrts/africa/comcases/allcases.html.

of supporting the policy of oil companies in Ogoniland. The oil companies are in the habitual practice of non-complying with minimum environment standards with respect to the pollution of Ogoniland, contaminating their water and destroying Ogoni farm produce with fumes from the oil companies' operations. The African Commission not only made Nigerian government conduct investigations into the violations, it also made the government ensure that adequate compensation was paid to the victims of human rights' violations.

(B) Endorois Welfare Council v Kenya

This is a case where the Kenyan government evicted the Endorois community, an indigenous community, from their ancestral land in the 1970s for the purpose of using their land for a natural reserve and tourist facilities. The African Commission in its ruling stated that the eviction of the Endorois people violated their rights as an indigenous people to property, health, culture, religion and natural resources. The Commission ordered the Kenya government to restore the Endorois peoples back to their historical land and also compensate them.[356] The case signifies the first time that the African Commission would recognize indigenous peoples' land rights and their right to development under the African Charter.[357]

2.6.3.3 Indigenous Peoples and Their Relationship to the Land

According to Erica Daes in her final working paper reports and statements by indigenous peoples from all parts of the world delivered at the fifty-third session of the working group on indigenous populations established the fact that land and resources rights are of urgent and fundamental nature.

Various instruments such as the UN Declaration on the Rights of Indigenous Peoples, the International Covenants on Human Rights, the International Labor Organization Convention No. 169 concerning indigenous and peoples in independent countries, and other relevant international and regional human rights instruments also highlighted the importance of the land to the indigenous peoples. The establishment of the

356   Centre for Minority Rights Development (Kenya) and Minority Rights Group International on behalf of Endorois Welfare Council v. Kenya, 276/2003, *available at* http://www.escr-net.org/caselaw /caselaw_show.htm?doc_id=1216218.

357   Human Rights Watch, Kenya: Landmark Ruling on Indigenous Land Rights (February 4, 2010), *available at* http://www.unhcr.org/refworld/docid/4b71215bc.html.

working people on the indigenous population gave the indigenous peoples the opportunity to emphasize the fundamental nature of their relationship to their homelands. This relationship reflects the spiritual, social, cultural, economic and political significance to indigenous societies of their lands, territories and resources.

Jose R. Martinez Cobo in the study of the problem of discrimination against indigenous populations suggested that "It is essential to know and understand the deeply spiritual special relationship between indigenous peoples and their lands as basic to their existence as such and to all their beliefs, customs, traditions and culture."[358] This goes to show that land has become part of indigenous peoples' life and they cannot exist or be functional without it.

He went further to state that indigenous peoples' land is not merely a possession and a means of production, but that the relationship between their spiritual life and their land has many implications. Their land is not a commodity which can be acquired, but a material element to be enjoyed freely.[359] Their land cannot be acquired or sold because it is priceless to them. It is their economic base and spiritually they cannot abandon the age long practice of the ancestors; culturally, they cannot trade away the grave yards of their ancestors.

The importance of the cultures and the spiritual values of the indigenous peoples' relationship with their lands or territories was also emphasized by International Labor Organization Convention No. 169 concerning indigenous and tribal peoples in independent countries which states in its part II, "In applying the provisions of this part of the convention governments shall respect the special importance for the cultures and spiritual values of the peoples concerned of their relationship with the lands or territories."[360] It went further to denote that "lands" referred to shall include the concept of territories, which covers the total environment of the area which the people concerned occupied or used.

The United Nations Declaration on the Rights of Indigenous Peoples, in both its preambulary and operative paragraphs, also states that "indigenous peoples have the right to maintain and strengthen their

---

358   Study, *supra* note 15.
359   Cobo, *supra* note 283, at 26, para. 196-197.
360   International Labor Organization Convention No. 169, *supra* note 118, at Art. 13.

distinctive spiritual and material relationship with the lands, territories, water and coastal seas and other resources which they have traditionally owned or otherwise occupied or used, and to uphold their responsibilities to future generations in this regard."[361]

In its preamble the United Nations Declaration showed its support for the rights of indigenous peoples to their land because the majority of the indigenous peoples, especially those in Nigeria, live traditional lives whereby their survival is dependent on their land. This is because the majority of them are herdsmen, farmers and fishermen. These occupations are so land-dependent that the peoples' relationship cannot be severed from their land, otherwise their means of livelihood and survival will be threatened. The indigenous peoples see their land and territories as the only legacy they can bequeath to their children and coming generations. Any attempt to trade away this legacy will be seen as a failure and disservice to their ancestors and their coming generations.

The proposed American Declaration on the Rights of Indigenous Peoples, drafted by the Inter-American Commission on Human Rights, also contains the following preamble which recognizes the relationship of indigenous peoples and their lands:

"Recognizing the respect for the environment accorded by the cultures of indigenous peoples of the Americas, and considering the special relationship between the indigenous peoples and the environment, lands, resources and territories on which they live and their natural resources."[362]

More importantly, Article 26 of UNDRIP expressly stated that Indigenous Peoples have the rights to the lands, territories and resources which they have traditionally owned, occupied or otherwise used or acquired.

Besides the above quotation taking notice of the environment and cultures of the indigenous peoples, it also recognizes the relationship they have with their lands. This goes to show that the issue of indigenous peoples and their lands and territories is one which concerns the international community and it deserves urgent attention.

---

361   U.N. Declaration, *supra* note 90, at Art. 25.
362   Proposed American Declaration, *supra* note 307.

The American Declaration further pointed out that the traditional collective system is the means by which indigenous peoples control and make use of their lands, territory and resources and this system is a necessary condition for their survival, social organization and development both as individuals and as a group.[363]

Erica Daes revealed in her final working paper some elements which are unique to indigenous people in respect of their relationship to land. She stated that:

(a) There is a strong bond between indigenous peoples and their lands, territories and resources;
(b) The indigenous relationship with their lands is attached with various dimensions and responsibility ranging from social, cultural and economic to political;
(c) The collective dimension of indigenous peoples' relationship to land is symbolic; and
(d) The preservation of the relationship is crucial to the indigenous peoples' identity, survival and cultural feasibility.[364]

According to the Erica Daes report, the colonization of indigenous territories greatly affected indigenous peoples in several ways which resulted in the deterioration of their territories through maltreatment, enslavement, suicide, punishment for resistance, warfare and over-exploitation of natural resources.

Erica Daes further pointed out that the attitudes, doctrines and policies developed to justify the taking of lands from indigenous peoples were and continue to be largely driven by the economic agendas of nation states. A very good example is the Niger Delta area of Nigeria which had relative peace prior to the discovery of oil in the 1960s, but upon the discovery of oil, the activities of the oil companies in the process of extracting oil from the land had brought untold hardship to the people and adversely affected the means of sustenance of the Ogoni people and other groups in the Niger Delta area who are predominantly farmers and fishermen. This insensitivity to the plight of the indigenous peoples was driven by the economic factor which gives priority over the well being of the people just because of the

---

363   Id.
364   Daes, "Indigenous Peoples and Their Relationship to Land," *supra* note 340, at para. 34.

economic dividends from the oil corporations' operations.

Daes showed that the colonizer secured ownership of the land through rationalization and military domination and this practice is very glaring in the countries that were colonized in Africa, Nigeria inclusive. The scholar also stated that most territories were diminished by forcible or coerced removal, relocation and allotment. Severing of indigenous peoples from their lands and territories and the failure by states to recognize the social, cultural, spiritual and economic significance of land to the indigenous peoples had both short-and-long term impacts on indigenous communities. An example of such an impact is the negative effect on the occupation of indigenous peoples. For instance, the Ogoni people of Nigeria could no longer practice their occupations as they used to, as these people were farmers and fishermen whose occupations are land-dependent and without the land their continued existence is not guaranteed.

The doctrine of *terra nullius* holds that indigenous lands are legally unoccupied until the arrival of a colonial presence gives the "discovery" colonial power free title to indigenous lands subject only to the indigenous peoples' use and occupancy.[365] Nevertheless, in the case of *Western Sahara*[366] the International Court of Justice ruled that the doctrine of *terra nullius* had been erroneously and invalidly applied against the tribal people of the Western Sahara. In 1992 the High Court of Australia while discussing the legal and other effects of the doctrine of *terra nullius* denounced the doctrine by concluding that the doctrine is unjust and is a discriminatory doctrine and can no longer be accepted.

Erica Daes also pointed out the current problems regarding indigenous land rights and these are as follows:

(a) Refusal of nation states to recognize existence of indigenous use, occupancy and ownership of land;[367] and
(b) Refusal of nation states to accord appropriate legal status and other legal rights in connection with indigenous people's ownership of land.[368]

---

365   J. L. BRIERLY, THE LAW OF NATIONS 151 (Oxford Univ. Press, 1960).

366   Western Sahara, Advisory Opinion, 1975 I.C.J. 12.; ("derivative title" from indigenous peoples)..

367   Daes, *supra* note 340.

368   *Id.* at para. 36.

Due to refusal of nation states to recognize the existence of indigenous use, occupancy and ownership, Erica Daes indicated that there exist numerous examples of unilateral state action whereby indigenous lands were regarded as public or government lands and examples of the treatment meted out to indigenous people were cited. Amongst others, the San or Bushmen in Africa countries face difficulties because of the lack of national legislation safeguarding their land use and tenure.[369] The Sami of Norway's land and resources are also threatened by governmental actions which includes the conveyance of indigenous lands in Finnmark to a state-owned company for commercial purposes.[370] The report pointed out that similar situations are reported in Indonesia, Thailand, India and most African countries.[371]

On the issue of the states' failure to accord appropriate legal status, appropriate judicial capacity and other legal rights, Daes states that many states do not acknowledge that the indigenous peoples concerned have legal entitlement or rights to the land or resources despite the fact that such states know that the indigenous communities, nations or groups exist and have exclusive use and occupancy of an area. This lack of recognition is usually manifested in the various indiscriminate manners with which most nation states treat indigenous peoples' land. A very good example is the Ogoni people of the Niger Delta area of Nigeria who had long been making good use of their land before the intrusion.

In many British commonwealth countries, exclusive use and occupancy of the land from time immemorial gives rise to aboriginal title which can be exercised against all except the state government.[372] The reason for this is not unconnected to the fact that states, especially in Nigeria are trustees of all land which means they hold the lands in trust. The title is often subject to the illegitimate assumption of state power to extinguish such title and this often leads to the overwhelming majority of human

---

369   Kristyna Bishop, *Squatters on Their Own Land: San Territoriality in Western Botswana*, 31 Comp. and Int'l L. J. S. Afr. 92 (1998).

370   Nazila Ghanea-Hercock, Alexandra Xanthaki & Patrick Thornberry, Minorities, Peoples and Self-Determination: Essays in Honour of Patrick Thornberry 81 (Martinus Nijhoff Pub., 2004).

371   Alan Thein Durning, *Guarding of the Land: Indigenous Peoples and the Health of the Earth*, 112 World Watch Paper 21-22 (December, 1992).

372   Nell Jessup Newton, *At the Whim of the Sovereign: Aboriginal Title Reconsidered*, 31 Hastings L. J. 1215 (1980).

rights problems affecting indigenous peoples. Such a problem could be an arbitrary dispossession of indigenous peoples from their lands for good or bad reasons or for no reason at all.

The Supreme Court of Canada,[373] recognized the aboriginal title and emphasized that it is a right to land, a property interest and a collective right that is unique; however the court pointed out that the right is limited to the extent that it cannot be used in an arbitrary manner. The indigenous peoples still have to deal with the state supreme authority which could be exercised to take away the aboriginal title at will. The state or sovereign could be the colonial government, or nowadays the state.

Erica Daes pointed out in her report that in 1971, the U.S. Congress relied on the aboriginal title doctrine to extinguish all the land rights and claims of practically every one of the 226 indigenous nations and tribes in the Alaska Native Claim Settlement Act.

Erica Daes noted that failure of the states to demarcate the indigenous land had compounded the indigenous peoples' problems. Demarcation becomes necessary because purely abstract or legal recognition of indigenous lands, territories or resources can be practically meaningless without a physical identity of the property. An example of this is the case of *Mayagna Indigenous Community of Awas Tingni v. Nicaragua*, where the government of Nicaragua granted a concession to a Korean timber company to log lands traditionally held by Awas Tingni without taking the interest of the people and their rights into consideration.

The state's assertion that it has complete rights to subsurface resources has caused numerous unfortunate social, economic, environmental and economic, environmental and cultural consequences which most times does not favor the indigenous peoples. There are several government programs and policies adversely affecting indigenous peoples relationship to their lands, territories and resources and these are as follows:

(a) Government allots lands to individuals; for instance, commonly held allotment of a land to individuals or family tends to weaken the indigenous community because the practice also results in loss of land.[374]

---

373   Delgamuukw v. The Queen, (1997) 153 DLR (4th) 193.
374   Daes, *supra* note 340, at Art. 74.

(b) States usually assume trust title and such lands held in trust by the government on behalf of indigenous peoples are usually abused and with no remedy for such breach.[375]

(c) The government's practice of using indigenous land as collateral for loan programs is likely to result in the eventual loss of indigenous lands and resources. Governments often take risks with the indigenous peoples' land by using it as collateral for a loan and there is a tendency for such land to be lost if there is default.[376]

(d) Government handling of lands which are of great religious or cultural significance to indigenous people may be incompatible with the wishes and aspirations of the indigenous peoples' customs and religious beliefs.[377]

While the decision in *Mabo's* denounced the doctrine of *terra nullius*, it did not remove all the cultural biases, nor did it fully examine the assumed state authority and power to determine the extent of indigenous land rights. A clear example is the power that the sovereign has to revoke or take away aboriginal title.

Daes further identified that many countries are taking positive steps towards securing indigenous rights and this has been done by states to recognize and protect, to an extent, indigenous land rights through constitutional amendments, specific legislations, and sections with more general laws. Numerous countries have incorporated into their constitutions significant provisions calling for the demarcation and protection of indigenous lands. For instance, Canada recognized and affirmed the treaty and aboriginal rights of aboriginal peoples of Canada.[378] Ecuador also made provision for indigenous peoples' rights, where it not only provided for collective rights but also recognized the ancestral ownership of communal lands.[379] Additionally, the Venezuela Constitution recognizes the rights of native peoples to lands they ancestrally and traditionally occupy that are necessary to develop and guarantee their way of life.[380]

---

375   *Id.* at Art. 76.

376   *Id.* at Art. 77.

377   *Id.* at Art. 78.

378   Canada Constitution Act, 1982, Art. 35(1).

379   Political Constitution of the Republic of Ecuador, Art.84(3).

380   Constitution of the Bolivarian Republic of Venezuela, Art. 119.

The history of indigenous peoples has been in existence since the colonial era, and it has historical and cultural roots. This requires active dialogue and partnership. The efforts of Erica Daes on behalf of the indigenous peoples and their lands have shed more light on this. She said it is high time the expropriation of indigenous peoples' lands be examined, and the undermining of their land tenure system needs to be addressed. The displacement from their land needs to be addressed besides.

It has been pointed out that evidence of indigenous peoples' traditional and customary land tenure can be established through qualified expert and academic opinion. Oral accounts and documentation by indigenous communities concerned can also be helpful.[381]

Several nations now have common practices on indigenous peoples' land and resource rights; for instance, some members of the Organization of American States (OAS) such as Bolivia have in their constitution[382] regulations governing indigenous community lands and the sustainable use and exploitation of natural resources. Brazil also made a provision under Chapter VIII of its constitution for indigenous peoples' original rights to the lands they traditionally occupied.[383] Ecuador is another nation that has in its constitution a provision that recognizes and guarantees indigenous peoples' rights to their ancestral lands.[384] The importance of land and resources to the indigenous peoples' survival is also reiterated by Sarah Stevenson where she points out that land is necessary for the subsistence and cultural integrity of indigenous peoples.[385]

As stated earlier, right to land is an important right for which the indigenous peoples worldwide are agitating. Land is part of indigenous peoples' life that they cannot exist without. Continued denial of indigenous

---

381   Anaya and Williams, *supra* note 201, at 47.

382   Article 171 of Bolivia Constitution, 1994; *see also* National Plans of Action for the Promotion and Protection of Human Rights – Bolivia, Office of the UN High Commissioner for Human Rights, *available at* http://www2.ohchr.org/english/issues/plan_actions/bolivia.htm.

383   Article 231 of Brazilian Constitution, 1988.

384   Article 84 of Ecuador Constitution; *see also* "Ecuador Passes New Constitution Acknowledging Indigenous Rights," Rights and Resources Initiative, *available at* http://www.rightsandresources.org/blog.php?id=358.

385   Sarah Stevenson, *Indigenous Land Rights and the Declaration on the Rights of Indigenous Peoples: Implications for Maori Land Claims in New Zealand*, 32 FORDHAM INT'L J. 301 (2008-2009).

peoples' rights to their lands and its resources will amount to snuffing their life out of them.

2.6.4 Cultural Rights

Cultural rights are one of the rights to which the indigenous peoples are entitled. This position was buttressed by the International Covenant on Economic, Social and Cultural Rights (ICESCR), especially in its preamble where it states that in accordance with the universal declaration of human rights, the ideal of free human beings enjoying freedom from fear and want can only be achieved if conditions are created whereby anyone may enjoy his economic, social and "cultural rights."

Provisions of the instrument also pointed out that by virtue of the right to self-determination, the indigenous peoples are free to determine their political status and freely pursue their economic, social and "cultural development." [386] Wiessner in his article pointed out that Indigenous peoples' demand for preservation of their endangered culture, their language, and their land was due to the collective spiritual relationship they have with their land and this is one of the factors that separates them from other groups. Wiessner, therefore, recommends that the indigenous community should be allowed to govern itself in order to continue the life of its culture and its members and have it flourish. [387] The provision of the Covenant mandates state parties to the Covenant to under take to ensure the equal rights of men and women to the enjoyment of all economic, social and "cultural rights" set forth in the present Covenant. [388]

The Covenant states that the steps to be taken by state parties to achieve the full realization of these rights shall include technical and vocational guidance, training programs, policies, and techniques to achieve steady economic, social and "cultural development" and full and productive employment under conditions safeguarding fundamental political and economic freedoms to the individual. [389]

---

386   International Covenant on Economic, Social and Cultural Rights, *supra* note 155, at Art. 1.

387   Wiessner, *Cultural Rights of Indigenous People, supra* note 271, at 127, 129 & 140.

388   International Covenant on Economic, Social and Cultural Rights, *supra* note 155, at Art. 3.

389   *Id.* at Art. 6(2).

The Covenant also enjoins state parties to recognize the right of everyone to take part in cultural life[390] and the benefits to be derived from the encouragement and development of international contacts and cooperation in the scientific and "cultural fields."[391] This covenant reiterates the importance or significance of cultural rights to indigenous peoples and enjoins nation states to encourage and promote same.

Janusz Symonides in his article concluded that cultural rights are an underdeveloped category of human rights.[392] This statement may sound bitter, but it is the truth. It is a fact that cultural rights are in the same category as social and economic rights but when it is time for implementation, attention is often only focused on economic and social rights while cultural rights are neglected. This is generally the practice of most nations states. It is rarely heard that a nation state is implementing cultural rights, while its counterparts economic and social rights are always in the news. Cultural rights are embedded in most regional and international instruments.

Symonides further showed in his article that the reason for the downplaying of cultural rights by most nation states may not be far fetched. He opined that most nation states think some people might begin to agitate for identification which may eventually lead to secession and national disunity[393] if their request for actualization of their cultural right is granted. Symonides, however, denoted that in the absence of cultural rights, democratic societies cannot be guaranteed[394] since peoples' cultures permeate every sphere of life.

Various international instruments made adequate provision for this right and this includes the Universal Declaration of Human Rights which states that "every one has the right to freely participate in the cultural life of the community"[395] and this was supposed to be made possible by a national and international effort.[396] This put an obligation on the nation states to ensure the realization of this right.

390   Id. at Art. 15(1)(a).

391   Id. at Art. 15(4).

392   Janusz Symonides, *Cultural Rights: A Neglected Category of Human Rights,* 50,158 Int'l. Soc. Sci. J. 559 (1998).

393   Id. at 560.

394   Id. at 561.

395   Universal Declaration of Human Rights, G.A. res. 217A (III), U.N. Doc A/810 (1948) Art.27 at 71, *available at* http://www1.umn.edu/humanrts/instree/b1udhr.htm.

396   Id. at Art. 22.

The International Covenant on Economic, Social and Cultural Rights also stated that the "state party must recognize the right of everyone to take part in cultural life."[397] The provisions of the International Covenant on Civil and Political Rights gave persons belonging to ethnic, religious or linguistic minorities the right to enjoy their culture, practice their religion and use their language.[398]

The provision for cultural rights is not limited to universal instruments alone as regional instruments too are not left out. Regional instruments such as the American Declaration of the Rights and the African Charter on Human and Peoples' Rights have all in one way or the other provided that every individual should have the right to take part in the cultural life of their community. The cultural right does not apply to individuals alone as the provisions of ICCPR expressly state that persons belonging to communities where ethnic, religions or linguistic minorities exist should be allowed to enjoy the cultural right in community with other members of their group.[399]

It could be submitted that the existence of various cultures should not be used by the nation states to bar people or groups from enjoying their cultural rights. Cultural diversity should not be ruled out in any society, and the existence of numerous cultures should not pose any problem. Those cultures are meant to be practiced and enjoyed by its faithful, and thus, they should not be denied the right.

The Declaration in the provisions[400] of Articles 12 and 29 deal with indigenous peoples' cultural and intellectual property. Article 12 states the following:

> Indigenous peoples have the right to manifest, practice, develop and teach their spiritual and religious traditions, customs and ceremonies; the right to maintain, protect, and have access in privacy to their

---

397   International Covenant on Economic, Social and Cultural Rights, adopted and opened for signature, ratification and accession by General Assembly resolution 2200A (XXI) of 16 December 1966, Art. 15, entry into force 3 January 1976, in accordance with article 27.

398   International Covenant on Civil and Political Rights, adopted and opened for signature, ratification and accession by General Assembly resolution 2200A (XXI) of 16 December 1966, Art. 27, entry into force 23 March 1976, in accordance with Article 49.

399   *Id.*

400   U.N. Declaration, *supra* note 83, at Arts. 12 & 29.

religious and cultural sites; the right to the use and control of their ceremonial objects; and the right to the repatriation of their human remains.[401]

While article 29(1) states:

Indigenous peoples have the right to the conservation and protection of the environment and the productive capacity of their lands or territories and resources. States shall establish and implement assistance programmes for indigenous peoples for such conservation and protection, without discrimination.[402]

The provision took note of the indigenous peoples' culture and encourages them to protect it because it is their heritage.

Lorie Graham in her article[403] pointed out that children are the most vulnerable to change and are usually unable to resist such change. From the perspective of this author, the colonial system had a lot of influence on the culture of the colonized people. Some of this influence had both a positive and negative impact on the customs of the colonized people. An example of a positive effect is the modernization the system brought to the colonized peoples' primitive ways of life. An example of the negative effect of the colonized custom is the overbearing influence of the colonial culture on the colonized peoples, which easily made the children and the young members of the group to be swayed by the changes made by the colonialists to the colonized cultures. The writer also stated that the major channels through which the colonized cultures are influenced are colonial missionaries and education.[404] These colonial missionaries, in their bid to introduce their religion to the colonized peoples, always imposed their religion and ways of life. Therefore, the traditional religious practice of the colonized peoples are always relegated to the backseat.

The influence of education equally had a strong effect on the colonized cultures. This is because the introduced Western education not only brought knowledge to the colonized, but it also changed their orientation towards

---

401   Id.

402   Id.

403   Lorie Graham. *Reparations, Self-determination, and the Seventh Generation*: 21 HARV. HUM. RTS. J. 47 (2008).

404   Id. at 48.

their ways of life. This made the group cultures start dying natural deaths because of the great effect which the Western education and ways of life had on their cultures. In most societies in Nigeria for example, many people started abandoning their age-old traditional occupations such as farming, hunting, fishing, divination, and so forth for white-collar jobs in the city. Most people also started to abandon their traditional religions for now dominant religions such as Christianity and Islam. Thus most people no longer perform rituals and other traditional rites as they used to do before.

Several international instruments supported the cultural rights of the indigenous peoples. One of these instruments is the Convention on Indigenous and Tribal Peoples in Independent Countries which advocated the need for indigenous peoples to exercise control over their ways of life and to develop and maintain their identities. The cultural rights of indigenous people can also be seen as the peoples' right to determine and establish the cultural regime under which they want to operate and live.[405] John Henriksen while proffering reason for the agitation of indigenous peoples' for cultural rights stated that indigenous peoples pursue this right in order to prevent their heritage, values, cultural identity and ways of life from being destroyed or adversely influenced by external forces.[406]

The provisions of the United Nations declarations also expressly support the rights of indigenous peoples to establish and control their educational systems and institutions and to provide education in their own languages.[407] States are obligated to ensure that indigenous individuals, particularly children, have access to an education in their own culture and provided in their own language.[408] Indigenous peoples also have the right to establish their own media in their own language and must not be deprived of non-indigenous media,[409] while states are obligated to ensure that state-owned media duly reflects indigenous cultural diversity.[410]

Legacy and heritage are part of the important inheritance that any society could bequeath to their children and coming generations and this is what the indigenous peoples are striving to achieve in their effort to protect

---

405   Henriksen, *supra* note 311, at 10.

406   *Id.*

407   U.N. Declaration, *supra* note 83, at Art. 14(1).

408   *Id.* at Art. 14(3).

409   *Id.* at Art. 16(1).

410   *Id.* at Art. 16(2).

and preserve their cultures.

Michael Asch, while stressing the importance of indigenous peoples' rights, revealed that indigenous rights are the rights that aboriginal peoples possessed before European settlement, [411] and which they continue to possess unless such rights are explicitly extinguished by conquest, treaty, or an act of Parliament. According to Paul Havemann, [412] much of the discussion of indigenous rights reflected debates about power, the obligations of rulers to their subjects, and the rights of those subjects within the domestic politics of the imperial powers as they made the transition from feudal to liberal societies.

The African Nation states and their attitude to the indigenous peoples' cause and their agitation for rights shall be discussed in chapter three.

---

411   Michael Asch, *Aboriginal Self-Government and Canada Constitutional Identity,* in MICHAEL LEVIN, ETHNICITY AND ABORIGINALITY: CASE STUDIES IN ETHNONATHIONALISM 40 (Univ. of Toronto Press, 1993).

412   Haveman, *supra* note 227, at 13.

CHAPTER THREE

INDIGENOUS PEOPLES FROM AFRICAN GOVERNMENTS PERSPECTIVE

3.1 AFRICA AND INDIGENOUS PEOPLES

The view and attitude of the African nation states towards the indigenous peoples' issues concerning the definition and the rights to which they are entitled will be examined in addition to the rights proposed by the United Nations. This examination becomes necessary because this subject is focused on determining whether indigenous peoples do exist in Nigeria and whether these peoples are entitled to some rights. Since Nigeria is situated in the African continent, it is only logical to study the prevailing view of the African nation states on this subject.

The African continent is a vast one that covers 30,244,000 square kilometers.[413] And as of the year 2000, the African continent was home to some 771 million people residing in fifty-four separate countries. The people of Africa speak more than 2,011 (or some thirty percent) of the world's 6,073 distinct languages.[414] Some African countries are especially diverse. Sudan, for example, contains over two hundred ethnic groups who speak some 134 languages, while Nigeria has about three hundred and fifty or more ethnic groups speaking different languages. The above information established the fact that the African continent is a vast one in view of the size and the numbers of its inhabitants.

"Indigenous peoples" as a term in Africa is normally applied to tribes that are nomadic or farmers. There are millions of these indigenous peoples

---

413   *Continents of the World: Africa,* Mbendi Information Services, *available at* http://www.mbendi.com/land/ p0007.htm.

414   *Id.*

who are largely restricted and neglected by the various African governments. The African governments prefer the "modern world" at the expense of their pre-colonial heritage.[415] This preference is caused by the effect of colonization and the aftermath of the so called civilization brought by the colonialists. There are approximately 30 million nomadic peoples and millions more pastoralists in Africa. Most of these peoples would be designated as "indigenous" in other parts of the world.[416] As a result of this fact, it could be concluded that the refusal of the African nation states to identify indigenous peoples within their territory is not justified because they share the same characteristics with indigenous peoples in other continents.

Some African nation states are in the habit of using routine and arbitrary definitions in their bid to shy away from their obligations to indigenous peoples in their domain. They tend to lump them together with others who have the similar characteristic of residing in remote areas and being marginal in a socioeconomic sense. A good example of this is Botswana, a nation state with diverse cultures where the government prefers not to differentiate specific populations that are targets of development programs. This is because the government does not wish to be seen as segregating its multiracial peoples on the basis of ethnic identification.[417]

In Africa, it is difficult to differentiate people that are indigenous from those that are not because a variety of populations have moved in and out of local areas over time. The majority of Africans always identify themselves as belonging to specific tribal or ethnic groups. Even at that, there are internal subdivisions to which people pay heed, such as a clan affiliation.

The effect of the commercial world and of the western world has extremely influenced the African governments in their economic and developmental drives causing them to start displacing nomadic tribes off their lands without the peoples' consent. This was because the government needed their land for its developmental programs. The Tanzanian government is a good representative of this trend. The government dispossessed 30,000 Baribaigs from their grazing lands for the purpose of wheat production to

---

415   Alexander Ewen, *Africa and Eurasia, in* Voice of Indigenous Peoples, 145, 145-46 (Alexander Ewen, ed., Clear Light Publishers 1994).

416   *Id.* at 146.

417   Robert K. Hitchcock & John D. Holm, *Bureaucratic Domination of Hunter-Gatherer Societies: A Study of the San in Botswana,* 24.2 Development and Change 305-38 (1993); Saugestad, *supra* note 70, at 60.

be sold commercially.[418] The African governments have showed little regard for the indigenous peoples, their land and their cultures. This is evident by the conversion of the indigenous peoples' lands to parks and game reserves in their bid to preserve Africa's unique wildlife from extinction. The endangered African animals are mostly found on the indigenous peoples' lands. This is probably because of the lands' underdevelopment that the animals tend to use it for shelter.[419]

A myriad of indigenous peoples in Africa have been displaced by the worldwide and regional political struggles which has led to vast calamities for the indigenous peoples and has considerably worsened the peoples' situation.[420] This not only has had an adverse effect on the indigenous peoples, but it has also added to their burden. An example of such a regional political struggle is the bloody clash in Angola between the indigenous peoples and Portugal which led to the death of 100,000 Angolans and 750,000 refugees. This singular incident not only weakened the country, but it generated bitter ethnic rivalries.[421]

When almost all of the African colonies became independent in the 1960s, the general belief, that the dignity of the people of African descent that had been eroded by years of colonization would be restored, was never realized. It was extremely disappointing; however, that the heads of the new states were fashioned after the European models. These African governments and leaders are more interested in continuing with the arrangement left behind by the colonial masters than making any effort to alter this arrangement to continue their peoples' cultures, desires and ways of life.[422] It is equally sad that the European economic systems and related connections that were put in place during the colonization have continued with their bad and devastating effects. These effects tend to erode the African cultures which the locals have cherished so much. Also, through colonization numerous efforts were made to exterminate and replace the African indigenous institutions by social organization, self-determination, and cultural identity. These efforts were not only inherited by the independent nation states, but these states have

---

418   Ewen, *supra* note 415, at 146.

419   *Id.* at 147.

420   *Id.*

421   *Id.*

422   Moringe L. Parkipuny, *Native Leaders Address at the United Nations in 1992* in Voice of Indigenous Peoples, 77, 79 (Alexander Ewen, ed., Clear Light Publishers 1994).

vigorously supported and continued with this ideology.[423] This is evident in the African regimes and governments' failure to make any concrete effort to communicate with their citizens in order to rectify the anomalies caused by the colonization. Instead, they have closed their ears to any suggestion, no matter how insignificant and characterized any indigenous proposals as inspired by unpatriotic feelings.[424] Thus, the stance of the current African governments does not in anyway differ from the stance of the past colonial administrations that saw the African pre-independence desire as an ancient ideal which was only intended to cause disturbances within the law and administration.[425]

The endeavors of the African unity leaders to eliminate cultural diversity have produced problematic numbers of land border disputes and nationality conflicts over the indigenous peoples' rights to a national existence. The nation states felt that this right conflicted with the governments' priority drive for unity. It is on this stage that the indigenous peoples of Africa, the minority people, continued to be marginalized, "deprived of their fundamental freedoms, and having their basic rights violated with impunity through discrimination and prejudice."[426] The African governments of today are just like the colonialists who only see "the negative side of diversity" which they believe will ultimately lead to tribal hostilities.[427] For this reason, the African governments decline to address the inequity and harm caused by the imposition of foreign varieties of government and of culture. This led to the devastation of the indigenous peoples' African values and spawned "corruption, nepotism, irresponsibility and hatred."[428]

The African countries governments tend to take two different positions on the issue of indigenous populations within their territories. First, they claim that there are no indigenous peoples whatsoever, or second, they state that all of the groups in the country are indigenous.[429] The government is adamant to change its position even in the midst of oral histories, data from archaeological records and sometimes ethno-historic information that glaringly proves that indigenous peoples truly exist. The government tends

---

423   *Id.*

424   *Id.* at 80.

425   *Id.*

426   *Id.*

427   *Id.*

428   *Id.*

429   Mutume, *supra* note 74, at 2.

to be conservative about changing the status quo on the excuse that if they allow any group of people, it might cause segregation which might lead to disunity among the subjects. The socio-economic cultural and political act of domination that the indigenous peoples suffered during the colonial era still continued after the independence of most nation states, and this has led to a lack of recognition of indigenous peoples' status. Post-colonial Africa states are more interested in uniformity and denying the differences.[430] This attitude of not recognizing the difference represented by the indigenous peoples is a threat to their cultural survival.[431] It may even lead to the extinction of their culture if the issue is not urgently addressed.

Over the past two decades a number of different African groups have claimed to be indigenous, some of whom have attended the meeting of the Working Group on Indigenous Populations (WGIP) of the United Nations in Geneva. They have also taken part in a number of international forums on indigenous peoples' human rights and advocacy organizations.[432]

There has been a lot of awareness brought about on the issue of indigenous peoples in Africa. Regional meetings on African indigenous peoples' rights have been held in recent years. One example being a meeting held in Arusha, Tanzania, in January 1999, that was organized by the International Work Group for Indigenous Affairs and the Pastoralist Indigenous Non-Government Organizations Forum. At many of these meetings the participants, who are usually representatives of their groups, always outline the wishes of their people hoping this will help their cause. Examples of these causes are civil and political rights, including the right to life and the right to take part in decision making. The people are also concerned about their land rights, economic rights and cultural rights without which their existence may be threatened. For example, the indigenous peoples find it difficult to get access to the land because of various acts or laws enacted

430   Julian Kunnie & Maqhudeni Ivy Goduka, Wisdom and Power: Affirming our Knowledge through Narratives 252 (Ashgate Pub. 2006); see also Chidei Oguamanam, International Law and Indigenous Knowledge: Intellectual Property, Plant Biodiversity and Traditional Medicine 22 (University of Toronto Press, 2006).

431   Kunnie, supra note 440, at 252.

432   See Sidsel Saugestad, Contested Images: Indigenous Peoples in Africa, 2 Indigenous Affairs 6-9 (1999) concerning the identity of indigenous peoples in Africa; see also Africa's Indigenous Peoples: "First Peoples" or " Marginalized Minorities?" (Alan Barnard & Justin Kenrick, eds., Center of African Studies, University of Edinburgh, 2001).

by the nation states. In central Africa, for example, Batwa or Twa (Pygmies) generally had problems in gaining title over their land. Most groups have a history of hunting and gathering in eastern and southern Africa,[433] and are also experiencing this harrowing treatment from the government.

The issue for the indigenous peoples of Africa is complicated by the serious economic and political distress they must go through.

A combination of war, economic depression, environmental degradation, and poorly framed development policies have left many people, especially the poor, worse off over the past two decades. Structural adjustment programs (SAP) of the International Monetary Fund and the World Bank have led to cut backs in spending on health, education, and welfare.[434]

Nigeria is an example of countries where the implementation of SAP has failed woefully. Various African countries have had their sustenance systems together with their "social and physical infrastructures" crumble. Looking for a reversion of these movements, the indigenous peoples' groups and their advocates are agitating for opportunity to participate in the decision making, the abolishment of inequalities, and the wiping out of discrimination.[435] The indigenous peoples in Africa are pursuing change in their governmental policies and programs because they are not contented to be last on the socioeconomic hierarchy ladder. They are also trying to influence the government at the international level to instill additional programs and policies that are fairer, moral and virtuous.[436]

The World Bank and the Global Environmental Facility (GEF) have substantially "invested in both the environmentally and socially sustainable development projects at the local level in indigenous communities. The World Bank has also hosted several international meetings of indigenous peoples in Africa."[437] And part of its efforts is the World Bank policy on indigenous peoples. Despite all their progress, the major problem confronting the indigenous peoples in Africa is the failure of the nation-states, international institutions, and transnational corporations to comply with the human

---

433   Hitchcock, *supra* note 417, at 211.
434   *Id.* at 205, 214.
435   *Id.*
436   *Id.* at 215.
437   *Id.*

rights legislation and guidelines on indigenous peoples and the development project implementation,[438] which they have flagrantly disobeyed.

African indigenous peoples are generally not acknowledged as indigenous or as having rights that are definite and fixed because of the nature of their struggle and adversity. This is caused by a combination of social and political factors. Indigenous peoples in Africa are always denied their civil and political rights using the reasoning that certain groups would have greater rights than other people if the indigenous peoples were allowed to have their way. Most African governments have not only prohibited their citizens from attending international meetings on indigenous peoples' rights all in a bid to frustrate them, but most indigenous organizations are prevented from even gaining official recognition.[439]

The manner that countries of the world manage the indigenous peoples' issues is extremely diverse. For instance in North America, the Canadian First Nations and the American Indians are generally acknowledged as "domestic dependent nations"[440] with restricted autonomy.[441]

Indigenous peoples' civil rights, political rights, land rights, economic rights, and cultural rights are recognized in some nation states in Latin America where the governments are administered by indigenous

---

438   *Id.*

439   *Id.* at 220.

440   The phrase "domestic dependent nations" came up in the case of *Cherokee Nation v. Georgia* (30 U.S. 5 (Pet.) 1 (1831)) where the Supreme Court held that the Cherokee Nation was not a foreign nation but a "domestic dependent nation" that is subject to the sovereignty of the United States federal government. This is because the tribe was neither a state nor a foreign nation. This case was one of the three foundational cases (also referred to as the Marshall Trilogy) that established the field of federal Indian law. These are cases which arose due to the conflicts from the attempts of the government to assert their authority over the tribal governments. Justice Marshall in his opinion gave consensus that brought up the concept of Indian nations retaining their existing "nation status." Two other cases were used by the Supreme Court to establish their point. One case was *Worcester v. Georgia* (31 U.S. 515, 8 L. Ed. 483 (1832)) where the Supreme Court held that Indian tribes as separate nations had defined territorial boundaries within which state law was inoperative. The third case is that of *Johnson v. M'Intosh* (21 U.S. (8 Wheat) 543 (1823)) where Justice Marshall held that the Indians do not have enforceable title to the land acquired by the Europeans during their invasion. The Court further held that the Indians only enjoyed a right of occupancy (which was not deemed full title) as the ultimate title to land had passed to the United States government under the discovery doctrine.

441   *Id.*

peoples.[442] The situation in Africa is totally different from the situation in North America and Latin America as earlier mentioned. African indigenous peoples realize that they reside in areas that are lagging behind other regions of the world, notably North and South America, Europe, and the Middle East.[443] This conclusion was drawn based on the treatment being meted to them by various nation states in Africa. One of the numerous reasons for the predicaments of the African indigenous people is the ploy of the African governments to shy away from their responsibilities to indigenous peoples by using "cultural relativist arguments" to excuse the rejection of human rights reasoning that they are encouraging economic development and sustaining political stability.[444] In other words, the African governments feel their beliefs and activities should be determined or dictated by the nation's culture without taking into consideration the universal human rights standards. The African indigenous peoples, however, do not agree with the notion that the cultural values of nations and peoples should prevail over the universal human rights standards which often leads to conflicts between the indigenous groups and the nation states.[445]

African indigenous communities and organizations have made various efforts to get the governments of the states in which they reside to develop and enforce national legislation that is aimed at human rights promotion and protection, but there has been little or no progress. The situation in Nigeria is a good example where efforts of indigenous groups and human rights organizations are always frustrated. One of such instances was the case of Movement for the Survival of Ogoni People (MOSOP) whose leader Ken Saro Wiwa was killed by the government while championing the cause of his indigenous group. Indigenous groups and their supporters have banded together to protest human rights violations, and have sought redress in international fora and courts for nation states actions.

Most indigenous groups question the African governments' argument that the state beliefs and activities should be dictated by the state's customs and that the human rights standard should be subjected to such customs. The indigenous groups and human rights organizations have stressed the importance of being protected from governmental repression

---

442   ALISON BRYSK, FROM TRIBAL VILLAGE TO GLOBAL VILLAGE: INDIAN RIGHTS AND INTERNATIONAL RELATIONS IN LATIN AMERICA 127 (Stanford Univ. Press, 2000).

443   Id.

444   Hitchcock, supra note 417, at 220-21.

445   Id. at 221.

and the negative effects of globalization in Africa which leads most nation states to give priority to economic gain rather than the well-being of the indigenous groups. For instance, the government of Nigeria gives priority to encouraging Shell BP, a Royal/Dutch corporation in extracting oil in the Niger Delta area where indigenous communities lands and territories have been degraded at the expense of the well-being of the indigenous groups that rely on the land and territory for their means of livelihood. It has also been observed that African governments and the companies working in Africa endorse economic development at the expense of civil, political, social, and cultural rights and in fact violate international law and the various United Nations instruments such as the International Covenant on Civil and Political Rights and the Covenant on Economic, Social, and Cultural Rights.[446]

The international indigenous rights movement has had significant impacts on the ways in which African indigenous peoples have attempted to establish their own identities and promote their rights. African governments have always shown their opposition to indigenous peoples and their supporters who are seeking greater recognition of indigenous peoples' rights. The government position is usually shown by arresting and detaining indigenous leaders and by suspending the operations of nongovernmental organizations that are seeking to promote indigenous rights and social and environmental justice.[447]

Some indigenous groups have actively resisted state efforts to promote development or bring about cultural assimilation which they think will erode their age-old customs which govern their everyday affairs, in some cases using nonviolent tactics and in other cases seeking to bring about self-determination through military means. The danger of confronting the government with the use of force is that they will be facing the military might of their own government which is in most cases much more sophisticated than that of the indigenous peoples.

The argument of African governments is that all peoples within their domain are indigenous in the sense that they are populations whose ancestors have inhabited the continent since time immemorial and that they do not see the need to distinguish some groups as "more indigenous" than

446   HANNE VEBER, JENS DAHL, FIONA WILSON, ESPEN WAEHLE: "... NEVER DRINK FROM THE SAME CUP." PROCEEDINGS OF THE CONFERENCE ON INDIGENOUS PEOPLES IN AFRICA. TUNE, DENMARK, 11 (1993) (IWGIA DOC. No.74, Copenhagen 1993).

447   INTERNATIONAL WORK GROUP FOR INDIGENOUS AFFAIRS, THE INDIGENOUS WORLD, 2000-2001.

others. The government thinks this might lead to strife or internal conflict. The conflicts and the problems characteristic of indigenous peoples are real and very glaring despite the various attempts made to proffer a working definition to define people that are truly indigenous and to find permanent solutions to conflicts and problems in which differences of culture and ethnicity are involved.[448]

The indigenous peoples of Africa are seen as populations that voluntarily neglected, or were schemed out from participating in modern development. Indigenous peoples were put in a position of marginal importance during the colonial period and this marginalization was continued against indigenous peoples by the post-colonial governments. While marginalization is part of the historical experience of indigenous peoples, it cannot serve as a sole characteristic but only serve as a complement to other characteristics. Thus, marginalization alone will not qualify any group as indigenous. Therefore, people or groups of people who are marginalized can not be considered indigenous solely on that factor, and the question of whether the peoples or groups of people in question will cease to be indigenous should they succeed in liberating themselves from their marginalized condition will not arise.[449]

Africa's indigenous peoples' struggles are not asking for control of state power or state institutions or to aspire to independent statehood, but they claim rights to territory and self-determination in order to secure their own existence.[450]

The indigenous peoples' claims in Africa center mainly on the issue of collective rights and the paramount one is the indigenous peoples demand for their rights to territory and land.[451] The major reason for this is that their livelihood and existence totally depends on their lands and natural resources. The expropriation of their land by the government of nation states is causing them great hardship. A very good example is the case of Nigeria where the lands of indigenous people of the Niger Delta area of Nigeria were granted to the foreign company Shell BP for oil exploration at the expense of

---

448   Veber, *supra* note 446, at 11.

449   *Id.* at 15.

450   *Id.*

451   Jeremy Swift, *The Future of African Hunter-Gatherer and Pastoral Peoples,* 13.2 DEVELOPMENT AND CHANGE 159, 159-181 (April 1982).

the inhabitants.[452] The proceeds from the natural resources extracted from the territory were put on a legislative list which automatically stopped the inhabitants from having control of the commercial gains made from their land. The inhabitants, therefore, suffered a double tragedy. Their land was degraded through the activities of the foreign oil companies and they could no longer practice their ancient occupations which included farming and fishing. The second loss is that they were not compensated for the loss of their land which is their means of sustenance. They are, therefore, not able to benefit from the economic gains made from the oil company's activities.

In establishing the indigenous peoples as the first comer in a place, the term "from time immemorial" is usually used to show that an inhabitant is regarded as the first settler in a territory. It is always very difficult in Africa to prove the connection of the indigenous peoples to the land when compared to what is necessary in Europe where the process is very simple.[453]

Despite the African government's contention that there are no indigenous peoples in Africa, there are several instruments stating that indigenous peoples not only exist in Africa but they are entitled to some rights.

3.2 AFRICAN INSTRUMENTS SUPPORTING INDIGE-NOUS PEOPLES AND THEIR RIGHTS

There are several Acts made for the protection of the African people, and this includes, but is not limited to the Constitutive Act of the African Union. This states that one of the objectives of the union shall be to "[P]romote and protect human and peoples' rights in accordance with the African Charter on Human and People's Rights and other relevant human rights instruments."[454]

While the provisions of the Constitutive Act does not expressly mention the "indigenous peoples," it could be deduced from the words that

452   PRADYUMNA PRASA KARAN, THE NON-WESTERN WORLD: ENVIRONMENT, DEVELOPMENT, AND HUMAN RIGHTS 525 (Routledge, 2004); see also LAURA WESTRA & BILL LAWSON, FACES OF ENVIRONMENTAL RACISM: CONFRONTING ISSUES OF GLOBAL JUSTICE 195 (Rowman & Littlefield Pub. Inc, 2001).

453   RICHARD J. PERRY, FROM TIME IMMEMORIAL: INDIGENOUS PEOPLES AND STATE SYSTEMS 8 (Austin: University of Texas, 1942).

454   Constitutive Act of the African Union, Art. 3(h), available at http://www.africa-union.org/root/au/AboutAu/Constitutive_Act_en.htm.

the phrase "human and peoples' rights" encompassed the indigenous peoples. The provision also recognized the relevant human rights instruments and it is a fact that the majority of the international and regional instruments made adequate provisions for indigenous peoples and the rights to which they are entitled.

The Assembly of the African Union in January 2007 showed its support and welcomed the efforts by the international community to allow the rights of indigenous peoples and expresses full support and solidarity with indigenous peoples of the world.[455]

3.2.1 African Charter on Human and Peoples' Rights (Banjul Charter)

The African Charter on Human and Peoples' Rights (also known as Banjul Charter) came into being on the 28th June 1981 in Nairobi and entered into force on the 21st October 1981.[456] The African Charter consists of a preamble and sixty-eight articles. The charter was to amongst others reaffirming the pledge in the Organization of African Unity (OAU) Charter to eradicate all forms of colonialism from Africa[457] and to promote international cooperation, having due regard to the charter of the United Nations and the Universal Declaration of Human Rights (UDHR).[458]

The charter imposes duties on both the state and individuals. In the Charter, the state is mandated to promote and protect morals and traditional values recognized by the community.[459] The state is also obligated to take care of the physical and moral health of the family,[460] and assist the family.[461] Moreover, the state has the obligation to ensure the exercise of the right to

---

455   Decision on the United Nations Declaration on the Rights of Indigenous Peoples, U.N. Doc. Assembly/AU/9(VIII) Add.6, Assembly of the African Union, Eighth ordinary session, January 29-30, 2007, Addis Ababa, Ethiopia, Assembly/AU?DEC. 134-164 (VIII).

456   Malcolm Evans & Rachel Murray, The African Charter on Human and Peoples' Rights: The System in Practice, 1986-2006, 8 (2008).

457   OAU Charter, Art. 2(d), *available at* http://www.iag-agi.org/bdf/docs/oau_charter.pdf.

458   *Id.* at Art. 2(e).

459   African [Banjul] Charter on Human and Peoples' Rights, adopted June 27, 1981, OAU Doc. CAB/LEG/ 67/3 rev. 5, 21 I.L.M. 58 (1982), entered into force Oct. 21, 1986, Art. 17, *available at* http://www.africa-union.org/official_documents/treaties_%20 conventions_%20protocols/banjul%20charter.pdf.

460   *Id.* at Art. 18(1).

461   *Id.* at Art. 18(2).

development.[462]

The charter mandates the state parties to the charter to promote and ensure rights and freedoms contained in the Charter through teaching, education and publication.[463] Individuals, on the other hand, have duties toward their families and society, the state and other legally recognized communities and the international community.[464] Individuals are also obliged to respect and consider other fellow beings without discrimination.[465] The individual is required to contribute to the best of his abilities, at all times and at all levels, to the promotion and achievement of African Unity.[466]

In addition to these rights and duties, the Charter made provision for the establishment of the African Commission on Human and Peoples' Rights.[467] The Charter also listed the functions of the commission,[468] its procedures,[469] ways to handle communication from the states,[470] applicable principles[471] and general provisions.[472]

It is important to point out that most of the provisions of the International Covenant on Civil and Political Rights (ICCPR) and the International Covenant on Economic, Social and Cultural Rights (ICESCR) correspond with the provisions of the African Charter. For instance, the following tables show the similarities between the African Charter and the above mentioned instruments.

---

462   *Id.* at Art. 22(2).
463   *Id.* at Art. 25.
464   *Id.* at Art. 27.
465   *Id.* at Art. 28.
466   *Id.* at Art. 29.
467   *Id.* at Art. 30.
468   *Id.* at Art. 45.
469   *Id.* at Art. 46.
470   *Id.* at Art. 47.
471   *Id.* at Art. 60.
472   *Id.* at Art. 64.

AFRICAN CHARTER	ICCPR
Art. 4- Respect for life and integrity.	Art. 6- Right of everyone to the opportunity to gain his living by work which he freely chooses
Art.6- Right to liberty and security of individual	Art.9- State parties to recognize everyone's right to social security.
Art. 20- All people shall have right to self-determination.	Art. 1- All people have the right of self-determination.
Art. 3- Every individual shall be equal before the law	Art.14- All are equal before the courts and tribunals .
Art.8- Everyone shall have freedom of conscience and religion.	Art. 18- Everyone has the right to freedom of thought, conscience and religion.
Art. 10- Every individual shall have the right to free association.	Art. 21- Everyone has the right to freedom of peaceful assembly and association.

AFRICAN CHARTER	ICESCR
Art. 20- All people shall have right to self-determination.	Art.1- All peoples have the right to self-determination
Art. 17- Every individual shall have the right to education.	Art. 12- State shall recognize the right of everyone to education.
Art. 15- Every individual have the right to work under equitable and satisfactory conditions.	Art. 7- state parties to recognize right of everyone of the enjoyment of just and favourable conditions.
Art. 3- Every individual shall be equal before the law	Art. 3- State parties to ensure the equal right of men and women to the enjoyment of all economic, social and cultural rights.

The African Charter also made provision for the third generation rights which require the cooperation of all people.[473] One example of these is the right to self-determination which provides that people shall freely determine their political, economic and social development.[474]

The collective rights of peoples (indigenous peoples included) have been affirmed by the African Charter on Human and Peoples' Rights to which Nigeria is a signatory. This charter grants peoples unquestionable and inalienable rights to self-determination,[475] the right to freely dispose

473   U. O. Umozurike, The African Charter on Human and Peoples' Rights 51 (Martinus Nijhoff Pub., 1997).

474   African [Banjul] Charter on Human and Peoples' Rights, adopted June 27, 1981, OAU Doc. CAB/LEG/67/3 rev. 5, 21 I.L.M. 58 (1982), entered into force Oct. 21, 1986, Art. 20, *available at* http:// www. africa-union.org/offical_documents/treaties_%20 convention_%20protocols/banjul%20charter.pdf.

475   *Id.* at Art. 20.

of their wealth and natural resources,[476] the right to economic, social and cultural development;[477] and the right to an environment favorable to their development.[478]

In Africa, these rights have been applied to indigenous peoples by ACHPR in the landmark cases of SERAC[479] which involve the Ogoni peoples of Nigeria and the Nigerian government. ACHPR also recently recognized the indigenous peoples' status of Endorois in Kenya,[480] whereby ACHPR recommended that Kenya must recognize the ownership rights of the Endorois and restore them back to their ancestral lands and pay them adequate compensation for the loss suffered.

3.2.2 African Commission on Human and Peoples' Rights

The African Commission on Human and Peoples' Rights was established by the African Charter on Human and Peoples' Rights (also known as Banjul Charter) which came into force on 21st October 1986 after its adoption in 1981 by the Assembly of Heads of State and Government of the Organization of African Unity (OAU). The mission of this commission is to ensure promotion and protection of human and peoples' rights throughout the African continent.[481]

3.2.2.1 Functions of the African Commission on Human and Peoples' Rights

The Commission has the duty to promote human and peoples' rights, particularly to collect documents, undertake studies and researches on African problems in the field of humans and peoples,[482] and formulate principles and rules aimed at solving legal problems relating to human and peoples' rights.[483]

---

476   *Id.* at Art. 21.

477   *Id.* at Art. 22.

478   Id. at Art. 24.

479   Social and Economic Rights Action Center & the Center for Economic and Social Rights v. Nigeria. Communication No. 155/96.

480   Centre for Minority Rights Development (Kenya) and Minority Rights Group International on Behalf of Endorois Welfare Council v Kenya (276 / 2003).

481   African Commission on Human and Peoples' Rights: History, *available at* http://www.achpr.org/ english/_info/history_en.html.

482   *Id.* at Art.45(1) (a),

483   *Id.* at Art. 45(1) (b).

Art. 62 of the charter mandates the Commission to handle the state reports which the states are expected to send to the Commission every two years on the measures they have taken to implement the provisions of the character. The Commission also has the duty to draw inspiration from international law on human and peoples' rights in their operation[484] and the Commission shall take into consideration general or special international conventions in the operation. These will serve as applicable principles.[485]

The commission has been very operative. At its 30th ordinary session in Gambia[486] the African Commission on Human and Peoples' Rights welcomed the establishment of the African Union following the adoption of the Constitutive Act of the African Union. It resolved to accept the requests of the Assembly of Heads of State and Government to submit proposals on the incorporation of the African human rights mechanism into the structures of the African Union.[487]

Additionally in 2002, at its 31st ordinary session in Pretoria, South Africa,[488] the Commission apart from considering communication from nation states, adopted the resolution on:

(1) The ratification of the protocol on the establishment of the African Court on Human and Peoples' Rights; and
(2) The ratification of the statute on the International Criminal Court by OAU/AU member states.[489]

3.2.3 The African Union Attitude

The African Union (AU) is the principal organization for the promotion of socio-economic integration across the continent. It includes

---

484   *Id.* at Art. 60.

485   *Id.* at Art. 61.

486   Final Communiqué of the 30th Ordinary Session of the African Commission on Human and Peoples' Rights, 30th Ordinary Session of the African Commission on Human and Peoples' Rights, 13th – 27th October 2001, Banjul, The Gambia, *available at* http://www.achpr.org/english/communiques/ communique30_en.html.

487   *Id.* at Para. 11.

488   31st Ordinary session of the African Commission on Human and Peoples' Rights, 2-16 May 2002: Pretoria, South Africa.

489   Final Communiqué on the 31st Ordinary Session of the African Commission on Human and Peoples' Rights, May 2-16, 2002, Pretoria, South Africa.

53 African countries as member states. The AU was inaugurated on July 2002 in South Africa. The body replaced the Organization of African Unity (OAU) and its creation is consistent with the spirit of Pan-Africanism.[490] The African Union has been instrumental to the quelling of political unrest in the form of secession and threat to the sovereignty of the nation states. The Union was more interested in reconciliation than warfare.

The Union was in support of the Nigerian federal government against the secession bid of the Igbo of eastern Nigeria which resulted into a civil war that lasted for thirty months.[491] The AU also played a significant role in the independence war between Eritrea and Ethiopia, despite the fact that Eritrea eventually achieved its independence from Ethiopia in 1993, after thirty years of intermittent armed conflict.[492] The AU was part of the body responsible for bringing a cease-fire between Eritrea and Ethiopia by making both parties sign the cessation of Hostilities Agreement. The Union was involved during the secession of Katanga from the Congo. The Katanga case was a big test for the AU because the case was inherited by the Union since the problem was already in existence before the formation of AU. The general expectation was that the union would oppose the secession in clear terms, but because of the interest of the Western neocolonial forces, the white South African mining interest, and the lack of trust in Lumumba's commitment to democracy, the secession was able to materialize.[493]

The Katanga case illustrated the capacity of the African state system.[494] On July 11, 1960, Katanga seceded from the Congo.[495] The Katanga province was geographically and economically an integral part of the multinational corporate empire in Southern Africa after the First World War.[496] The integration of the mineral-rich Katanga province into the Southern African

---

490   Timothy Murithi, The African Union: Pan-Africanism, Peacebuilding and Development 3 (Ashgate Pub., Ltd., 2005).

491   Charles Robertson, International Politics since World War II: A Short History 327 (M.E. Sharpe, 1997).

492   John Tessitore and Diana Ayton-Shenker, A Global Agenda: Issues Before the 56TH Assembly of the United Nations 20 (Rowman & Littlefield, 1991).

493   On the Way to Statehood: Secession and Globalization 72 (Aleksandar Pavkovic & Peter Radan, eds., Ashgate Pub., 2008).

494   Francis Mading Deng & William Zartman, Conflict Resolution in Africa 337 (Brookings Institution Press, 1991).

495   Georges Nzongola-Ntalaja, The Congo from Leopold to Kabila: A People's History 99 (Zed Books, 2002).

496   Id.

economic complex was a major part of the reason for the Katanga secession.

Early years of mining exploitation revealed that most of the skilled workers were white settlers from the south. They tried to propagate the racism of the Belgian colonial system[497] and they tried to create a colonial settler system and subordinate the economy of the province to their interest.[498] The forces of Britain, France and South Africa gave active support to the secession because they did not trust Lumumba's commitment to democracy. The above cases are part of the involvement of the African Union in the activities of the African nation states.

The African Union[499] (AU) at its eighth African Union Summit made some decisions which concerned indigenous peoples. The AU commented on the United Nations Declaration on the Rights of Indigenous Peoples concerning their decisions.[500] The AU took note of the UN Declaration of the Rights of Indigenous Peoples adopted by the UN Human Rights Council on June 29, 2006, and welcomed the efforts of the international community to address the rights of indigenous peoples and expressed its support and solidarity with indigenous peoples of the world.

It is, however, sad to note that Namibia,[501] a member of African Union, successfully lobbied other countries represented at the United Nations to frustrate the adoption of the United Nations rights resolution by delaying a declaration on the rights of indigenous peoples, thus dampening the hope of rights advocates that have been campaigning for a resolution at the initial stage for about twenty-two years.[502] It was Namibia that proposed amendments, on behalf of several African nations, to put off consideration of the Declaration until the end of the General Assembly session in September 2007 to allow for further consultations. The fifty-three African member states thus voted as a bloc to delay the adoption of the Declaration and this portrayed them as supporters of continuing colonization and subjugation of

---

497   *Id.*

498   *Id.* at 101.

499   The principal organization for the promotion of socioeconomic integration across the continent, and this includes 53 African countries as member states.

500   Decision, *supra* note 455.

501   Namibia is an African country.

502   Christof Maletsky. *Namibia Slammed for "Killing" UN Rights Resolution*, INDIG-ENOUS PEOPLES CAUCUS, 1 December 2006, *available at* http://www.ipcaucus.net/HRday/Namibia.html.

indigenous peoples.[503]

The act of Namibia was based on the premise that some provisions in the draft declaration contradicted the national constitutions of a number of African countries. The matter was tabled to allow time for careful consideration of the matter. The act of Namibia goes to show the attitude of most African governments to the indigenous peoples issue. It is even more disturbing that an African country could lead a revolt against the European Union on the issue of whether the Declaration should be delayed or not, especially with an African country leading the move for the delay. Namibia, which championed the opposition against the United Nations Declaration's adoption, stated that some provisions of the then UN draft declaration of the indigenous peoples' rights was inconsistent with the national constitutions of a number of African countries. It could, therefore, be concluded that Namibia sees the declaration as a threat to the states' territorial integrity. The African group position paper (Aide mémoire) consistently referred to the threat of secession.[504] It could be deduced from history that part of the reason why Namibia was against the adoption of the United Nations Declaration of indigenous peoples rights was the threat of secession by the Caprivi Strip.[505] The Caprivi Strip is an elongated segment of land which extends the Namibian territory into the center of the African continent. The Caprivi Strip shares borders with the states of Botswana, Angola and Zambia and its geographic location could facilitate secession.[506]

In the view of Inuit Circumpolar Council and Saami Council (Arctic Caucus), the vote against the Declaration by African states displayed the fact that they could not accept a human rights instrument that supports and is consistent with international law and its progressive development in the specific context of the world's indigenous peoples. There are, however, insinuations that the African states were not working alone but were aided

---

503   Statement by Indigenous Peoples Caucus, *UN's Human Rights Record Challenged by Indigenous Peoples,* INDIGENOUS PEOPLES CAUCUS, 9 December 2006, *available at* http:// www.ipcaucus.net/ HRday/HRday.html.

504   Press Release, *Indigenous Peoples of Africa Co-ordinating Committee IPACC, INDIGENOUS PEOPLES CAUCUS,* 5 December 2006, *available at* http://www.ipcaucus.net/ HRday/IPACC.html.

505   EDMUND JAN OSMAŃCZYK & ANTHONY MANGO, ENCYCLOPEDIA OF THE UNITED NATIONS AND INTERNATIONAL AGREEMENTS 1507 3d ed. (Routledge, 2004).

506   Krzysztof Trzcinski, *The Significance of Geographic Location for the Success of Territorial Secession: African Example,* 11 MISCELLANEA GEOGRAPHICA 213-14 (Warszawa, 2004).

and abetted by Canada, Australia, New Zealand and the United States, each of which believed to be against the declaration.[507]

The Assembly reaffirmed and ended up voting the resolution[508] that member states of the OAU pledged to respect borders existing at the time of their achievement of national independence. The Assembly also reaffirmed the resolution[509] concerning the Declaration on the Granting of Independence to Colonial Countries and Peoples.

In addition to the above, the Assembly welcomed efforts by the international community to address the rights of indigenous peoples and expressed full support and solidarity with indigenous peoples of the world.

Also included in the decisions reached was the support by the Assembly of the decision of the UN General Assembly to defer consideration and action on the Declaration to allow for further consultations on the numerous matters of fundamental political and constitutional concern. Amongst the most important of these matters are questions about the definition of indigenous peoples; self-determination; ownership of land and resources; establishment of political and economic institutions; and national and territorial integrity. The Assembly decided to maintain a united position in the negotiation on amending the Declaration and constructively work alongside other UN member states in finding solutions to the concerns of the African states.

The Assembly mandated the African Group at the UN to continue to ensure that Africa's interests in this matter are safeguarded. However, as good as the decisions were, the decision of the African Union Assembly to support the decision of the UN General Assembly to defer consideration and action on the United Nation Draft Declaration of Indigenous Peoples' Rights was a big setback for the people seeking indigenous peoples' international legal status before the Declaration was eventually adopted in 2007. This singular act showed that the African governments have not changed from their rigid position that indigenous peoples do not exist in Africa. It is the contention

---

507   Press Statement of the Inuit Circumpolar Council and Saami Council (Arctic Caucus), *Africans Deny Inuit and Saami Human Rights, INDIGENOUS PEOPLES CAUCUS, available at* http://www.ipcaucus.net/ HRday/Saami.html.

508   Resolution AHG Res-17/ of 1964.

509   United Nations General Assembly Resolution 1514 (XV) of 14 December 1960 on the Declaration on the Granting of Independence to Colonial countries and Peoples, 947th Plenary Meeting, 14 December 1960, Art. 7.

of the author that the decision to defer supported by nation members of the African Union Assembly was a disservice to the indigenous peoples' cause.

It is, however, important to point out that the Draft Declaration was eventually voted for in 2007 and it became the United Nation Declaration of the Rights of Indigenous Peoples. 143 member states voted in support of the declaration while only 4 voted against and 11 abstained. This includes African states, to their credit. Nigeria, however, together with Burundi and Kenya abstained.

3.3 HUMAN RIGHTS SITUATION IN AFRICA

The human rights situation in Africa is diverse, complex and varies from country to country and from one community to another. According to the report of the African Commissions Working Group on indigenous populations, most areas occupied by pastoralists, hunter-gatherers and other peoples who have identified with the indigenous peoples movement are under-developed with poor infrastructure.[510] This is due to the care-free attitude of governments or nation states towards the plight of the indigenous peoples. Most times, these people are either evicted from their land or denied access to the natural resources upon which their survival as peoples depends for the benefit of others.[511] When eventually the natural resources are extracted, the indigenous peoples do not benefit from the economic gain made from the resources. They are more or less the goose that laid the golden egg, but gains nothing in return.

The African Commission in its report confirmed that dispossession of land and natural resources are the major problems with which the indigenous peoples have to battle.[512] This is because most of the indigenous peoples had been forced to migrate from their traditional land against their wishes. The excuse by governments and nation states was that such lands were needed for economic development, but this cause has not in any way helped the indigenous peoples' situation, but rather it has made their situation worse. Some of them have lost their heritage, some could not

---

510   Report of African Commission on Human and Peoples' Rights (ACHPR) Working Group of Experts on Indigenous Populations/ Communities, adopted by the African Commission on Human and Peoples' Rights at its 28th Ordinary session, 20 (TWGIA, 2005).

511   *Id.*

512   *Id.*

practice their occupation because their land had been degraded, while some had lost connection with their customs and religions. This is a violation of the African Charter which states that every people has the right to its natural resources, wealth and property.[513]

The dispossession of land and natural resource from the indigenous peoples contravenes the provisions of African Charter which expressly states that all peoples have the right to freely dispose of their wealth and natural resources.[514] The dispossession act threatens the economic, social and cultural survival of the indigenous pastoralist and hunter gatherer communities. This is because the land and other natural resources are critical for the survival of any subsistence community and Africa is no exception. The African Charter made provision for the protection of rights to land and natural resources[515] which is fundamental for the survival of indigenous communities in Africa.

The African Commission showed in its report that indigenous pastoralist and hunter-gatherer communities in Africa have been losing their land incrementally over the years. This was caused by the assumption of the "*terra nullius*" principle[516] which indicates "land belonging to no one." This rule, ignoring indigenous possession, has allowed nation-states to take over lands from hitherto occupied communities that rely on farming and hunting.

The Commission Report equally indicated that the pastoralist and hunter-gatherer communities are usually the target of nation-states because such communities have little or no legal title since the indigenous peoples are governed in their everyday affairs by customary law which are largely unwritten and not recognized or respected by the various national legislations which do not make any provisions for collective title to land.

Many pastoralist and hunter-gatherer communities had been dispossessed. For instance, the Batwa of Rwanda were dispossessed from their land[517] in 1988 for the purpose of establishing a military zone and a national park on the land. The same fate also befell the Batwa in Burundi and

---

513   African Charter, *supra* note 459, at Art. 21(1) & (2).

514   *Id.* at Art. 22(1).

515   *Id.* at Art. 20,21,22 &24.

516   *Id.* at Art. 21.

517   Report of African Commission, *supra* note 510, at 22.

Uganda as they were driven out of their ancestral forest areas which resulted in their loss of land. This dispossession was responsible for the poverty, marginalization and discrimination being experienced by the Batwa today. This was against the peoples' wishes, but since they have no representative in the government that could present their wishes, they are more or less voiceless and have to comply with whatever the government wants. This practice of dispossession by the nation states has created myriads of social and cultural problems for the indigenous peoples. For example, it renders the displaced people homeless because in most situations, the government never provides alternative accommodations for these peoples.

In Nigeria, concessions of indigenous lands to oil companies for exploration has seriously affected the livelihood of indigenous communities. They also lose their means of sustenance and connection with their customs and religions which are generally closely tied to their land. The case of the Ogoni people of Nigeria is another example where people have been denied rights to the rich oil resources found on their land and they have found themselves extremely vulnerable, as they were defenseless against the dominant groups of the society who are in control of the government and had access to military might and resources to achieve their aims.

The drilling operation of Shell, an oil company whose operation in Nigeria started in 1958, has led to the decline of Ogoni agricultural production and fishing occupations.[518] A series of complaints made to Shell and to government authorities about the anomaly has not yielded any positive results. Instead, the government of Nigeria only fortified Shell with more security so that their activities would not be disturbed by the indigenous peoples. All the while, the inhabitants, who are at the receiving end of this environmental abuse, were left to their fate.

Shell's increased operation led to an increase in oil spillage which intensified the environment pollution problem for the Ogoni people. Protests from the Ogoni people have over the years led to massive human rights abuses in the area and this culminated in the execution of one of the Ogoni leaders, Ken Saro Wiwa.[519]

518   Beverly Wright, *Race, Politics and Pollution: Environmental Justice in the Mississsippi River Chemical Corridor, in* JULIAN AGYEMAN, ROBERT DOYLE BULLARD, & BOB EVANS, JUST SUSTAINABILITIES: DEVELOPMENT IN AN UNEQUAL WORLD 141 (MIT Press, 2003).

519   *Id.; see also* IKE OKONTO & ORONTO DOUGLAS, WHERE VULTURES FEAST: SHELL, HUMAN RIGHTS, AND OIL 169 (Verso 2003).

The human rights situation of the indigenous peoples in Africa is not all negative as there are some positive sides, too. The African Commission has enumerated in its report some positive action by some of the African governments in the midst of the distressing picture of land alienation, dispossession and impoverishment of indigenous communities. A very good example is South Africa, where the country's Constitution Act 108 of 1996[520] provides for restitution of rights in land to persons or communities who were dispossessed of property after 19 June 1913 as a result of racially discriminatory laws or practices.

The Restitution of Land Rights Act 22 of 1994, which was passed within seven months of the establishment of the new democratic government in 1994, established the Commission on Restitution of Land Rights which has the responsibility to investigate and process all land claims lodged by the 31st December 1998.[521] Amongst the Khoesan Communities that have benefited from the land restitution program are the Riemvasmank community, the Mier community, the Kleinfonteintjie community in Schmidtsdrift, as well as the Khomani San community of the Southern Kalahari. Thabo Mbeki[522] at the handing over of claimed land to the Khomani San of the Southern Kalahari explained that the government action was an example to the world that South Africa is fulfilling its pact with the United Nations on the issue of indigenous peoples.

3.4 CULTURAL RIGHTS IN AFRICA

Apart from land rights, cultural rights are one of the rights enshrined in the African Charter. Cultural rights is another form of rights enshrined in the African Charter as the Charter expressly states that "All peoples shall have the right to their economic, social and cultural development with due regard to their freedom and identity and in the equal enjoyment of the common heritage of mankind."[523]

---

520   The Constitution of the Republic of South Africa Act 108 of 1996 Section 25(7) *available at* http://www.info.gov.za/documents/constitution/1996/a108-96.pdf.

521   Cairo Resolution of 1964, Organization of African Unity, OAU doc, AHG/Res. 17(1) Section 4-6, The Restitution of Land Rights Act 22 of 1994, *available at* http://www. info.gov.za/acts/1994/a22-94.pdf.

522   The then Deputy President of South Africa.

523   African Charter, *supra* note 459, at Art. 22.

This provision recognized and appreciates the essence of culture of every group, indigenous peoples inclusive. Under the African Charter, the nation states in Africa are obligated to observe the provision.

It is a fact that the loss of productive resources has impacted negatively on the indigenous people's culture and this has denied them the freedom to maintain a livelihood of their choice and to develop their culture and cultural identity. This is so because most indigenous peoples have been dispossessed of or driven away from their land and as a result have been cut off from their age-old traditional religions, since most indigenous societies live religiously and without it they cannot function as they had been since time immemorial.

The reason for the failure of African governments to recognize this right is not far fetched. There is the fear that cultural diversity could lead to separatist demands within a unitary state, thus leading to tribalism and ethnic uprisings. According to the African Commission report, the promotion of national languages and dominant cultures has led to the suppression of indigenous languages and cultures. The report pointed out Morocco as an example of where the government continues to suppress the Tamazight language as a symbol of Berber identity and cultural rights. Nigeria is another good example where English is the official language at the expense of indigenous languages as a symbol of Berber identity.

In all, there have been positive responses from some African governments on the issue of cultural rights. For instance, in Morocco the Amazigh cultural identity was recognized 45 years after independence.[524] The South African government has also through the Constitution[525] obliged the state to take practical and positive measures to elevate the status and advance the use of indigenous languages. Also, the Khoi, Nama and San languages were protected by the constitution.[526] Moreover, the constitution of most nation states makes reference to religious, cultural and linguistic communities.

---

524   Report of African Commission,supra note 510, at 43

525   South African Constitution, *supra* note 520, at Section 6(2).

526   *Id.* at Section 6(5).

3.5 COMPLIANCE WITH INTERNATIONAL HUMAN RIGHTS INSTRUMENTS

The African Commission Report stated that most African governments have shown little interest in recognizing indigenous rights within the context of the United Nations human rights instruments despite the fact that some of them have ratified international instruments relating to human rights.

The essence of the African Charter was for the member states of the African Union to be bound by its Article which recognize the rights, duties and freedom enshrined in the charter. The present situation and various studies on indigenous peoples in Africa show that African governments do not comply with the provisions of the Charter as they should.

The Working Group on Indigenous Peoples or Communities in Africa at its 28th ordinary session, amongst other resolutions, resolved to establish a working group of experts on the rights of indigenous peoples or communities in Africa.[527] Another positive step taken by the African Charter is its resolution to expressly recognize and protect collective rights. It used the term "people" in its preamble and provisions as was indicated by its use of "people's right" which showed that is was meant to protect collective rights. The charter indicates that it was against the idea of one people dominating or oppressing another. The Constitutive Act of the African Union[528] also expressly states that one of the objectives of African Union (AU) is the promotion and protection of human and "peoples" rights which indicates that the African human rights system is tailored towards protecting collective rights.

The African Commission Report that the African Charter makes provision for collective rights that can be conceivably enjoyed only in a collective manner such as the right to self-determination. It is the submission of this author that self-determination can only be enjoyed as a group. This another major support for indigenous peoples' cause.

The African Charter made provision for the right to self-

527   Fourteenth Annual Activity Report (2000-2001) of the African Commission to the Assembly of Heads of State and Government of the OAU, 37th Ordinary session/Fifth ordinary session of the AEC, 9-11 July 2001, Lusaka, Zambia, AHG/229 (XXXVIII).

528   Constitutive Act, *supra* note 454, at Art. 3(h).

determination, but this self-determination right[529] can only be exercised within the inviolable national boundaries of the state with due regard to the sovereignty of the nation-state. The Charter also made recourse to international law principles on human and peoples rights by stating that

> the commission shall draw inspiration from international law on Human and Peoples' Rights, particularly from the provisions of various African instruments on Human and Peoples' Rights, the Charter of the United Nations, the Charter of the Organization of African Unity, the Universal Declaration of Human Rights, other instruments adopted by the United Nations and by African countries in the field of human and peoples' rights as well as from the provisions of various instruments adopted within the specialized agencies of the United Nations of which the parties to the present charter are members.[530]

This provision showed clearly that the African Charter is in alliance with the provisions and objectives of the various human rights instruments.

The African Commission reports listed characteristics of indigenous peoples in Africa. The report summarized the overall characteristics of the groups identifying themselves as indigenous peoples by stating that their cultures and ways of life differ considerably from the dominant society and that their cultures are under threat in some cases to the extent of extinction. This is just one of the threats that indigenous peoples face. Their cultures are being threatened and are at the verge of being submerged and consumed by the foreign cultures of the dominant groups of the society which has little or no respect for indigenous peoples' culture.

In addition, the report raised a point on the issue of definition of indigenous peoples in Africa to the extent that the definition should not be limited to the aboriginal factor alone, but should include self-identification and similar situations. Otherwise it will be very difficult to apply the concept in Africa. In Africa, dominant groups have, after independence, continued the oppressive system entrenched by the colonialists through suppressing marginalized groups and this sort of present-day internal suppression within African states is one of the problems which the present African indigenous movement seeks to address.

---

529   African Charter, *supra* note 459, at Art. 20(2).

530   *Id.* at Art. 60.

The African Commission report laid emphasis on the fact that focusing on aboriginality is difficult and not very constructive except in cases of the San of Southern Africa and the Pygmies of Central Africa when discussing this issue in African context. It notes that effort should be placed on self-identification as indigenous which is distinctively different from other groups within a state on the ground of subjugation, marginalization, dispossession, exclusion or discrimination because these people claiming indigenous peoples' status have different cultures, ways of life or modes of production that are radically different from those of the national and dominant society.[531] The African Commission report supported the four elements advocated by Erica-Irene Daes in 1982. They, however, see the four elements as only guiding principles to characterize indigenous peoples and that all the four elements need not be present at the same time in a given situation. The four elements are as follows:

(1) The occupation and use of a specific territory;
(2) The voluntary perpetuation of cultural distinctiveness, which may include the aspects of language, social organization, religion and spiritual values, modes of production, laws and institutions;
(3) Self-identification, as well as recognition by other groups, as a distinct collectivity; and
(4) An experience of subjugation, marginalization, dispossession, exclusion or discrimination.[532]

The four elements supported by the African Commission are all in alliance with most of the "attempt at definitions" discussed in chapter one. For instance, "occupation and use of a territory" is similar to "being regarded as the first or original inhabitants," marginalization and discrimination is similar to the vulnerability of the indigenous peoples to the society. The cultural difference from the dominant society and self-identification by other groups are also in alliance with the earlier discussed position on indigenous peoples definitions in chapter one.

Indigenous peoples of Africa have attracted international attention to their plight and African indigenous representatives had been participating

---

531   African Commission on Human and Peoples Rights, Report of the African Commission's Working Group on Indigenous Populations/Communities, 92-93 (IWGIA; Bilingual edition, 2005).
532   Id.

in various international forums which include amongst others:

(1) The international decade of the world's indigenous peoples, which had been in existence since 1993;

(2) The Working Group on Indigenous Populations (WGIP) established in 1982, by the UN sub-commission on prevention of discrimination and protection of minorities;

(3) Permanent Forum on Indigenous Issues established within the United Nations in 2000;

(4) Special UN rapporteur for indigenous people nominated by the commission on human rights in 2001. The report of the Special Rapporteur takes positive note of the resolution on indigenous people/ communities in Africa adopted by the Africa Commission on Human and Peoples' Rights;

(5) The Working Group on Indigenous Populations which prepared a draft UN Declaration on the Rights of Indigenous Peoples; and

(6) The UN's Voluntary Fund for support to indigenous peoples with active participation of African representative.

The above forums that Africa indigenous peoples are associated with shows that they are very serious about their aspirations to enjoy the rights which they feel they are entitled.

Efforts of the indigenous peoples were manifested at an Arusha seminar[533] where participants presented a range of issues and problems. It was concluded that indigenous peoples "could be characterized as non-dominant, vulnerable and disadvantaged." It was suggested that indigenous peoples had an attachment to a particular land or territory and or had a way of life which was threatened by current state policy and affected by the inevitable extinction of their traditional resource base if urgent steps are not taken to arrest the situation.

---

[533]   Report on the Seminar on "Multiculturalism in Africa: Peaceful and Constructive Group Accommodation in Situations Involving Minorities and Indigenous Peoples" held in Arusha, United Republic of Tanzania, 13-15 May 2000, COMMISSION ON HUMAN RIGHTS,Sub-Commission on the Promotion and Protection of Human Rights Working Group on Minorities, Sixth session. Para. 28. E/CN.4/Sub.2/AC.5/2000/WP.3 *available at* http://www.unhchr.ch/huridocda/huridoca.nsf/(Symbol)/E.CN.4.Sub.2.AC.5.2000. WP.3.En?Opendocument.

3.6 THE IMPORTANCE OF THE RECOGNITION OF INDIGENOUS PEOPLES IN AFRICA

The African Commission report emphasizes that the principle of self-identification as provided in the ILO Convention 169 and by the Working Group on Indigenous Populations is a key principle which the Commission believes will help in guiding further deliberations of the African Commission on the indigenous peoples subject. The African Commission pointed out that all African states host a rich variety of different ethnic groups, some of which are dominant while some are not.

The report also warned that the term "indigenous peoples" should not be abused with the aim of achieving rights and positions over and above other ethnic groups or members of the national community as a term by which to nourish tribalism or ethnic strife and violence. This shows the delicate nature of indigenous peoples' issues. That is why the report emphasized that the indigenous status should not be employed by a group of people in order to gain undue advantage over other ethnic groups.

The Commission report observed that "indigenous" is the term the concerned groups used to dialogue with the government of their countries about enforcement of fundamental individual and collective human rights and that they should be recognized as peoples who have the right to participate in decisions that will affect them and to be allowed to determine their future and destiny.

In its conclusion, the African Commission report affirmed that the African indigenous peoples have their own distinctive features that differentiate them from the specific features of the African state and its roles. They also have a specific attachment to their land and territory. They have specific cultures and modes of production that are distinct from the groups that dominate political, economic and social power. They have their own governance and laws which are in the form of customary laws which are largely unwritten, as well as modes of distinctive productions and culture. The African Charter made provision for both the individual and collective rights of indigenous peoples which are for the promotion and protection of the human rights of indigenous peoples.

The admission of existence of indigenous peoples by the African Commission shows that indigenous peoples are not alien to the African continent as being claimed by most African nation states.

In a nutshell, the relationship of Africa nation states and the indigenous peoples is not a cordial one. While some countries such as South Africa and Tanzania and a host of others could be commended, the majority of the nation states still maintain that they do not have indigenous peoples within their territory, or at best, that everybody is indigenous. This attitude has made the situation of indigenous peoples in Africa a precarious one.

The majority of African nations only pay lip service to most of the international instruments enacted in support of the rights of indigenous peoples. While most of them ratified the instruments, their actions and attitudes toward the indigenous peoples are contrary to the provisions of the international instruments.

The situation of the African indigenous peoples will only improve when the nation states change the notion they have about indigenous peoples of the continent. It is only then that rights to which indigenous peoples are entitled to will be respected by the various nation states.

Professor van Genugten, while pointing out the various problems confronting indigenous peoples in Africa and the need for proper attention to indigenous issues, opined that consistent cases of injustice against indigenous peoples could make judges and commission members of the African Commission of Human and Peoples' Rights challenge legislators to enact legislation that will strengthen the position of indigenous peoples.[534] He was convinced that if indigenous peoples are recognized and allowed to operate in a democratic manner according to their desire, there will be little or no conflict between them and the nation states.

---

534   Willem van Genugten, *Protection of Indigenous Peoples on the African Continent: Concepts, Position Seeking, and the Interaction of Legal Systems*, 104 Am. J. Int'l L. 64 (2010).

CHAPTER FOUR

NIGERIAN HISTORICAL, SOCIAL AND ANTHROPOLOGICAL CONTEXT

4.1 THE HISTORY OF NIGERIA

The topic of this subject revolves around the people in Nigeria and it is necessary to look into the history of the West African country called Nigeria and its people.

There is no concrete evidence on the point in time when Nigeria came into existence. This is because at the time Nigeria came into existence, people were not yet versed in the art of writing. Thus, they relied only on oral history for centuries which get faded with age, but it was through this medium that the history was passed on from generation to generation.[535] The country of Nigeria however, came into formal existence in 1914 following the amalgamation of the Northern and Southern protectorate.[536] The name "Nigeria" was suggested by Lord Lugard's wife, Flora Shaw.[537] The problem of the lack of documented history was, therefore, responsible for the unavailability of a precise history of the land so denominated. The origins of the lands, however, go much deeper. For example, pebble tools were found in the north of Old Bussa in Nigeria. This was in association with more sophisticated stone tools suggesting that they represent a culture of a time

---

535   ANTHONY OYEWOLE & JOHN LUCAS, HISTORICAL DICTIONARY OF NIGERIA 3, 2d ed. (African Historical Dictionaries, No. 40, The Scarecrow Press, 2000).

536   INTERNATIONAL SECURITY AND THE UNITED STATES: AN ENCYCLOPEDIA 545 (Karl R. DeRouen & Paul Bellamy, eds., Praeger Security International, 2008); see also C.C. Aguolu, The Role of Ethnicity in Nigerian Education, 48.4 THE JOURNAL OF NEGRO EDUCATION 517 (1979).

537   A. J. FAJANA, NIGERIA AND HER NEIGHBOURS 41 (Afr. Univ. Press, 1964); DANIEL E. HARMON & RICHARD E. LEAKEY, NIGERIA: 1880 TO THE PRESENT: THE STRUGGLE, THE TRAGEDY, THE PROMISE (EXPLORATION OF AFRICA: THE EMERGING NATIONS) 43 (2000).

immemorial.[538] Various other pieces of evidences of a history dating back to the African Stone Age include hand axes found on the Jos, Plateau. These hand axes were actually stones probably used for cutting and digging. This evidence showed the type of tools which the Nigerian ancestors used for their occupation. It also gave an insight into the types of occupation the ancestors might have engaged in. For instance, hand axes are normally used for cutting and digging. This could mean that Nigerian ancestors were predominantly farmers. Crowder pointed out that the hand axe culture, which is also referred to as the Acheulian culture, had been found during research in many parts of Africa, but such evidence exists only in Jos Plateau in Nigeria where tools used by early settlers as far back as 8 B.C. were found.[539] There is evidence of tools used by men living in the African Middle Stone Age which was found in Asejire, near Ibadan in Western Nigeria.[540]

Archaeological research also shows that people were already living in Iwo-Eleru[541] in South-western Nigeria as early as 9000 B.C.[542] Microlithics, which are small finely-made stone tools and ceramic industries were developed by Savanna pastoralists from at least the fourth millennium B.C. and were continued by subsequent agricultural communities. In Southern Nigeria, hunting and gathering were the earlier occupations and this gave way to subsistence farming and the cultivation of staple foods in the first millennium B.C. Some other evidence found which signifies early human habitation in Nigeria are artifacts such as stone choppers. These were found at Beli in Northern Nigeria.[543] Hand axes and cleavers were excavated in Jos, Plateau state.[544]

There is evidence of Early Stone Age sites in the Jos Plateau area and Middle Stone Age sites in the northern area of the Niger, Taraba, Benue rivers, the Jos Plateau, and Okigwe.[545] The Stone Age was the period associated with hunter-gatherers who searched frantically for food and eventually settled

---

538   MICHAEL CROWDER, THE STORY OF NIGERIA 19 (FABER AND FABER, LONDON 1962).

539   *Id.*

540   *Id.* at 20.

541   Iwo-Eleru is a city, near Akure, Ondo State, Nigeria.

542   T. Shaw & S.G.H. Daniells, *Excavations at Iwo-Eleru, Ondo State, Nigeria*, 14 WEST AFRICAN JOURNAL OF ARCHAEOLOGY ix-xiv (1984).

543   APRIL GORDON, NIGERIA'S DIVERSE PEOPLES: A REFERENCE SOURCEBOOK 5 (ABC-CLIO, 2003).

544   ROLAND OLIVER, THE AFRICAN EXPERIENCE 21 (Westview Press, 2000).

545   TOYIN FALOLA, THE HISTORY OF NIGERIA 16 (Greenwood Press, 1999).

for agriculture. The use of tools such as microliths, bows, arrows and spears was associated with the late Stone age during which human beings put the tools to good use.[546] There is evidence of Stone Age people in Nigeria who engaged in agriculture, tending wild fruits, yams and palms and in Northern Nigeria, people engaging in millet and sorghum farming and also herding cattle, sheep, and goats.[547] The Metal Age began with iron, and later copper, brass, and bronze. The use of iron and other metals improved the practice of agriculture and promoted the emergence of cities. The knowledge of iron spread to so many places, and transformed peoples' agriculture and welfare.[548] Evidence of few skeletal remains has been found and these show some resemblance with as well as differences from today's people. These remains suggest that there has been a long and ancient pattern of moving and mixing of people throughout Nigeria.

Prior to 1500, much of now modern-Nigeria was divided into states identified with contemporary ethnic groups. The states included the Yoruba kingdoms, the Igbo kingdom of Nri, the Edo kingdom of Benin, the Hausa cities, and Nupe.

The Portuguese navigators were the first Europeans to visit Nigeria in the late fifteenth century.[549] A desire to trade, understand Africa's geography, and spread Christianity were among the numerous factors motivating their visits. When the Portuguese arrived in the Kingdom of Benin in the fifteenth century, they met a monarchy with an ancient system of government that had chiefs and palace officials presiding over a kingdom that was expanding in all this directions.[550] It was apparent that it was a progressive form of government. This goes to show that the inhabitants had their own government, ways of life and organized ways of running their affairs long before the coming of the Europeans. The Portuguese dominated trading activity with the Kingdom of Benin to the exclusion of other Europeans. This dominance was, however, short lived in the sixteenth century as other European countries such as the British, French, and Dutch joined the trade.[551] These countries then shifted their focus to slave trade. The slave transaction thrived because manpower

---

546   Id.

547   Id.

548   Id. at 18.

549   Gordon, *supra* note 543, at 46.

550   MICHAEL CROWDER & GUDA ABDULLAHI, NIGERIA: INTRODUCTION TO ITS HISTORY 58 (Longman, 1979).

551   Id.

was needed by these Europeans to work on plantations overseas and they figured out that it is only in Africa that they could get the supply for the needed manpower. The Europeans engaged in the purchase of slaves who had been captured from inland together with agricultural produce from coastal middlemen. The Portuguese were joined in this trade by the British, French, and Dutch traders. Bonny, Owome, and Okrika were some of the city-states established by individuals who had become wealthy by engaging in the slave trade.

4.2 THE ATLANTIC SLAVE TRADE

The Atlantic slave trade was part of the factors that brought attention to West Africa and to Nigeria in particular. It was a trade which blossomed while it lasted and the object of the trade was human beings. During the trade, contact with the outside world was across the great sea of sand. The Sahara and the trade supplied Nigerians with salt as well as cloth, beads, horses, copper and other related materials in exchange for gold, slaves, ostrich-feathers, leather and ivory which they sold to the Arab merchants of North Africa.[552]

As earlier stated, the Portuguese were the first Europeans to have direct contact with Nigeria.[553] By the end of the fifteenth century, in furtherance of the trade in slaves, the Portuguese had explored the whole of the west coast of Africa and had started to trade with Benin. The Portuguese engaged in transactions of human beings whom they used as slaves for labor at their plantations on the island colony of São Thomé.[554]

By the seventeenth century, slave trade had become established between Europe and Africa and this lasted for forty years culminating in transportation of over ten million Africans across the Atlantic to work on their plantations as slaves.[555] The slave trade was successful because of the parochial thinking and the traditional way of life of the Africans, who attached so much importance to European goods and products that they exchanged human beings which they could sell to Europeans as slaves.[556] In most situations, the people sold as slaves were usually criminals or prisoners

---

552   *Id.* at 57.

553   Gordon, *supra* note 543, at 14.

554   Crowder and Adbullahi, *supra* note 550, at 58.

555   *Id.*

556   *Id.* at 59.

of war from other ethnic groups and often the slaves sold were just people of which the seller wished to get rid.

The slave trade had a great impact on African societies.[557] The trade brought profit to some African societies in terms of goods, guns and gun powder which they got in exchange for human beings sold as slaves. These European products, particularly the guns and gun powder encouraged war and slave raiding. This made people live in constant fear and led to the loss of able-bodied men and women who would had been productive citizens[558] who would contribute to the society development.

Crowder and Abdulahi pointed out that the slave trade reduced human life to the level of a merchandise. The result was the spread of the black race across North and South America and the Caribbean where they now form a substantial part of the population[559] with some of them still preserving their culture and religion,[560] especially in Brazil and Cuba where many black people still follow the religion of their Yoruba ancestors.[561]

Since Europeans brought firearms as items of trade, the imported firearms enabled Africans to secure more slaves for sale and this brought tales of woes as these activities brought sorrow and sadness to families who lost their loved ones to this unholy trade.[562] Some African merchants that engaged in the slave trade prospered greatly from the trade and some societies expanded considerably on the basis of the profits gained from it. The slaves sold from the Delta area of Nigeria to the Europeans did not come from these states but were imported from the hinterland, particularly from among the Igbo-speaking peoples. These slaves were obtained through several means which included kidnapping, which led to loss of many children and adults who were usually caught on the road and sold into slavery. Also, debtors and criminals who otherwise would have been executed were made another source of the slave supply. Another source of the slave supply is warfare which was necessitated by the quest for slaves and this created a general state of insecurity in Igboland. The relevance of slave trade in the

557   PHILIP D. CURTIN, THE ATLANTIC SLAVE TRADE 269-70 (Univ. of Wisconsin Press, 1969).
558   Crowder and Adbullahi, *supra* note 550, at 60.
559   *Id.*
560   *Id.*
561   *Id.*
562   DEBORAH VESS, AP WORLD HISTORY (REA) - THE BEST TEST PREP FOR THE AP WORLD HISTORY 288 (Research & Education Assoc., 2006).

history of Nigeria to this inquiry is to show what influenced the coming of Europeans into Nigeria which later culminated in colonialism.

4.3 THE BRITISH COLONIZATION

The European scramble for territories in Africa was one of the reasons that influenced the British acquisition of Nigeria.[563] The Napoleonic Wars in Europe saw Britain's land empire expand through a series of conquests of French allied territories. These advents of the British led to their establishment of outposts on the West coast of Africa. These stations initially served as trading posts, then for emancipated slave settlements and for military base purposes which led to an ever increasing area of jurisdiction being established. The creeping influence of the British over the black tribes led to a number of race wars in West Africa, amongst which is the one with the Ashanti tribesmen. In the Niger delta area of Nigeria, the British took control of the increasing trade in palm oil. In 1807, the British abandoned the slave trade while other countries continued it until about 1875. In an effort to finally put an end to the slave trade, the British annexed Lagos in 1861 as a crown colony and also claimed Southern Nigeria at the Conference of Berlin.[564] In 1862, the British established their rule in Southwestern Nigeria partly by signing treaties and by use of force. By 1906, the Britain took over the control of Nigeria, and the Protectorates of both Southern Nigeria and Northern Nigeria were amalgamated in 1914 and this culminated in the colony and Protectorate of Nigeria.[565]

4.3.1 Administration under Colonial Rule

The colonial administration of Nigeria was based on an indirect rule government devised by Lugard.[566] Under the indirect rule government, Britain did not discard the existing political institutions but ruled through them. In the Southeast new African officials similar to the traditional rulers in other parts of the country were set up. Although they did not enjoy support of the majority of the people, they were able to rule courtesy of

---

563   Oyewole, *supra* note 535, at 108.

564   Gabriel Palmer-Fernandez, Encyclopedia of Religion and War 7-8 (Routledge, 2004); *see also* Paul Stoller, Embodying Colonial Memories: Spirit Possession, Power and the Hauka in West Africa 57 (Routledge, 1995).

565   Oyewole, *supra* note 535, at 6.

566   Falola, *supra* note 545, at 70.

the British power that stood behind them.[567] Important decisions were made by the British governor and this undermined the African ruler's traditional authority. There are times when the decisions of the colonial administration did not satisfy the local populace and one of such was a decision made in 1929 which led to the Aba riot.[568]

In 1947 Britain in a bid to give the native representative a voice promulgated a constitution that gave the traditional authorities a greater voice in national affairs. The constitution was not given total support because it excluded the western educated elite and this led to the denunciation of the said constitution. In 1951, a new constitution called the Macpherson Constitution was enacted[569] which made provision for elected representation on a regional basis and this created a more representational colonial system.

This constitution provided for a central house of representatives, but friction between the central and regional legislatures related to the question of where supreme party authority lay soon caused a breakdown. In response to the yearnings of nationalists, the Lyttleton constitution was promulgated in 1954[570] and this created a fully federal system, comprising the three geographic regions of Nigeria, the Southern Cameroons, and the Federal Territory of Lagos. Each region had a governor, premier, cabinet, legislature, and civil service, and the federal government was represented in Lagos by a governor-general, bureaucracy, house of representatives, and senate. In 1954 Nigeria was reconstructed into a federal state divided into three regions namely Northern, Western and Eastern regions, and in 1960 Nigeria gained independence.[571]

---

567   *Id.*

568   *Id.* at 72.

569   Oyewole, *supra* note 535, at 7.

570   MARTIN P. MATHEWS, NIGERIA: CURRENT ISSUES AND HISTORICAL BACKGROUND 105 (Nova Publishers, 2002).

571   Oyewole, *supra* note 535, at 1.

PRE-COLONIAL NIGERIA[572]

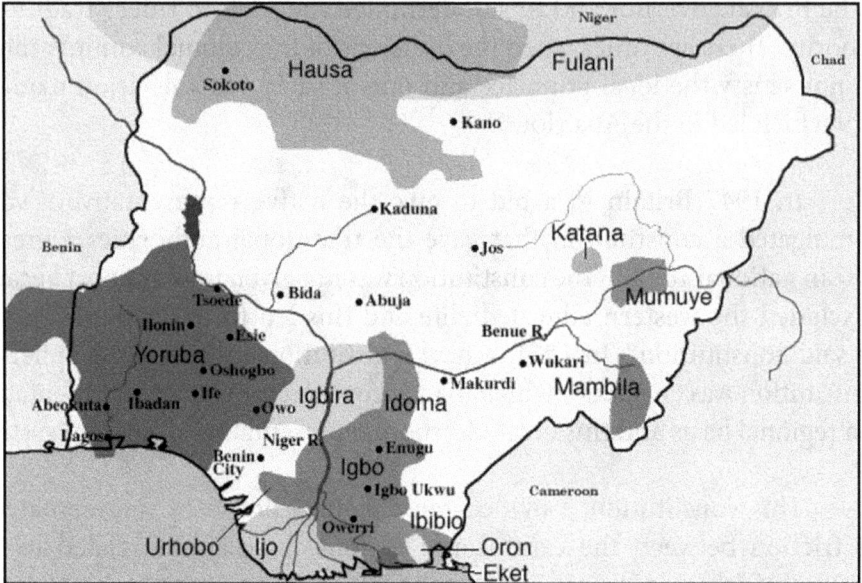

Niger
Hausa
Fulani
Chad
Sokoto
• Kano
•Kaduna
Katana
•Jos
Benin
•Bida
•Abuja
Mumuye
Tsoede
Benue R.
Honin•
•Esie
Yoruba
•Oshogbo
•Wukari
•Oshogbo
•Makurdi
Mambila
Abeokuta•
Ibadan
•Ife
•Owo
Igbira
Idoma
Lagos
Niger R.
Benin
City
•Enugu
Igbo
Cameroon
•Igbo Ukwu
Owerri
Ibibio
Urhobo
Ijo
Oron
Eket

MAP OF COLONIAL NIGERIA[573]

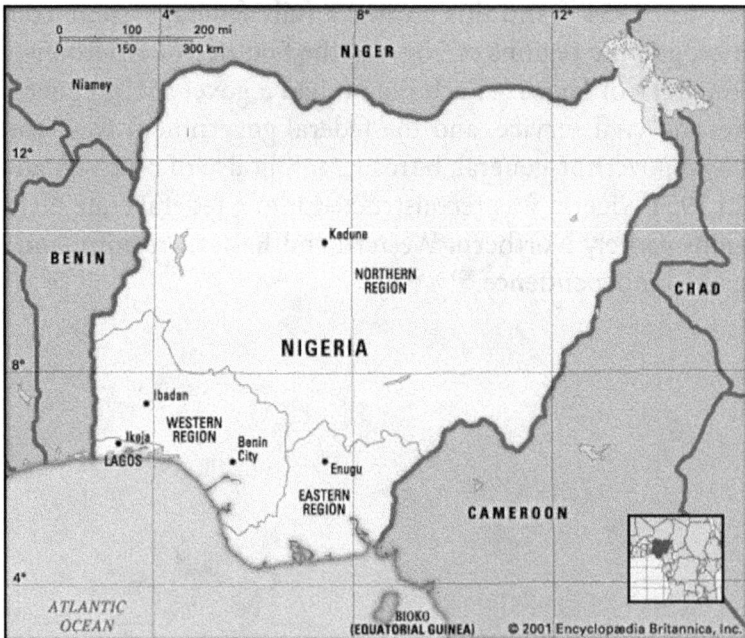

0   100   200 mi
0   150   300 km
NIGER
Niamey
12°
•Kaduna
NORTHERN
REGION
CHAD
BENIN
8°
NIGERIA
•Ibadan
WESTERN
REGION
Benin
•Ikeja
REGION
•City
LAGOS
•Enugu
EASTERN
REGION
CAMEROON
4°
ATLANTIC
OCEAN
BIOKO
(EQUATORIAL GUINEA) © 2001 Encyclopædia Britannica, Inc.

572   Map showing pre-colonial peoples, and the particular domination of the region by the Yoruba, Igbo, Fulani and Hausa, *Nigeria Information,* ART & LIFE IN AFRICA (revised October 1998), *available at* http://www.uiowa.edu/%7Eafricart/toc/countries/Nigeria.html.

573   Encyclopedia Britannica. 2001, *available at* http://media-2.web.britannica.com/eb-media/23/61723-004-4EDF3E92.gif.

MAP OF MODERN NIGERIA[574]

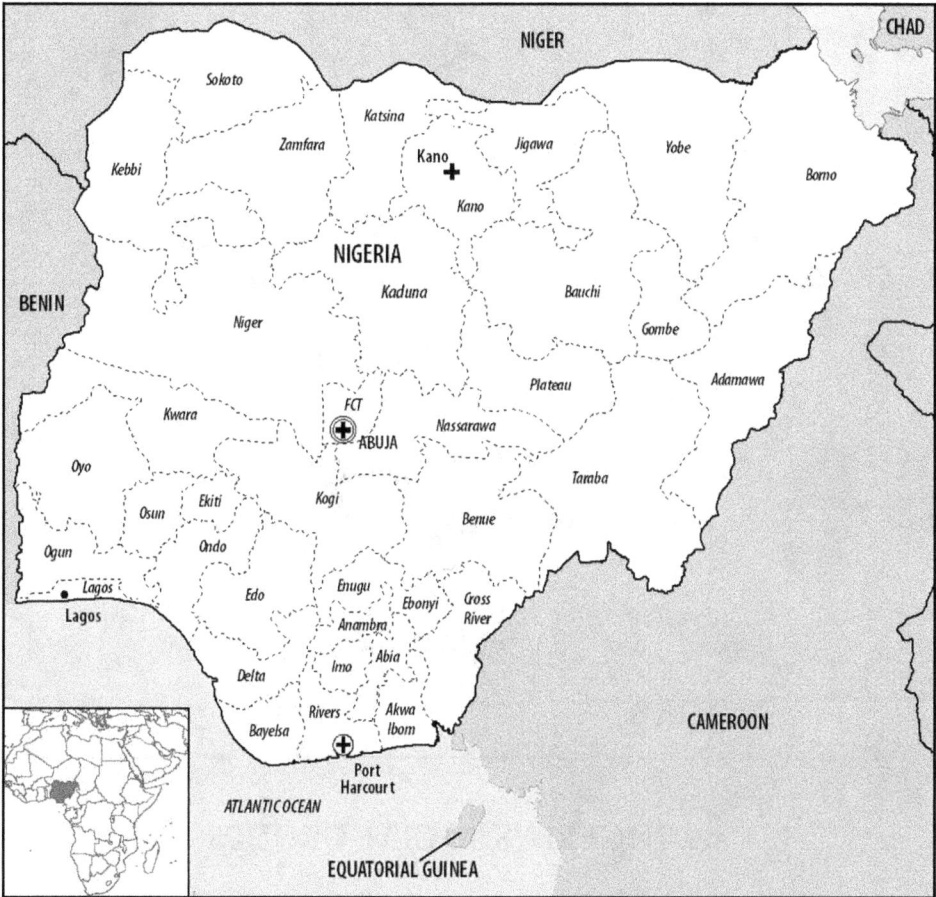

574   ENCYCLOPEDIA BRITANNICA, 2001, *available at* http://media-2.web.britannica.
com/eb-media/24/61724-004-1356B3C1.gif.

NIGERIA'S ETHNIC GROUPS[575]

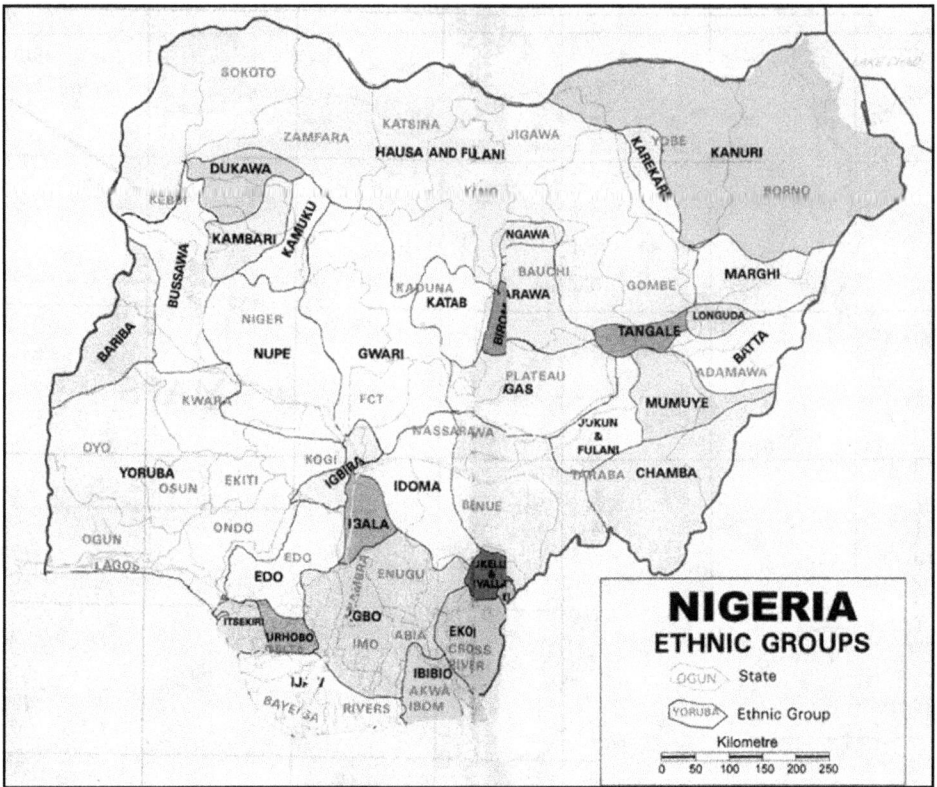

4.4 NIGERIA'S SOCIAL GROUPS

Nigeria's social groups shall be examined in the course of this book and the features of the various groups scrutinized in order to determine whether any of them have the features associated with indigenous peoples as defined above.

Nigeria is a large and diverse country. It has an area of 356,669 square miles.[576] The country is composed of ethnic groups whose histories date to historic times, and remains of ancient civilizations have been discovered in

---

575   Ethnic Map of Nigeria - ONLINENIGERIA.COM, *available at* http://www.onlineni-geria.com/mapethnic.asp.

576   *Id.*

some locations. Various archaeological findings have also revealed evidence of ancient civilizations and examples of these are the various discoveries in locations such as Ile-Ife in the southwest, Igbo-Ukwu in the east, and Nok in the Middle Belt.[577]

4.4.1 Ethnic Groups

Ethnicity is believed to be equivalent of a blood relationship.[578] Siegfried Wiessner has also defined ethnicity as cultural attributes that link individual human beings, such as a common language, religion, social rituals and routines, and a feeling of togetherness.[579] The people recognize each other as belonging to the same ethnic group and feel like distant kin, loosely related to each other through common descent.[580] The ethnicity of such a group is the idea of a group distinguishing themselves from others and most times are based on a sense of common history, usually combined with other characteristics, such as sharing the same race, religion language or culture. There are situations where groups may have a common ethnicity imputed to them, without feeling or recognizing it themselves. A classic example is the "Indians" of the Americas, a diverse series of distinct populations who were lumped together by governments and authorities that are new to the system of the people.[581] Ethnicity is a sense of connection that is ascribed to peoples, either by themselves or by others or both.

Part of the characteristics of ethnic groups is that they must have a shared sense of their past, but that past is open to interpretation in a variety of ways that may have good or bad effects on their present tragic consequences in the present situation.[582] Ethnic groups do not come into being because people belong to the same race or share the same language or culture, but it is based on the peoples' conviction that their characteristics make them a

---

577   Falola, *supra* note 545, at 9.

578   Encyclopedia of Educational Psychology 363 (Neil J. Salkind and Kristin Rasmussen, eds., Sage 2008

579   Siegfried Wiessner, *Ethnic Groups, in* 1 Encyclopedia of Genocide and Crimes Against Humanity 304 (Dinah Shelton, ed. 1999).

580   David Maybury-Lewis, Indigenous Peoples, Ethnic Groups, and the State 59 (Allyn & Bacon, 1997).

581   Murray Lionel Wax, Indian Americans: Unity and Diversity 174 (Prentice-Hall, 1971).

582   National Geographic Society (U.S.), Peoples of the World 10 (National Geographic Society, 2001).

distinct group from others.[583]   However, the danger of doing so is that it may lead to several interpretations which may cause confusion. It is, therefore, a fact that all indigenous peoples are ethnic groups, but not all ethnic groups are indigenous.

Nigeria has about three hundred and fifty different ethnic groups[584] with their various languages. The four largest groups are the Hausa, Yoruba, Igbo and Fulani. These groups are divided into three main ethnic groups – the Hausa accounts for twenty- one percent of the ethnic groups, the Yoruba accounts for another twenty-one percent, the Igbo accounts for eighteen percent of the ethnic groups, while the Fulani were responsible for nine percent of the ethnic groups.

As stated earlier, what is now known as Nigeria came into existence when the Northern and Southern protectorates were combined in 1914. Nigeria used to be a loose geographical area before becoming a British colony and it was made up of many diverse groups with different cultures and political systems. Their societies varied from highly independent, small villages to large, and complex states. In many cases, some ethnic groups in Nigeria are related to groups in surrounding countries. For instance, the Yoruba tribes were split between Nigeria and the neighboring country of Dahomey, while we also have the Hausas in neighboring Niger country. This explained the reason for the existence of groups of same ethnics in different countries which was caused by the boundary adjustment of nation states.

When the British colonized Nigeria, they arbitrarily fixed the boundaries without regard to the territorial claims of the various groups and this had adverse effects on these groups. This was responsible for the existence of people of different tribes in a region which they did not originally belong.

In Nigeria, ethnic groups are sometimes created by inter-marriages, intermingling and assimilations. Thus, groups that originated from these fusions maintain a limited individual identity. The groups are thus composed of smaller groups with various differences among them.

---

583   MAYBURY-LEWIS, *supra* note 580, at 61.
584   There is no clear-cut figure but the ethnic groups in Nigeria is not less than 250.

4.4.2 List of Nigerian States

Nigeria is divided into 36 states which accommodates over 350 ethnic groups; the list of the states are as follows:

Abia State
Adamawa State
Anambra State
Akwa Ibom State
Bauchi State
Bayelsa State
Benue State
Borno State
Cross River State
Delta State
Ebonyi State
Edo State
Ekiti State
Enugu State
Gombe State
Imo State
Jigawa State
Kaduna State
Kano State
Katsina State
Kebbi State
Kogi State
Kwara State
Lagos State
Nasarawa State
Niger State
Ogun State
Ondo State
Osun State
Oyo State
Plateau State
Rivers State
Sokoto State
Taraba State
Yobe State
Zamfara State
Federal Capital Territory

4.4.3 List of Nigerian Ethnic Groups

The ethnic groups earlier discussed represent only a small fraction of Nigeria's total number. A comprehensive, though not exhaustive, list of the groups[585] and their locations are listed below.

As stated earlier in this book, the 36 states accommodate the over 350 ethnic groups. It must, however, be noted that some ethnic groups may be found in more than one or two states. Below is the list of some of the ethnic groups and the states where they could be found.

1. Abayon - Cross River
2. Abua (Odual) - Rivers
3. Achipa (Achipawa) - Kebbi
4. Adim - Cross River
5. Adun - Cross River
6. Affade - Yobe
7. Afizere - Plateau
8. Afo - Plateau
9. Agbo - Cross River
10. Akaju-Ndem (Akajuk) - Cross River
11. Akweya-Yachi - Benue
12. Alago (Arago) - Piateau
13. Amo - Plateau
14. Anaguta - Plateau
15. Anang - Akwa lbom
16. Andoni - Akwa lbom, Rivers
17. Angas - Bauchi, Jigawa, Plateau
18. Ankwei - Plateau
19. Anyima - Cross River
20. Attakar (ataka) - Kaduna
21. Auyoka (Auyokawa) - Jigawa
22. Awori - Lagos, Ogun
23. Ayu - Kaduna
24. Babur - Adamawa, Bomo, Taraba, Yobe
25. Bachama - Adamawa
26. Bachere - Cross River
27. Bada - Plateau
28. Bade - Yobe
29. Bahumono - Cross River
30. Bakulung - Taraba
31. Bali - Taraba
32. Bambora (Bambarawa) - Bauchi
33. Bambuko - Taraba

---

585   Nigerian Peoples and Cultures 14 (Akinjide Osuntokun & Avodeji Olukoju, eds., 1997).

34. Banda (Bandawa) - Taraba
35. Banka (Bankalawa) - Bauchi
36. Banso (Panso) - Adamawa
37. Bara (Barawa) - Bauchi
38. Barke - Bauchi
39. Baruba (Barba) - Niger
40. Bashiri (Bashirawa) - Plateau
41. Bassa - Kaduna, Kogi, Niger, Plateau
42. Batta - Adamawa
43. Baushi - Niger
44. Baya - Adamawa
45. Bekwarra - Cross River
46. Bele (Buli, Belewa) - Bauchi
47. Betso (Bete) - Taraba
48. Bette - Cross River
49. Bilei - Adamawa
50. Bille - Adamawa
51. Bina (Binawa) - Kaduna
52. Bini - Edo
53. Birom - Plateau
54. Bobua - Taraba
55. Boki (Nki) - Cross River
56. Bkkos - Plateau
57. Boko (Bussawa, Bargawa) - Niger
58. Bole (Bolewa) - Bauchi, Yobe
59. Botlere - Adamawa
60. Boma (Bomawa, Burmano) - Bauchi
61. Bomboro - Bauchi
62. Buduma - Borno, Niger
63. Buji - Plateau
64. Buli - Bauchi
65. Bunu - Kogi
66. Bura - Adamawa
67. Burak - Bauchi
68. Burma (Burmawa) - Plateau
69. Buru - Yobe
70. Buta (Butawa) - Bauchi
71. Bwall - Plateau
72. Bwatiye - Adamawa
73. Bwazza - Adamawa
74. Challa - Plateau
75. Chama (Chamawa Fitilai) - Bauchi
76. Chamba - Taraba
77. Chamo - Bauchi
78. Chibok (Chibbak) - Yobe
79. Chinine - Borno
80. Chip - Plateau
81. Chokobo - Plateau

82. Chukkol - Taraba
83. Daba - Adamawa
84. Dadiya - Bauchi
85. Daka - Adamawa
86. Dakarkari - Niger, Kebbi
87. Danda (Dandawa) - Kebbi
88. Dangsa - Taraba
89. Daza (Dere, Derewa) - Bauchi
90. Degema - Rivers
91. Deno (Denawa) - Bauchi
92. Dghwede - Bomo
93. Diba - Taraba
94. Doemak (Dumuk) - Plateau
95. Ouguri - Bauchi
96. Duka (Dukawa) - Kebbi
97. Duma (Dumawa) - Bauchi
98. Ebana (Ebani) - Rivers
99. Ebirra (lgbirra) - Edo, Kogi, Ondo
100. Ebu - Edo, Kogi
101. Efik - Cross River
102. Egbema - Rivers
103. Egede (lgedde) - Benue
104. Eggon - Plateau
105. Egun (Gu) - Lagos,Ogun
106. Ejagham - Cross River
107. Ekajuk - Cross River
108. Eket - Akwa Ibom
109. Ekoi - Cross River
110. Engenni (Ngene) - Rivers
111. Epie - Rivers
112. Esan (Ishan) - Edo
113. Etche - Rivers
114. Etolu (Etilo) - Benue
115. Etsako - Edo
116. Etung - Cross River
117. Etuno - Edo
118. Palli - Adamawa
119. Pulani (Pulbe) - Bauchi, Borno, Jigawa , Kaduna, Kano, Katsina, Kebbi , Niger, Sokoto, Taraba, Yobe, etc.
120. Fyam (Fyem) - Plateau
121. Fyer(Fer) - Plateau
122. Ga'anda - Adamawa
123. Gade - Niger
124. Galambi - Bauchi
125. Gamergu-Mulgwa - Bomo
126. Qanawuri - Plateau
127. Gavako - Borno
128. Gbedde - Kogi

162

129. Gengle - Taraba
130. Geji - Bauchi
131. Gera (Gere, Gerawa) - Bauchi
132. Geruma (Gerumawa) - Plateau
133. Geruma (Gerumawa) - Bauchi
134. Gingwak - Bauchi
135. Gira - Adamawa
136. Gizigz - Adamawa
137. Goernai - Plateau
138. Gokana (Kana) - Rivers
139. Gombi - Adamawa
140. Gornun (Gmun) - Taraba
141. Gonia - Taraba
142. Gubi (Gubawa) - Bauchi
143. Gude - Adamawa
144. Gudu - Adamawa
145. Gure - Kaduna
146. Gurmana - Niger
147. Gururntum - Bauchi
148. Gusu - Plateau
149. Gwa (Gurawa) - Adamawa
150. Gwamba - Adamawa
151. Gwandara - Kaduna, Niger, Plateau
152. Gwari (Gbari) - Kaduna, Niger, Plateau
153. Gwom - Taraba
154. Gwoza (Waha) - Bomo
155. Gyem - Bauchi
156. Hausa - Bauchi, Borno, Jigawa, Kaduna,Kano, Kastina, Kebbi, Niger,Taraba, Sokoto, etc
157. Higi (Hig) - Borno, Adamawa
158. Holma - Adamawa
159. Hona - Adamawa
160. Ibeno - Akwa lbom
161. Ibibio - Akwa lbom
162. Ichen - Adamawa
163. Idoma - Benue, Taraba
164. Igalla - Kogi
165. lgbo - Abia, Anambra, Benue, Delta, Ebonyi,Enugu, Imo, Rivers
166. ljumu - Kogi
167. Ikorn - Cross River
168. Irigwe - Plateau
169. Isoko - Delta
170. lsekiri (Itsekiri) - Delta
171. lyala (lyalla) - Cross River
172. lzondjo) - Bayelsa, Delta, Ondo, Rivers
173. Jaba - Kaduna
174. Jahuna (Jahunawa) - Taraba
175. Jaku - Bauchi

176. Jara (Jaar Jarawa Jarawa-Dutse) - Bauchi
177. Jere (Jare, Jera, Jera, Jerawa) - Bauchi, Plateau
178. Jero - Taraba
179. Jibu - Adamawa
180. Jidda-Abu - Plateau
181. Jimbin (Jimbinawa) - Bauchi
182. Jirai - Adamawa
183. Jonjo (Jenjo) - Taraba
184. Jukun - Bauchi, Benue,Taraba, Plateau
185. Kaba(Kabawa) - Taraba
186. Kadara - Taraba
187. Kafanchan - Kaduna
188. Kagoro - Kaduna
189. Kaje (Kache) - Kaduna
190. Kajuru (Kajurawa) - Kaduna
191. Kaka - Adamawa
192. Kamaku (Karnukawa) - Kaduna, Kebbi, Niger
193. Kambari - Kebbi, Niger
194. Kambu - Adamawa
195. Kamo - Bauchi
196. Kanakuru (Dera) - Adamawa, Borno
197. Kanembu - Bomo
198. Kanikon - Kaduna
199. Kantana - Plateau
200. Kanufi - Kaduna, Adamawa, Bomo, Kano,Niger, Jigawa, Plateau, Taraba, Yobe
201. Karekare (Karaikarai) - Bauchi, Yobe
202. Karimjo - Taraba
203. Kariya - Bauchi
204. Katab (Kataf) - Kaduna
205. Kenern (Koenoem) - Plateau
206. Kenton - Taraba
207. Kiballo (Kiwollo) - Kaduna
208. Kilba - Adamawa
209. Kirfi (Kirfawa) - Bauchi
210. Koma - Taraba
211. Kona - Taraba
212. Koro (Kwaro) - Kaduna, Niger
213. Kubi (Kubawa) - Bauchi
214. Kudachano (Kudawa) - Bauchi
215. Kugama - Taraba
216. Kulere (Kaler) - Plateau
217. Kunini - Taraba
218. Kurama - Jigawa, Kaduna, Niger, Plateau
219. Kurdul - Adamawa
220. Kushi - Bauchi
221. Kuteb - Taraba
222. Kutin - Taraba
223. Kwalla - Plateau

224. Kwami (Kwom) - Bauchi
225. Kwanchi - Taraba
226. Kwanka (Kwankwa) - Bauchi, Plateau
227. Kwaro - Plateau
228. Kwato - Plateau
229. Kyenga (Kengawa) - Sokoto
230. Laaru (Larawa) - Niger
231. Lakka - Adamawa
232. Lala - Adamawa
233. Lama - Taraba
234. Lamja - Taraba
235. Lau - Taraba
236. Ubbo - Adamawa
237. Limono - Bauchi, Plateau
238. Lopa (Lupa, Lopawa) - Niger
239. Longuda (Lunguda) - Adamawa, Bauchi
240. Mabo - Plateau
241. Mada - Kaduna, Plateau
242. Mama - Plateau
243. Mambilla - Adamawa
244. Manchok - Kaduna
245. Mandara (Wandala) - Bomo
246. Manga (Mangawa) - Yobe
247. Margi (Marghi) - Adamawa, Bomo
248. Matakarn - Adamawa
249. Mbembe - Cross River, Enugu
250. Mbol - Adamawa
251. Mbube - Cross River
252. Mbula - Adamawa
253. Mbum - Taraba
254. Memyang (Meryan) - Plateau
255. Miango - Plateau
256. Miligili (Migili) - Plateau
257. Miya (Miyawa) - Bauchi
258. Mobber - Bomo
259. Montol - Plateau
260. Moruwa (Moro'a, Morwa) - Kaduna
261. Muchaila - Adamawa
262. Mumuye - Taraba
263. Mundang - Adamawa
264. Munga (Mupang) - Plateau
265. Mushere - Plateau
266. Mwahavul (Mwaghavul) - Plateau
267. Ndoro - Taraba
268. Ngamo - Bauchi, Yobe
269. Ngizim - Yobe
270. Ngweshe (Ndhang.Ngoshe-Ndhang) - Adamawa, Borno
271. Ningi (Ningawa) - Bauchi

272. Ninzam (Ninzo) - Kaduna, Plateau
273. Njayi - Adamawa
274. Nkim - Cross River
275. Nkum - Cross River
276. Nokere (Nakere) - Plateau
277. Nunku - Kaduna, Plateau
278. Nupe - Niger
279. Nyandang - Taraba
280. Ododop - Cross River
281. Ogori - Kwara
282. Okobo (Okkobor) - Akwa Ibom
283. Okpamheri - Edo
284. Olulumo - Cross River
285. Oron - Akwa Ibom
286. Owan - Edo
287. Owe - Kwara
288. Oworo - Kwara
289. Pa'a (Pa'awa Afawa) - Bauchi
290. Pai - Plateau
291. Panyam - Taraba
292. Pero - Bauchi
293. Pire - Adamawa
294. Pkanzom - Taraba
295. Poll - Taraba
296. Polchi Habe - Bauchi
297. Pongo (Pongu) - Niger
298. Potopo - Taraba
299. Pyapun (Piapung) - Plateau
300. Qua - Cross River
301. Rebina (Rebinawa) - Bauchi
302. Reshe - Kebbi, Niger
303. Rindire (Rendre) - Plateau
304. Rishuwa - Kaduna
305. Ron - Piateau
306. Rubu - Niger
307. Rukuba - Plateau
308. Rumada - Kaduna
309. Rumaya - Kaduna
310. Sakbe - Taraba
311. Sanga - Bauchi
312. Sate - Taraba
313. Saya (Sayawa Za'ar) - Bauchi
314. Segidi (Sigidawa) - Bauchi
315. Shanga (Shangawa) - Sokoto
316. Shangawa (Shangau) - Plateau
317. Shan-Shan - Plateau
318. Shira (Shirawa) - Kano
319. Shomo - Taraba

320. Shuwa - Adamawa, Borno
321. Sikdi - Plateau
322. Siri (Sirawa) - Bauchi
323. Srubu (Surubu) - Kaduna
324. Sukur - Adamawa
325. Sura - Plateau
326. Tangale - Bauchi
327. Tarok - Plateau, Taraba
328. Teme - Adamawa
329. Tera (Terawa) - Bauchi, Bomo
330. Teshena (Teshenawa) - Kano
331. Tigon - Adamawa
332. Tikar - Taraba
333. Tiv - Benue, Plateau, Taraba
334. Tula - Bauchi
335. Tur - Adamawa
336. Ufia - Benue
337. Ukelle - Cross River
338. Ukwani (Kwale) - Delta
339. Uncinda - Kaduna, Kebbi, Niger, Sokoto
340. Uneme (Ineme) - Edo
341. Ura (Ula) - Niger
342. Urhobo - Delta
343. Utonkong - Benue
344. Uyanga - Cross River
345. Vemgo - Adamawa
346. Verre - Adamawa
347. Vommi - Taraba
348. Wagga - Adamawa
349. Waja - Bauchi
350. Waka - Taraba
351. Warja (Warja) - Jigawa
352. Warji - Bauchi
353. Wula - Adamawa
354. Wurbo - Adamawa
355. Wurkun - Taraba
356. Yache - Cross River
357. Yagba - Kwara
358. Yakurr (Yako) - Cross River
359. Yalla - Benue
360. Yandang - Taraba
361. Yergan (Yergum) - Plateau
362. Yoruba - Kwara, Lagos, Ogun, Ondo, Oyo, Osun, Ekiti, Kogi
363. Yott - Taraba
364. Yumu - Niger
365. Yungur - Adamawa
366. Yuom - Plateau
367. Zabara - Niger

368. Zaranda - Bauchi
369. Zarma (Zarmawa) - Kebbi
370. Zayam (Zeam) - Bauchi
371. Zul (Zulawa) - Bauchi

The population of Nigeria has been much influenced by geography.[586] There are several geographical factors responsible for this, and they include population density, subsistence strategies and a host of other factors. For instance, the Yoruba and the Igbo together with the Ibibio tribe, among others, are found in the forest belt and they specialize in farming, especially cultivating root crops and tubers.

Some of the Nigerian ethnic groups will be examined in detail, basically to look at their features, characteristics, their government, and their way of life to determine whether they possess indigenous peoples' characteristics according to the definition arrived at in chapter one.

4.4.3.1 Efik/Ibibio

There is no clear cut fact about when the Efik/Ibibio ethnic group came into existence. The Ibibio are mostly found in Uyo, Etinam, Ikot Abasi, Eket and Oron, Ikot Ekpene, Abak, and Ukanafun which are all in the Akwa Ibom state, while the Efik are based in Cross River state.[587]

As far back as the fifteenth century, the Ibibio lived at the river-side, a geographical setting that facilitated contact with the Portuguese and British traders. The Ibibio's major occupations are fishing and farming which are for local consumption. They are also into poetry, woodwork and raffia mat weaving. Another important trade that they engage in is palm-oil and kernel transaction with the Europeans.[588] While it is a fact that Efik/Ibibio ethnic group are non-dominant in Nigeria, there is no sufficient fact to show to what extent.

---

586   Crowder, *supra* note 538, at 4.

587   Emma S. Etuk, *Efik/Ibibio*, in ETHNIC AND CULTURAL DIVERSITY IN NIGERIA 9 (Marcellina U. Okehie-Offoha & Matthew N. O. Sadiku, eds., 2004).

588   *Id.* at 16.

4.4.3.2 Fulani

The Fulani ethnic group came into the Hausa states in the thirteenth century.[589] They are predominantly Muslim and it was due to their religious difference between them and their Hausa host that a jihad or holy war was fought which led to the Fulani conquest of the Hausa states. The Fulani government practiced an emirate system, which is a developed style of government with a carefully organized fiscal system.[590] The judiciary also comprised of learned men and this assisted them and gave them a reputation of integrity and ability in administering Islamic law.

The Fulani of Nigeria are often identified by their location, for example, Fulanin Yola,[591] Fulanin Jos.[592] or Fulanin Katsina.[593] The immediate surrounding cultures of the Fulani groups have a strong influence on them and this usually leads to cultural differences. They are found scattered all over West Africa.[594] Some people believed that the Fulani are a mulatto intermixture of Phoenician colonists from Syria with Wangara women of Pre-Tuareg Berber origin.[595] Another version of history stated that the Fulani are from Central Sudan and came to Northern Nigeria, specifically Sokoto in thirteenth century. The major cities where the Fulanis settled after the jihad include Yola, Bauchi, Kano, Hadja, and some parts of Adamawa and Yawure. A Fulani empire was established until the British took over Northern Nigeria in 1903. The Fulani can be classified into two groups. The first is the town or settled Fulani and is the superior class, while the second group is the cow Fulani who are predominantly herdsmen and are also called "Fulani Mbororo."

One fact that is very clear and important about Fulani history is that they are migrants and based on this assertion, they cannot lay claim to being original inhabitants of their territory. Due to the above fact, they cannot

---

589   CHIMAH EZEOMAH, THE EDUCATION OF NOMADIC PEOPLE: THE FULANI OF NORTHERN NIGERIA 2 (Nafferton Books, 1983); *see also* RICKY ROSENTHAL, THE SPLENDOR THAT WAS AFRICA 68 (Oceana Publications, 1967).

590   ABU BAKARR BAH, BREAKDOWN AND RECONSTRUCTION: DEMOCRACY, THE NATION-STATE, AND ETHNICITY IN NIGERIA 39 (Lexington Books, 2005).

591   Meaning Fulani based in Yola.

592   Meaning Fulani based in Jos.

593   Meaning Fulani based in Katsina.

594   George Moses, *Fulani,* in ETHNIC AND CULTURAL DIVERSITY IN NIGERIA 24 (Marcellina U. Okehie-Offoha & Matthew N. O. Sadiku, eds., 2004).

595   J. R. WILSON-HAFFENDEN, THE RED MEN OF NIGERIA 139 (Routledge, 1967).

make an argument of age-old means of sustenance, although the tribe is primarily associated with cattle rearing.

4.4.3.3 Hausa

The history about when the Hausa ethnic group of northern Nigeria came into existence is not clear. One school of thought stated that the Hausa people came from the Far East beyond Mecca,[596] while another school of thought claimed that the history and origin of Hausa as a language is closely linked to Arab traders.[597] This was influenced by the Trans-Sahara trade between the Arabs and the Hausa.[598] Hausa is organized into states and emirates ruled by an emir.[599] The political history of the Hausa people dates back to the twelfth century and was dominated by warfare and the colonization of the Hausa land.

The Hausa ethnic group is in Northern Nigeria and has a comprehensive, rich and diverse culture.[600] Hausaland is a great commercial center and Kano is one of the strongest commercial centers of Hausaland.[601] Hausa is used both as the name of the ethnic group as well as a language.[602] In other words, the ethnic language is the Hausa language. The Hausa speaking groups could also be found in Togo, Benin, BurkinaFaso, Cameroun and Ghana.[603]

In the sixteenth century, warfare was the political problem that plagued the Hausa ethnic group as there was constant warfare within the Hausa community at large. This situation arose because of the ambitious

---

596   CHARLES HENRY ROBINSON, NIGERIA, OUR LATEST PROTECTORATE 22 (H. Marshall and Son, 1900).

597   Ibraheem Khaleel, *Hausa*, in ETHNIC AND CULTURAL DIVERSITY IN NIGERIA 40 (Marcellina U. Okehie-Offoha and Matthew N. O. Sadiku, eds., 2004).

598   THOMAS LEONARD, ENCYCLOPEDIA OF THE DEVELOPING WORLD 1140 (Routledge, 2006).

599   MABEL OLUFUNMILAYO AJALA, NIGERIAN PROVERBS AND WISDOM: EXPLAINED 50 (Seaburn, 2007).

600   Khaleel, *supra* note 597, at 37.

601   BASIL DAVIDSON & F. K. BUAH, A HISTORY OF WEST AFRICA TO THE NINETEENTH CENTURY: WITH F. K. BUAH AND THE ADVICE OF J. F. ADE AJAYI 90 (Anchor Books, 1966).

602   M. ADAMU, THE HAUSA FACTOR IN WEST AFRICAN HISTORY 31 (Oxford University Press, 1978).

603   PHILIP J. JAGGAR, HAUSA 1 (John Benjamins Publishing Co., 2001).

attitude of the Hausa states to dominate one another.[604] This was because each state was eager to have the upper hand in the Trans-Saharan trade, but despite the competition among them in establishing the Hausa states, none of them was able to establish permanent military supremacy over Hausa land.[605]

There are no sufficient facts about the traditional occupation of the Hausa ethnic groups apart from the fact that they engaged in trans-Atlantic trade with Arab traders. This made it difficult to make an argument for Hausa having an age-old means of sustenance.

4.4.3.4 Igbo/Ibo

The Igbo/Ibo ethnic groups are located in the eastern part of Nigeria. The names "Igbo" and "Ibo" are used interchangeably, with the Government choosing to use "Ibo" exclusively. The main home land of the Ibo people is the hinterland of the Niger Delta to the east of the great river. Also, across the Niger to the West live the Western Ibos, some of whom were for many years situated within the Benin Empire. In the Delta itself, there were considerable numbers of Ibos who had lived and worked for centuries alongside the Delta peoples. The Ibos constitute the most numerous single group of the peoples in Southern Nigeria east of the Niger.

Archaeological research revealing the prehistory[606] of south-eastern Nigeria has shown evidence of human habitation as early as 3000 B.C. Archaeological evidence in parts of Igboland reveals that the early occupants of the region were mainly Late Stone Age hunter-gatherers and foragers hunting wild animals and gathering wild fruits, leaves, and tubers.[607] This fact showed that the ancient occupations of the Igbo/Ibo are farming and hunting.

---

604   R. A. Adeleye, *Hausaland and Borno, 1600-1800*, in History of West Africa, ch. 14. (J.F.A. Ajayi & Michael Crowder, eds, NY: Columbia Univ. Press, 1972).

605   Oduwobi Tunde & Iwuagwu Obi, *Nigeria: An Ethno-Historical Survey*, in Nigerian Peoples and Cultures 6 (Akinjide Osuntokun & Avodeji Olukoju, eds., 1997).

606   In this context, "prehistory" refers to the time prior to written documents; "protohistory" refers to the time during written history but before any particular areas were documented.

607   A. Ikechukwu Okpoko & A. Maduabuchi Ibeanu, *Igbo Civilization: An Archaeological and Historical Ethnographic Profile*, in Toyin Falola, Precolonial Nigeria: Essays in Honour of Toyin Falola 188 (Akinwumi Ogundiran, ed., 2005).

The prehistory of Southeastern Nigeria is less well known and this problem is peculiar to most West African states. This is because specialists tend to concentrate more on the history of East and South Africa. It is only the Ugbo Ukwu history that is well known, as all other archaeological research, for example the Nok culture, Ife, and Benin, was confined to the site where they were found.[608]

Cultural convergence in Igboland began sometime during the Late Stone Age, at a time when food production began to be developed. The Ezi-Ukwu Ukpa rock shelter, the oldest site excavated thus far, characterizes this period.[609] The excavations of the several sites discussed show a new understanding of the deep cultural history in Southeastern Nigeria.[610] The Igbo ethnic group is one of the largest ethnic groups in Nigeria.[611]

Archaeological studies and excavations in Igboland began only in the 1960s[612] and were revealing exciting results when they were interrupted by the Nigerian civil war and its aftermath. Consequently, little or no research could be done about the prehistoric culture of the Igbo/Ibo. What we have is scanty data which only provide minor insights on the subject. However, the scanty data available does provide interesting revelations. Research showed that the earliest signs of human presence were found at the Ezi-Ukwu Ukpa rock shelter in Afikpo, an area of wooded grassland.[613] Another site, in the same ecological environment that showed early human habitation, is at Nsukka. Both sites were associated with fired and unfired pottery sherds and crude stone tools. This is also referred to as early Neolithic cultures.[614]

---

608   Nkem Hyginus M. V. Chigere. Foreign Missionary Background and Indigenous Evangelization in Igboland 15 (Lit. Verlag, 2002); see also Don Ohadike, Igbo Culture and History, in Chinua Achebe, Things Fall Apart 15 (Heinemann, 1996).

609   Donald D. Hartle, Archaelogy East of the Niger: A Review of Cultural-Historical Developments, in West African Culture Dynamics: Archaeological and Historical Perspectives 195 (B. K. Swartz, Jr. & Raymond E. Dumett, eds., The Hague: Mouton Pub. 1980).

610   Id.

611   S.J.S. Cookey, An Ethnohistorical Reconstruction of Traditional Igbo Society, in West African Culture Dynamics: Archeological and Historical Perspectives 327 (B. K. Swartz, Jr. and Raymond E. Dumett,   The Hague: Mouton Pub., 1980).

612   Kelvin Shillington, Encyclopedia of African History 676 (2005).

613   Mathias Chinonyere Mgbeafulu, Migration and the Economy 1900 to 1975, 10 (iUniverse, 2003).

614   Cookey, supra note 611, at 328.

The archaeological findings at Igbo-Ukwu dated to the ninth century[615] They include excavations in 1959-1960 and 1964 that revealed large quantities of pottery with artistic work, ivory tusks, iron objects, bead ornaments and bronze objects amongst others. This excavation revealed that earlier inhabitants of the land engaged in artwork as part of their occupation since pottery and bead objects are artistic products. It could also be deduced from the findings that earlier inhabitants were blacksmiths who molded iron objects into farming tools. Such objects could be a machete, a hoe and a host of other tools which could indicate that these tools were used for farming.[616] These findings showed that the Igbo-Ukwu of Igbo/Ibo society is one that sustained a sophisticated culture. The copper and beads could have been imported, but these materials are evidence that the region was in contact with the outside world, probably through trade with the Europeans, amongst others.

The Igbo/Ibo system of government is a self-ruled and independent one that is based on the customs of the people. The village constitutes the Ibo's only effective political, social and economic unit and it serves as an entity in itself. It is possible for a group of villages to have a number of common interests. Each village has a council of elders who directs its general affairs, but the entire village assembles on occasion to discuss and make decisions on some vital issues.

The Ibos are extremely egalitarian and independent-minded. The Ibo society confers honorary titles on those that merit them by virtue of deeds of manly courage or on those successful in a special business. Their community was made up of various age groups, with each having special responsibilities for the good of all. The Igbo village society has its social norms and concepts which govern and guide the members in their daily lives and gives them a sense of belonging.

Prior to the advent of Europeans in Nigeria, the Igbo lived in compounds which indicate that a group of houses are usually occupied by one large family in the same area, and the oldest man is made the headman. The Igbos despised and disliked the dictatorship associated with colonialism, but because of their willingness to accept new ideas and new ways of life, they were submissive to the British rule which led to the creation of a colonial

---

615   Shillington, *supra* note 612, at 676.
616   Cookey, *supra* note 611, at 332.

establishment.[617]

The Igbo community is an essentially rural one which survived largely by subsistence agriculture.[618] The high incidence of tsetse fly infestation prevents a pastoral occupation, but the society was able to keep livestock such as sheep, goat, fowls and dwarf cattle which played a complementary role in the domestic economy. Despite all these specializations, the Igbos still value their land so much that it is not uncommon to see an Igbo family retain a piece of patrimonial land which could be either small or large depending on the social structure. Farming is the predominant occupation of the Igbo and Igbo life is always scheduled around a farming calendar.

4.4.3.5 Nupe

The Nupe ethnic groups are located in the Northern part of Nigeria. It is not known exactly when the group came into existence. The Nupe live in an area of transition from the southern forest belt to the dry Savannahs of the North. Their culture was greatly influenced by modern technology and communication and intermarriage with other Nigerian cultures. Nupeland lies generally in the geographic heart of Nigeria, in the low basin that is formed by the valleys of two rivers, the Niger and the Kaduna.

The largest Nupe emirate is the Bida emirate and it has been the core of the ancient Nupe Kingdom since 1857, whose ruler still bears the title "Etsu Nupe" meaning King of Nupe. Other Nupe emirates are smaller than Bida, but they are also independent. These are the Patigi and Lafiagi in Kwara state, and the Agaie and Lapai in Niger State.[619] There are some smaller Nupe under the rulership of Hausa, Yoruba and Gbira kings. For instance, the Zugurma under the Hausa emir of Kontagora, the Tsonga and Tsaragi under the Fulani-Yoruba emir of Ilorin, and Egga and its hinterland under the Atta of Gbira.

---

617   Marcellina U. Okehie-Offoha, Igbo, in ETHNIC AND CULTURAL DIVERSITY IN NIGERIA 64 (Marcellina U. Okehie-Offoha and Matthew N. O. Sadiku, eds., Africa World Press 1995).

618   S.J.S. COOKEY, KING JAJA OF THE NIGER DELTA: HIS LIFE AND TIMES, 1821-1891, 5-6 (NY: NOK, 1974).

619   Jerry Okolo, Nupe, in ETHNIC AND CULTURAL DIVERSITY IN NIGERIA 82 (Marcellina U. Okehie-Offoha and Matthew N. O. Sadiku, eds., AFRICA WORLD PRESS 1995).

Before the advent of Europeans, the Nupe were scattered over four or five emirates and chieftainships and the number rose to seven in the 1940s. The group, however, was not limited to the ancient Nupe kingdoms as the majority of them lived outside its boundaries and most of the Nupe citizens had been influenced by other cultures.[620] The Nupe were involved in a series of wars. History alludes to ten major wars waged by the Nupe ethnic group in the thirty years that preceded the British conquest, between 1864 and 1895.

The Nupe had a formidable army. Twice in the 1880s the Nupe army helped their Hausa allies, the emirs of Kontagora and Gwandu, to quell rebellions in their territories. Nupe's citizens specialize in the cultivation of oil palm, yam, maize, shea nut tree, and millet crops. The Nupe economy practices two principles of labor organization, namely individual work and family work. Collective labor among the Nupe is based on a system of mutual assistance among the villagers, an institution similar to that of other Nigerian cultures.[621]

4.4.3.6 Tiv

The Tiv are a Sudano-Bantu people found mostly in Benue, Cross River, Plateau, and the Taraba states of Nigeria,[622] but there are no cogent facts to establish when the group came into existence. They inhabit the central plain formed by the basins of the Benue, the Katsina Ala and the Cross Rivers and form one of the largest ethnic groups in the middle belt of Nigeria.[623] They also populate the lower slopes of the Adamawa and Jos plateaus in Nigeria and the Cameroun Republic.

The Tiv are prosperous subsistence farmers, and they exchange their farm produce and handicrafts at indigenous markets where they carry

---

620   Siegfried F. Nadel, A Black Byzantium: The Kingdom of Nupe in Nigeria (NY: Oxford Univ. Press, 1942); Ayo Bamgbose, *Issues in the Analysis of Serial Verbal Constructions,* 12.2 Journal of West African Languages 3-21 (October 1982).

621   Okolo, *supra* note 619, at 88.

622   J. Greenberg, *Studies in African Linguistic Classification: The Niger-Congo Family,* 2 Southwestern J.Anthropology 79-100 (1949).

623   Akpe Mbaatyo, *The Tiv,* in Ethnic and Cultural Diversity in Nigeria 101 (Marcellina U. Okehie-Offoha and Matthew N. O. Sadiku, eds., Africa World Press 1995).

out local trade.[624] The Tiv economy can be divided into three spheres.[625] The first is the one associated with subsistence in which the commodities involved are all locally produced foodstuffs, such as staple yams and cereals together with small livestock. Money is not involved in this economy as the transactions are done by barter.[626] The second type of economy is one where the commodities of trade are slaves, cattle and metal rods.[627] Here, the economy is not associated with markets and the actual shift of goods takes place at ceremonies where wealth is displayed.[628] The Tiv economy is also linked through the trading companies to the economy of outside world. Here, the companies buy Tiv cash crops and supply Tiv with imported goods. This economy is monetized and goods sold through a network of dependent African traders, which, in other words, is their link to international trade.[629]

4.4.3.7 The Koma

Although there are no specific facts about when the Koma people came into existence, there is an avalanche of evidence deduced from the peoples' way of life that shows that they have been in existence from time immemorial. As pointed out, much of the history of the Koma people was largely unwritten and some of the obtainable information about these people was transmitted through oral traditions.[630] Francis Jauro Nass states that interviews with somebody knowledgeable about Koma history showed that the people were the only original inhabitants of both the hilly and plain areas of Koma from creation.[631] The Koma are made up of two closely related sub-groups namely, the Beiya and Damti.[632]

The Koma people are a tribe in the Taraba state in northern Nigeria. These people live on mountain tops and do not wear clothes, but only use

624   Paul Bohannan, *The Impact of Money on an African Subsistence Economy*, in JOHNNETA B. COLE, ANTHROPOLOGY FOR THE NINETIES: INTRODUCTORY READINGS 276 (Simon and Schuster, 1988).

625   *Id.*

626   Trade by barter.

627   Bohannan, *supra* note 624, at 277.

628   *Id.*

629   *Id.* at 282.

630   FRANCIS JAURO NASS, MISSIONARY ENTERPRISE AMONG THE KOMA PEOPLE OF ADAMAWA STATE 4 (1996).

631   *Id.* at 5.

632   Joe Eboreime and Joe Ekpere, *The Koma of Gongola State, Nigeria: A Preliminary Ethnographic Report*, 53 THE NIGERIAN FIELD 89, 91 (1988).

leaves to cover their body. The Koma people are so much engaged in their age-old customs and traditions that they do not believe in any form of civilization. The elderly Koma walk around naked with leaves and animal skins barely covering their private parts.[633] The majority of the Koma people are so traditional that they still retain their old ways of making fire by striking two stones, instead of using matches.[634]

The people eat with certain special oils and other forms of food items that are not common to other communities in the state. The only source of drinking water for the Koma people is a river which they share with the animals. In other words, they do not have nor drink pipe borne or treated water. In the entire community, there are no signs of modern life as there are no recreation facilities, restaurants or chemist shops. The only provision store available functions only when there are visitors. The people still depend on a natural cooling system. They half bury a clay pot of water in the ground.[635] This shows that these people have their traditional way of doing things, which they not only believe in but which they still practice today. While the majority of the dominant group of the society is using modern ways of refrigeration, such as refrigerators and freezers, these peoples have stuck to their old natural cooling system.

The ancient occupation of the Koma people is farming, cattle-rearing, hunting and fishing, which they combine with trading. These occupations were all land-dependent and it has sustained their economy.[636] These people are, therefore, predominantly farmers and hunters.[637] The fertile soils of their area support drought-resistant crops like sorghum and millet. This shows that they not only have means of sustenance, they specialize in crops that can withstand or survive any situation. Other crops such as groundnut, rice and plantain are cultivated on the plain. The Koma also rear goats and chickens and they keep dogs to protect their homes. The Koma peoples occupations have a great influence on their social and political life. For instance, the people engage in communal labor to help one another during the harvest period.[638]

633   Sule Lazarus, *20 Years After: Koma People Still Naked,* DAILY INDEPENDENT ONLINE, Saturday May 13, 2006.

634   *Id.*

635   *Id.*

636   Nass, *supra* note 630, at 7.

637   *Research,* INDIGENOUS KNOWLEDGE AND DEVELOPMENT MONITOR, November 2000, *available at* http://www.iss.nl/ikdm/IKDM/IKDM/8-3/res-macdonald.html.

638   Nass, *supra* note 630, at 7-8.

The Koma settlement has no sign of modernization, as it has no electricity or safe drinking water, and the roads leading to the settlements are not motorable. This means that their roads were not tarred with asphalt as it was in other developed areas of the world. The inability of the people to fully accept civilization is connected with the failure of the governments to include the Koma people in their developmental programs. This is where the Koma's vulnerability comes into play as the people have no representative in the government and therefore, there is no way they could influence decision making at the center or federal level.

Nass pointed out that the urge for expansion of Adamawa Emirates has had a great impact on the Koma people, because the expansion led to the destruction of traditional structures which includes, but is not limited to, hamlets and families.[639] The Koma people are very religious, apart from their belief in Almighty God, they still have other lesser divinities that they worship such as Kholu, a native spirit. The Kene,[640] to which believers report theft cases and the Yagnri which is a family.[641] The Koma people perceived Christianity as a threat to their existing traditional religion. Francis Nass concluded that the insensitivity and exploitation of the ruling class was among the factors responsible for the underdevelopment of the Koma people.[642]

The Koma people are so attached to their culture that their culture is now seen as an impediment to their civilization. It was even claimed that it was based on their cultural attachment to the mountains. Since they have no intention to come down or change their location, civilization and education as understood by the western culture of progress and modernity has eluded them.[643]

The language of the Koma people is very distinct, and different from the language of the dominant group of the society. The language issue was even one of the obstacles faced by the missionaries who made an effort to

---

639   *Id.* at 13.

640   *Id.* at 16.

641   Eboreime, *supra* note 632, at 94.

642   Nass, *supra* note 630, at 33.

643   Kola Omojola, At the Crossroads: Challenges and Options for Nigeria 116 (1992).

introduce Christianity to the Koma people.[644] The Koma language is divided into three parts, namely the Koma-Beiya, the Koma-Damti and the Koma-Vomni.[645]

Mohammed Ahmed Moddibo and Alkasum Abba pointed out that the Koma people had been so neglected that no school was provided for the Koma community nor any form of essential amenities extended to them, despite the fact that schools have existed in Yola, which is close to Koma, as far back as 1920.[646]

The Koma people are, however, not worried about the absence of basic amenities as they have their own ways of solving their problems. The people stick to their age-old ways of herbal remedies, while shunning orthodox medicine. Those that refuse modern civilization had their natural means of healing and would have nothing to do with orthodox medicine. The Koma people see themselves as distinct from the dominant groups of the society and in spite of their dire material situation they decided to remain distinct.[647]

4.4.3.8 Yoruba

The Yoruba ethnic group is located in the Southwest area of Nigeria.[648] The term "Yoruba" is both the name and the language of this ethnic group. The term "Yoruba" was what the Hausas called Oyo dialect speakers and this was extended to other groups by the Christian missionaries in the nineteenth century.[649]

Ile-Ife, a town in Southwest Nigeria, is considered by the Yoruba as the place where life and civilization began because it is the place where

---

644   Nass, *supra* note 630, at 30.

645   *Id.; see also* Eboreime, *supra* note 632, at 91.

646   Mohammed Ahmed Moddibo & Alkasum Abba, *Education and National Integration Problems and Prospects,* in Okello Oculi, Nigerian Alternatives 90 (Nigeria: Ahmadu Bello Univ., 1987).

647   *Id.*

648   Raymond Scupin & Christopher Decorse, Anthropology: A Global Perspective 436 (Prentice Hall, 1991).

649   Samuel Johnson, The History of the Yorubas: From the Earliest Times to the Beginning of the British Protectorate 3-9 (Routledge, 1921).

archaeologists discovered a variety of terracotta and bronze sculptures.[650] Historians affirmed that the Yoruba ethnic group originated from Ile-Ife as the oldest fossilized skeleton was found in Iwo Elerun which is forty seven miles west of Ife. Physical evidence such as pottery fragments, tools and quartz flakes reflect that the site was occupied as early as 350 B.C. The Yoruba is made up of smaller collections of peoples which include the Egba, the Oyo, the Owu Ijesha, the Ekiti, the Eguns, the Ilaje, the Ijebu Ogun and so on.[651] The Yoruba society is organized into kingdoms and the greatest of these was Oyo, whose empire at a point stretched even to Ghana in the West and banks of the Niger to the East.

For centuries, most of the Yoruba ethnic group lived in towns,[652] some of them very large and fortified against attack while some were small. The traditional buildings are made with mud bricks and thatched roofs. These are built as large compounds where a number of families live, in blocks of single story apartments looking out onto rectangular courtyards. These are built in such a way that it would accommodate not only the nuclear family, but also the extended family which means that they are all in unity.

Yoruba people are usually related to one another in one way or the other.[653] They form a type of family group known as a "lineage," the descendants of the same ancestors through fore-fathers. The Yoruba social system allows polygamy.[654]

According to the Yoruba custom, the land belongs to the lineage and not to the individual.[655] The lineage, not its individual members, owns the land. Its members form a group which runs its own affairs and sticks together against outsiders. The oldest man is usually made the leader. The members of ethnic groups always solidarize with one another. For instance, they all join in celebrating family occasions such as marriages, the naming

---

650   Trudy Ring & Robert M. Salkin, International Dictionary of Historic Places 350 (Chicago: Fitzroy Dearborn Publishers,1994).

651   Johnson, *supra* note 649, at121.

652   Gordon, *supra* note 543, at 26.

653   Edward John Lake, The Church Missionary Atlas: Containing an Account of the Various Countries in which the Church Missionary Labours and of its Missionary Operations 34 (Church Missionary House, 1879).

654   Ifa Karade, The Handbook of Yoruba Religious Concepts 78 (Weiser, 1994).

655   Toyin Falola & Akanmu Gafari Adebayo, Culture, Politics and Money among the Yoruba 88-89 (Transaction Pub., 2000) [hereinafter *Culture*].

of babies, and funerals. Some lineages are so large that their members live in several compounds, but they still see themselves as one and they always come together when occasion demands.[656]

In the pre-colonial era, the Yoruba economy relied on the traditional way of farming referred to as "sedentary hoe farming," craft specialization, and trade. Hunting, fishing, animal husbandry, and the gathering of wild fruit are also practiced.[657] The Yoruba food diet consists of starchy food such as tubers which could be yams or cassava, grains, and plantains grown on their farms. The starchy foods are, however, supplemented by vegetables, meat and fish.[658] Chickens, guinea fowl, pigeons, ducks, and turkeys are kept as domestic birds, while goats, sheep, pigs, cattle, horses, dogs, cats, rabbits, and guinea pigs as domestic animals. Wild birds and game are hunted in the forests and in the open grasslands while fish and shrimp are caught in the larger rivers, the lagoons, and along the ocean.

4.4.3.9 People of the Niger Delta

The people of the Niger Delta can be divided into two main groups. The first are those inhabiting the creeks and salt water swamps of the huge delta of the river Niger which stretches from Arogbo in the West to Nkoro in the East, while the second are those living in its hinterland in an area stretching from the Eastern borders of Benin in the West to the Crossriver in the East.[659] In the Niger-Delta there is evidence to suggest that the city states that grew so spectacularly during the era of the slave trade were already in existence before the coming of the European traders.[660] Crowder and Abdullahi substantiate this fact by pointing out that the list of kings of Bonny and Nembe[661] was so long that it could concretely be deduced that there was a pre-European foundation or existence. The conversation with kings, trading skills of the people and oral traditions concerning the Niger-Delta people as well as reports by European visitors suggests that the people had long been in existence before they came into contact with the Europeans.

656   Ben Burt, The Yoruba and their Gods 4 (London: British Museum Pub., 1977).

657   William Russel Bascom, The Yoruba of Southwestern Nigeria 18 (Holt, Rinehart and Winston, 1969); *see also* John Ferguson, The Yorubas of Nigeria 79 (Open Univ. Press, 1970).

658   Id.

659   Crowder & Abdullahi, *supra* note 550, at 64.

660   Id. at 65.

661   These are towns in Niger-Delta.

The people of the Niger-Delta engaged in fish and salt production in large quantities by boiling sea-water to obtain salt through evaporation or by boiling mangrove shoots and roots and then mixing their ash with water. After filtering, the solution is evaporated to obtain its high salt content.[662] The majority of the people inhabiting the Niger-Delta were Ijaw speaking,[663] that is, they speak the Ijaw language.

To corroborate the fact that the Niger-Delta had been in existence before colonization, the comment of Pachero Pereira, a Portuguese trader was reiterated by Crowther and Abdullahi. They stated that the Niger-Delta was already an established industry with great organization, as salt and fresh produce were obtained from its ports and villages. It also provided easy access to dry land farming, and its inland waterway system, that links Porto Novo with Bonny and passes through the Lagos Lagoon, and brought large numbers of different peoples into trading relationships with each other, both before and after the arrival of the Europeans.[664]

4.4.3.9.1 The Ogoni

The Ogoni nation is situated in the Niger-Delta area of Nigeria[665] which is part of the Rivers State of Nigeria. Its approximate boundaries are the Aba-Port Harcourt highway to the west, the big bend and mouth of the Imo River in the North and East respectively, and the coastal flats occupied by the Andonis to the South. The Ogoni nation consists of three groups and these are the Khana, the Gokana and the Eleme. The main source of income for the people is farming and fishery, products of which they sell for profit. They are also into poetry and palm wine tapping.

Most Ogoni people are traditionalists, worshipping a common deity called Bari, (Obari-Eleme) other immediate gods and ancestral spirits are also worshipped in the various villages and kingdoms. The Ogoni nation has a culture of it own. This culture is very rich, although the group has shown great skill in adapting aspects of Ijaw and Ibibio customs.

---

662   Crowder and Abdullahi, *supra* note 550, at 65.

663   *Id.*

664   *Id.* at 66.

665   Julian Agyeman, Robert Doyle Bullard, & Bob Evans, Just Sustainabilities: Development in an Unequal World 137 (MIT Press, 2003).

The Ogoni have a distinct culture where they see land as god and worship it as such, although they still rely on their Shamans to cure illnesses.[666] The Ogoni's religion and everyday life revolves around their land which they use for their worship, production and reference for their ancestors. The land represents a bond to their ancestors buried there.[667]

Central to the Ogoni issue is the question of land use and ownership, and this is one big problem not confined to Ogoniland alone. Various communities are forcibly made to relinquish their rights to their lands. In the case of the Ogoni, land acquisition and use by Shell[668] and the government was done through force without the consent of the local people. And in situations where the people consented, the local people were not paid any compensation for the loss of their farmlands and damaged crops.[669] The governments are in the habit of exploiting the provision of the Land Use Act to take over peoples' land either for a genuine reason or none.[670] Most times, the government does not compensate the Ogoni people for the destruction that usually occur on their land during the laying of oil pipelines. Their farmland and crops are usually destroyed in the process. This has not only caused untold hardship to the indigenous peoples, it has also increased their poverty level to an intolerable level.[671]

The consistent exploitation of Ogoniland and their resources consequently led to economic hardship for the people.[672] The economic

666   MARY KATE SIMMONS, UNREPRESENTED NATIONS AND PEOPLES ORGANIZATION YEARBOOK 499 (Martinus Nijhoff Pub., 1996).

667   Mary Harvan, *The Gods of the Delta: Ken Saro-Wiwa and the Literature of the Ogoni Struggle* in MAPPING THE SACRED: RELIGION, GEOGRAPHY AND POST COLONIAL LITERATURE 244 (Jamie S. Scott and Paul Simpson-Housley, eds., Rodopi Pub., 2001)

668   Shell is a global group of oil, gas and petrochemical companies with a broad portfolio of hydrogen, biofuels, wind and solar power interests.

669   ALAN THOMAS, SUSAN CARR & DAVID HUMPHREYS, ENVIRONMENTAL POLICIES AND NGO INFLUENCE: LAND DEGRADATION AND SUSTAINALE RESOURCES MANAGEMENT IN SUB-SAHARAN AFRICA 152 (Routledge, 2001).

670   An Act to Vest all Land compromised in the territory of each State (except land vested in the Federal government or its agencies) solely in the Governor of the State, who would hold such Land in trust for the people and would henceforth be responsible for allocation of land in all urban areas to individuals resident in the State and to organisations for residential, agriculture, commercial and other purposes while similar powers will with respect to non urban areas are conferred on Local Governments. (27th March 1978 was the commencement of the Act).

671   OGONI, TRIALS, AND TRAVAILS 8 (Lagos: Civil Liberties Organisation, 1996).

672   *Id.* at 105.

activities have declined because the people cannot carry out their occupations of farming and fishing as they could before and the continued oil exploration has led to the degradation of the land. The exploitation of the Ogoni land and its resources without any return or benefit from the process is threatening their means of survival, since their means of sustenance is land dependent.[673] The government is more or less likely to betray the people, as they tend to provide security for the oil companies to carry out their activities to the detriment and expense of Ogoni people.

The Ogoni people are an ethnic minority in the Nigerian Federation[674] and have been oppressed and discriminated against just like many other minority groups in Nigeria. Since Nigerian independence in 1960, economic and political power has been concentrated at the national level by the dominant groups of the society. This has relegated the minority groups, among which are Ogoni peoples, to the backseat. The Ogoni are more or less a subordinate to the three large and dominant ethnic groups. They are scarcely heard and they never occupy any position of relevance. This is so because political offices in Nigeria are often distributed along ethnic lines, and since they are in the minority, their chances of getting relevant positions are very slim. The Ogonis are barely represented in the national government and on the few occasions that they were considered, they were given a mediocre position with minor, if any, significance.

To gain economic power and to ensure the viability of Ogoniland, the Ogonis realized that political power should complement their struggle to ensure a degree of autonomy. This led to the fashioning of the Ogoni Bill of Rights.[675] These rights are rights that cut across socio-cultural, economic and political lines. The provisions of the Ogoni bill of rights includes, amongst others, the following:

(1) That Ogoni be granted political autonomy while still remaining part of the federal Republic of Nigeria.
(2) The right of the control and use of a fair proportion of Ogoni economic resources for Ogoni development.

---

673   *Id.* at 10.

674   Joshua Cooper, *The Ogoni Struggle for Human Rights and a Civil Society in Nigeria,* in STEPHEN ZUNES, LESTER R. KURTZ & SARAH BETH ASHER, NONVIOLENT SOCIAL MOVEMENTS: A GEOGRAPHICAL PERSPECTIVE 189 (Wiley-Blackwell, 1999).

675   ADAM GEAREY, GLOBALIZATION AND LAW: TRADE, RIGHTS, WAR 48-49 (Rowman & Littlefield, 2005); *see also* NANCY PELUSO & MICHAEL WATTS, VIOLENT ENVIRONMENTS 211 (Cornell University Press, 2001).

(3) The right to protect the Ogoni environment and ecology from further degradation.

The authorities, however, turned deaf ears to the aspirations of the Ogoni nations. Instead, they decreed measures and implemented policies which further marginalized the Ogoni people, denying them political autonomy, the right to their resources, to adequate representation as the right in all Nigeria's national institutions, and to the protection of their environment and ecology from further degradation.

The Movement for the Survival of Ogoni People (MOSOP), formed by the Ogoni peoples to fight its cause, gained wider acceptance and was admitted into the world's Unrepresented Nations and Peoples Organisation (UNPO) in January 1993. The efforts of Mosop gave international attention to Ogoni's ecological problem and the problems facing ethnic minority rights.[676]

As part of its effort to attract attention to their plight, on 4th January 1993, 300,000 Ogoni celebrated the Year of Indigenous Peoples by peacefully protesting against Shell's activities and the environmental destruction of Ogoniland. The Ogoni people carried out a mass demonstration against the oil companies because their activities had devastated, polluted and degraded Ogoniland. The oil activities had also contaminated the peoples' lands and poisoned their crops. Their claim is for their environment to be restored and for the right of self-determination so that they can actively participate in the way and manner that they are being governed.[677]

The present situation in Ogoniland is not palatable as there is terror in Ogoniland. Their fundamental human rights have been trampled upon and violated by security operatives. According to Ledum Mitee, "the state of repression, makes it impossible for Ogonis to live. Ogoni now looks more of a huge concentration camp."[678] This statement is a narration of the situation on the ground in Ogoniland and it is a very pathetic one. MOSOP strongly believes that the oil companies, particularly the Shell BP, was responsible for

676   Ogoni, *supra* note 671, at 13.

677   C. Bakwuye, *Ogonis Protest over Oil Revenue*, DAILY SUNRAY, January 6, 1993, at 1 and 20, in Andrew Rowell & Stephen Kretzmann, The Ogoni Struggle - A Project Underground Report, Initial Research by Lowenstein Nigeria Project, Yale Law School. First Edition November 1, 1996, Last updated March 4, 1997.

678   Ogoni, *supra* note 671, at 25.

influencing the government to support them to the detriment of the Ogoni people because of the largesses that comes into the government purse from the oil companies' operations.[679]

This overview of Nigeria's social groups will be limited to only the above mentioned ethnic groups in Nigeria since it would exceed the bounds of this book to review all ethnic groups and identify all the indigenous peoples in Nigeria. A review of these major groups will show that indeed there are indigenous peoples in Nigeria. There are, however, some other popular ethnic groups such as the Urhobo, the Edo, the Itsekiri, the Isoko and the Yala in the Niger Delta Area, while the Bachama Ebira, the Igala, the Tapa, the Kaja, the Kataf, the Mumuye, the Idoma, and the Kanuri are all in the middle belt and the North, whose detailed analysis and characterization will still have to be undertaken.

The country comprises many different ethnic groups, speaking many different languages and practicing many different religions.[680] In pre-colonial times, these different groups were organized in communities which ranged from small hamlets of a hundred people to big cities of many thousands that were centre of states with a population of several million inhabitants.[681]

One peculiar thing about Nigerians is that its great majority still gains its living from the land.[682] The Ogoni are one of the many ethnic groups in Nigeria that have zealously preserved their traditional political structure despite the incursion of Western civilization and its occupation of the Niger delta dates beyond eighteenth century.[683] Since 1958, when Shell discovered oil in Ogoniland, the Ogoni have lost vast expanses of land to oil prospecting and have been forced into smaller land areas.[684] The Shell action has led to population density which has exacerbated hunger, disease, and has led to the unavailability of basic social amenities such as piped water, electricity, and good roads.

---

679   GLENN ADELSON, JAMES ENGELL, BRENT RANALLI & KEVIN VAN ANGLEN, ENVIRONMENT: AN INTERDISCIPLINARY ANTHOLOGY 714 (Yale University Press, 2008).

680   Crowder and Abdullahi, *supra* note 550, at 7.

681   *Id.*

682   *Id.*

683   Obiora Okwu-Okafor, *Self-Determination and the Struggle for Ethno-Cultural Anatomy in Nigeria: The Zangon Kataf and Ogoni Problems,* 6 ASICL PROC. 114 (1994).

684   Chinedu Ezetah, *International Law of Self-Determination and the Ogoni Question: Mirroring Africa's Post-Colonial Dilemma,*19 LOY. L.A. INT'L & COMP. L.J. 815 (1996-1997).

The Ogoni derive their identity from their relationship with their land and their survival depends on it.[685] This dependence ranges from a sense of shared ancestry, culture, spirituality and social relationships to land-dependent occupations. For example, the consistent pollution of Ogoni land and water had an adverse effect on their land and water, thus leaving them with no potable water and their crops (vegetables) were also damaged. These two elements (land and water) are vital to the Ogoni survival.

The new oil wells, extensive pipeline networks, and oil spills from the Shell operation have destroyed arable land necessary for agriculture, which is one of the main sources of income and this has led to a decline in food production. Just as the Yanomami of Brazil suffered from the activities of gold miners which includes, but is not limited to, poisoning their land with mercury used for the mining processes.[686] The Ogoni also suffered seriously from the exploration activity of the oil companies on their land.

4.5 THE BOND OF LINEAGE AMONG THE ETHNIC GROUPS

Nigeria's ethnic groups are composed of non-centralized societies. A non-centralized society is one held together by the bond of lineage with the basis of such societies being the extended family or lineage, and members of such societies owing their primary loyalty to their lineage.

Pre-colonial Nigeria was comprised of states which are small and large with various forms of governments. The states were divided into provinces, each one administered by a chief loyal to the king.[687] These states can be classified into centralized and non-centralized ones. Those centralized states have a large political unit with its territory increasing and decreasing on the basis of relative military strength and they are controlled by a powerful king and his chiefs. The king exercises direct control while allowing heads of kinship groups to govern their various wards. A province could have many villages and towns, and also many ethnic groups of people in the case of kingdoms like Oyo. The second category of states in pre-colonial Nigeria was the non-centralized states exemplified by the states of

685   Ogoni, *supra* note 671, at 191.
686   Daes, *supra* note 11, at 98-100.
687   Falola, History, *supra* note 545, at 86.

the Igbo, Isoko, Uhrobo and Ibibio in Eastern Nigeria and most states in the Middle Belt. They are usually small in size and organized around villages or small towns. The government was decentralized, thus power was distributed among the elders. The society was regulated by sanctions, religious influence and controlled by the clan heads.[688]

The Igbo society is traditionally a non-centralized one.[689] Their society was divided into many patrilineal clans,[690] each with its own founding ancestor. Hundreds of villages existed, not as members of one Igbo kingdom, but as autonomous units, each with its own government. In a typical Igbo village, there was a Council of Elders comprising heads of different families and a village assembly where the majority of the public was allowed to engage in free speech and to be involved in decision making. The administration of justice was democratic as the elders and citizens discussed offenses and the nature of the punishment to be meted out.[691] In the absence of a centralized government, the heads of different families are involved in decision making, and also involved in the deliberation on offenses and the nature of commensurate punishment.

As stated earlier, linguistic and cultural differences often exist within the groups and this forms the basis for the existence of sub-ethnic systems. This leads to occupational and class differentiation which is dependent on the level of production in the group, the level of growth of the productive forces, and the level of division of labor within the social formation.

Relations between ethnic groups within the same political system produce ethnicity,[692] and this is apparent in the case of Nigeria where there is intense competition and rivalry among the Nigerian ethnic groups. Relations between ethnic groups which are political systems themselves constitute international relations and this is referred to as nationalism. Although the colonialists referred to the war between the various ethnic groups as inter-tribal wars, this could not be so in actuality because the ethnic groups are

---

688   *Id.* at 23.

689   JEREMIAH DIBUA, MODERNIZATION AND THE CRISI OF DEVELOPMENT IN AFRICA: THE NIGERIAN EXPERIENCE 57 (Ashgate Pub., Ltd., 2006).

690   Adamu Kiyawa, Language and the Politics of Ethnicity in Nigeria: A Sociolinguistic Perspective (1983)(unpublished dissertation, University of Wisconsin-Madison) (on file with Univ. of Wisconsin-Madison Library).

691   Falola, History, *supra* note 545, at 24.

692   'RACE,' ETHNICITY AND NATION: INTERNATIONAL PERSPECTIVES ON SOCIAL CONFLICT 18 (Peter Ratcliffe, ed., UCL Press, 1996).

independent political entities in their own right, and thus, the war should be seen as more of an international war than a conflict between different entities within the same political unit.

Ethnicity is characterized by a common consciousness of being related to the other relevant ethnic groups. This factor more than any other defines the boundary of the group and this is relevant for understanding ethnicity at any historical point in time. It is a fact that the boundaries of most of these ethnic groups have changed over time. For instance, the Yoruba of western Nigeria had some part of their groups in the Benin Republic and some are in the Kogi state of Northern Nigeria. All of this came into being courtesy of boundary adjustments.

During the pre-colonial times the Yoruba-speaking peoples were organized in kingdoms which fought bitter wars against one another and shared no common consciousness, except the fact that they had the same ancestors. They have since acquired a common identity. This belief in common ancestry also applies to the Ibo ethnic groups. For instance, the pre-colonial distinction between the Olu and the Zigbo in Igboland has given way to a common Igbo consciousness.[693]

Each of these ethnic groups consists of smaller groups. For instance, the Yoruba consist of sub-groups with distinctive political structures such as the Ekiti, the Ijesha, the Oyo, the Egba, the Awori and so on.[694] The situation in the Igbo/Ibo and the Hausa ethnic group are not different as they also consist of several smaller groups.

It must be noted that two conflicting ethnic groups always underplayed their differences in other to present a united front against any external threat. This goes to show the unity and solidarity spirit that exist within each ethnic group. As long as the external threat continues, each group maintains its internal cohesion, but once this external common enemy is removed, the social components of each ethnic group will revert back to socio-cultural symbols to maintain their separate entity. Therefore, there are various social combinations and alliances between ethnic groups and their smaller internal systems depending on what unit is involved in a dispute or a particular situation at a particular time.

---

693   Bascom, *supra* note 657, at 6.

694   OLUFEMI VAUGHAN, NIGERIAN CHIEFS: TRADITIONAL POWER IN MODERN POLITICS, 1890S-1990S, 13 (Boydell & Brewer, 2006).

Each of the smaller social units has its own identifiable social system, which is a totally organized system of inter-relationships between various individuals and groups in a society. The social interactions not only have their own form or structure in the traditional culture, but they are also guided by normative roles and expectations. The Nigerian society is made up of widely different constituents. This was a result of diverse socio-cultural units. There are also various small units within an ethnic group[695] that share similar institutions and central areas of social relations like kinship, marriage and family, but may differ in their political organization and government.

The Nigerian states shared many things in common. This includes their economy which was dependent on agriculture, as seventy percent of the Nigerian population depends on agriculture and was in fact responsible for sixty percent of non-oil export before the rise in oil prices.[696] Trade, mining, and manufacturing are the other spheres of the Nigerian economy. People always use elements associated with production such as tools, capital, land, and labor to perform a variety of economic activities. Hoes and machetes are the tools commonly used for the farming occupation. These tools were manufactured locally, thus minimizing reliance on foreign technology and despite the use of traditional tools, large-scale production was still possible.[697] Finances for projects were made possible through family assistance and local savings clubs.[698]

Most people engage in polygamous marriages so as to have a large and complex family which will guarantee a large work force for the family[699] on the farm or in whatever occupation the family is involved. Additional labor could also be secured if a family teams up with other families in a cooperative work group. The wealthy and powerful people make use of slaves for the labor force. In most cases, some slaves will be freed after meeting certain conditions.

_____In Nigeria, most occupations are land related, thus the society always

695   Gordon, *supra* note 543, at 102.

696   T. Ademola Oyejide, The Effects of Trade and Exchange Rate Policies on Agriculture in Nigeria 11 (Int. Food Pol'y Res. Inst., IFPRI, 1986).

697   Falola, History, *supra* note 545, at 24.

698   *Id.*

699   Ethan Gorenstein and Ronald Comer, Scientific American Reader to Accompany Abnormal Psychology 20 (Macmillan, 2001).

ensures that all individuals had access to it. Prior to the enactment of the Land Use Act, land was a communal property which is inalienable out of which every family in the community has a share from which they could not be dispossessed. As a most valuable asset, it was also sanctified by way of using the religious factor to maintain the laws preventing sale. Land was also regarded as property belonging to the ancestors, the living, and the coming generation. This necessitates the strict rule of inalienability of the property either as gift or sale.[700]

4.6 THE SOCIO-ECONOMIC RELATIONSHIP AMONG NIGERIAN ETHNIC GROUPS

There is an inter-group relation among Nigerian ethnic groups. Inter-group relations are the interactions between two or more distinct cultural or linguistic groups. It could either be a peaceful one through trade, migration or marriage,[701] or it could be a violent one through war and conquest. The inter-group relation has led to the spread of some common traits such as religious ceremonies, names, dresses, titles, currencies, and so forth. It also led to socio-economic institutions among the interacting communities. For instance, the intermingling has led to joint participation by the various ethnic groups in arts, sports and entertainment industries.

The unequal allocation of resources in society during the colonial era gave rise to intense competition among the ethnic groups. The way and the manner that the ethnic groups compete among one another makes inequality among the groups inevitable. The effort of individuals and groups not to be relegated to redundancy has anti-social effects, as the competition dominates human interaction and there is hostility in every sphere of the competition.[702] This was evident in the case of the Nigerian ethnic groups who exhibited competitive rivalry in every sphere of life. This competitiveness runs through political, social and economic activities, too.

In Nigeria, ethnicity is associated with the belief in the cultural and linguistic diversity of the country. It is often regarded as an unavoidable effect

---

700   Falola, History, *supra* note 545, at 25.

701   L. C. Dioka, *Inter-Group Relations Among Nigerian Communities*, in Nigerian Peoples and Cultures 55 (Akinjide Osuntokun and Avodeji Olukoju, eds., 1997).

702   Nnoli Okwudiba, Ethnic Politics in Nigeria 5 (Enugu: Fourth Dimension Pub., 1978).

of socio-cultural differences.[703] The pre-colonial societies of Nigeria relied on their traditional resources which include labor and power for satisfying their immediate needs for food, shelter and clothing in accordance with their habits and traditional consumption patterns. Peasants and handicraft production dominated the pre-colonial systems, and the tools of production were their handiwork.[704]

Agriculture was the main source of livelihood of the ethnic groups as this ensures food supply and made population expansion and modernization possible. In the Savanna, large scale cattle rearing was added to farming.[705] Most especially, the people of the Niger delta relied on fishing and farming while a section of the population focused on trading, oil palm milling, productions of craft and so on, but all this changed with the discovery of oil.[706]

The ethnic groups engaged in manufacturing were dependent on animal, mineral and vegetable products. Their most common products were ceramics and leather items such as bags, saddle covers and so on, textile materials such as cotton, yarns, dyestuffs, and food. Their craftsmen and women also used clay to produce kitchen utensils and decorative items.[707]

The most significant impact of inter-group trade activities of the ethnic groups is that it enabled them to circulate products that they produced in large quantity and this led to the exchange of products of different ecological origin. This allows each of the ethnic groups to have access to commodities of other ethnic groups. Such commodities of exchange include salt, iron, tools and textiles. Within a group, producers were interdependent. For instance, the farmer relied on the blacksmith for their farming tools such as cutlasses and hoes, while the blacksmith and the people in other occupations relied on the farmers for their food supply.

Trade among diverse groups led to interdependence,[708] as those in the forest supplied kola nuts to those in the Savanna, while those in the

---

703   *Id.* at 107.

704   *Id.* at 108.

705   *Id.* at 25.

706   J. Wheeler & Peter Newell, Rights, Resources and the Politics of Accountability 207 (Zed Books, 2006).

707   Okwudiba, *supra* note 702, at 26.

708   Gordon, *supra* note 543, at 24.

Savanna supplied animal products in exchange. The circulating currencies of the ethnic groups and the good road networks facilitated an effective distribution system. The currencies allowed the groups to store their wealth, and they also created a capital market that made available a conducive atmosphere where lenders and creditors could negotiate.

The market places are the meeting points for diverse ethnic groups.[709] The marketplace with its open space and stalls is the usual place where the ethnic groups conduct their transactions. This enabled members of diverse group to interact, trade, share information and network among themselves. The government always collects dues to finance the running of the government. Such markets are held in the morning or in the evening to serve the needs of the people within a town or village and its surrounding environment. There are also periodic markets which are usually held at two or more day intervals where regional products are usually distributed, collected and exchanged.

The various states interacted with one another and the major channel for this is through trade. No state was self sufficient in its needs either of basic items or of luxuries as there is a tendency for them to need items and products from one another. This is largely a factor of ecological differences. Coastal communities had salt and fish in abundance to offer others. The forest communities had kola nuts in large quantities which they exchanged with other ethnic groups for rock salt, horses, and cattle products. Regional markets, with traders from various areas, emerged in many locations and they all served as zones of interaction. The inter-group relationship was also boosted by religious, social, and cultural agencies such as age-grade associations, secret societies, marriage ties, and oracle practices of the various ethnic groups.[710]

The ethnic groups generally lived in harmony with one another, but occasionally conflicts do arise. A good example is the situation in Ibadan in the 1930s wherein the Ibadan cattle market in southwest Nigeria of Yorubaland was largely patronized by the Hausas who are mostly the cattle landlords and butchers. The trade later developed into rivalry between the Yorubas and the Hausas. This led to the displacement of the Hausas, as the competition to control the trade became intense between the Yorubas and

---

709   Bahru Zewde, Society, State and Identity in African History 242 (Ethiopia: Forum for Social Studies, 2008).

710   Okwudiba, *supra* note 702, at 27.

the Hausas.

Before 1940, the comparatively narrow economic gap between the Hausa and Igbo indicates that their members competed for similar resources which are not limited to unskilled jobs and semi skilled jobs and petty trading. The collective interest of the groups was focused on the resources and this necessitated the intense competition.[711]

The Yoruba were given tough competition by the Igbo and Hausa for the available resources, since the collective interests of the Yoruba were focused at the top and juicy aspect of the economy. This is because the prestige, status and achievement were measured and determined by these economic activities and this fueled the struggle among the groups for posts at the higher levels of the public and private sectors. The socio-economic competition among the ethnic groups increased the feeling of ethnic identity as many people solidarize with their group and this enlarged the competing group sizes.

The colonial influence gradually shifted from the communal ownership of land to individual land ownership which caused a monetary value to be placed on land, a clear departure from what operated before.[712] This commercialization of land brought individualism into the use of land because the lands acquired by individuals are now being used for their personal benefit and the community and families could no longer make collective use of the lands.

The ethnic nationalism in Nigeria existed before the postcolonial period and it continued after independence as the competition for power and survival of each ethnic group became the focal point of the political leaders. The impending disunity and mistrust threatening ethnic politics triggered the lawmakers to address the issue in both the 1979 and the 1999 Constitution. Article 15(3) of the Constitution state as follows:

> For the purpose of promoting national integration, it shall be the duty of the state to- (a) provide adequate facilities for and encourage free mobility of people, goods and services throughout the federation;

711   *Id.* at 225.
712   T. C. Mbagwu, Oil Palm Economy in Ngwaland (Eastern Nigeria) (1970) (unpublished Ph.D dissertation, University of Ibadan).

194

(b) secure full residence rights for every citizen in all parts of the federation; (c) encourage intermarriage among persons from different places or origin, or different religious, ethnic or linguistic association or ties; and (d) promote or encourage the formation of associations that cut across ethnic, linguistic, religious or other sectional barriers.[713]

The provisions of this section encourage the unity of all the various ethnic groups and this greatly facilitates the inter-ethnic relationship among the groups.

Additionally, Article 15(4) states that "The state shall foster a feeling of belonging and of involvement among the various peoples of the federation, to the end that loyalty to the nation shall over-ride sectional loyalties."[714]

This provision states that all ethnic groups shall be given a sense of belonging. This is to foster a strong bond among them. This provision will only be effective if the government at the center distributes the public service positions and the resources equally. This will discourage the various ethnic groups from the unhealthy competition among themselves.[715]

4.7 NIGERIA ETHNIC GROUPS AND THEIR RELIGIONS

Religion is part of the social life of the Nigerian ethnic groups. The ethnic groups engage in three major religions and these are the Islamic religion, Christianity and other traditional religions.[716] Nigeria's religious demography indicates that Muslims account for nearly fifty percent of the population, while forty percent of Nigerians are Christian and the remaining ten percent practice indigenous beliefs.[717]

The major role that religion plays in Nigerian society cannot be underestimated. There is a strong relationship between ethnic and religious

713   CONSTITUTION OF THE FEDERAL REPUBLIC OF NIGERIA, 16 (1999) Art. 15 (3) (a), (b), (c) & (d).

714   Id. at Art. 15(4).

715   Ike E. Udogu, The Issue of Ethnicity and Democratization in Africa, Towards the Millennium, 29.6 JOURNAL OF BLACK STUDIES, 794 (July 1991).

716   ROBERT SCHINKE & STEPHANIE HANRAHAN, CULTURAL SPORT PSYCHOLOGY 167 (Human Kinetics, 2009).

717   Kathryn M. Coughlin, Nigeria in MUSLIM CULTURES TODAY: A REFERENCE GUIDE 119 (Kathryn M. Coughlin, ed., Greenwood Press, 2006).

identity in Nigeria. The Muslim or Islam faithful are in the majority in Northern Nigeria, which is heavily populated by the Hausa and Fulani ethnic groups.[718] Christianity is the prevalent religion in Southern Nigeria which is populated by the Yoruba and Igbo tribes.[719] Both Northern and Southern Nigeria also have part of their ethnic tribes that practice traditional religions. These are people who see Christianity and Islam as imported religions in which they do not believe. They rather prefer to practice their ancestor's religion. There are also those that remain neutral and do not believe in any religion.

Religion has a lot of influence on Nigeria's social life. It permeates the economy, politics, as well as education. For instance, there are missionary schools as well as Islamic schools. These missionary schools teach their students based on a Christian-oriented syllabus, while the Islamic schools teach their students based on a Islamic-oriented syllabus. Thus, it is not uncommon to see Christians enrolling their kids in missionary schools, while the Muslims enroll their kids in Islamic schools. The good thing, however, is that these religions schools are few in number when compared to schools that are neutral.

4.7.1 Islam

The Islamic religion was introduced to West Africa and later to Northern Nigeria by the Arab merchants who participated in the Trans-Saharan trade[720] by the fourteenth century.[721] Therefore, the spread of Islam was greatly influenced by the traditional economy.[722] The religion was also promoted by tribal leaders who discovered that the religion expanded their trade network. The unity brought by this religion greatly minimized tribal and ethnic rivalries. The religion metamorphosed into an emirate state

718   Fatima L. Adamu, *A Double-edged Sword: Challenging Women's Oppression within Muslim Society in Northern Nigeria,* in GENDER, RELIGION AND SPIRITUALITY 56 (Caroline Sweetman, ed., Oxfam Pub., 1999).

719   Alex Gboyega, *Nigeria: Conflict Unresolved* in GOVERNANCE AS CONFLICT MANAGEMENT: POLITICS AND VIOLENCE IN WEST AFRICA 152 (William Zartman, ed., Brookings Inst. Press, 1997).

720   KALU OGBAA, THE NIGERIAN AMERICANS 15 (Greenwood Press, 2003); see also CATHERINE COLES & BEVERLY MACK, HAUSA WOMEN IN THE TWENTIETH CENTURY 90 (University of Wisconsin Press, 1991).

721   Shillington, *supra* note 612, at 1101.

722   DAVID WESTERLUND & INGVAR SVANBERG, ISLAM OUTISDE THE ARAB WORLD 57 (Palgrave Macmillan, 1999).

structure with the emir as the leader. The Islamic religion permeates most public institutions in Northern Nigeria.[723]

In Northern Nigeria, public meetings and related activities always start and end with a Muslim prayer. The religion was popularized to the extent that the majority of residents in northern Nigeria are familiar with both Islamic prayers and the five pillars of Islam. The height of the religion is the yearly trip to Mecca, the Hajj, to worship with other Muslims from all over the world. This is a prestigious trip that every faithful Muslim must make at least once during his or her lifetime.

4.7.2 Christianity

Christianity is the religion of the majority of the ethnic groups in Southern Nigeria, majorly populated by the Yorubas and Ibos.[724] Christianity is further split into different denominations, thus we have a diverse group of churches such as the Roman Catholic, the Anglicans, the Baptists, the Methodists, the Presbyterians, the Evangelists, the Pentecostal Christians and the Africanized sects such as the Aladura. The Roman Catholics and the Methodists, however, dominate in the Southeastern area of Igboland, while the Protestants and the Anglicans dominate the Yorubaland in the Southwest. Just like its Islam counterpart, the introduction of Christianity to Nigeria has aided commerce through the Portuguese traders in the fifteenth century, who first introduced native Nigerians to the Christian faith, but yielded few long-term converts. The abolition of slavery also aided the transfer of Christianity.

Britain's colonial rule in the nineteenth century also helped formalize the geographic and religious differences between the North and the South which would have escalated to a serious problem. While the British government worked with the Muslim leaders in the north, who prohibited the spread of the Christian faith, the central power structures in the south enabled churches to create a system of religious institutions and schools. This led to the inculcation of Christian tenets and teaching in the school syllabus.

As in the northern part of Nigeria, religion provided a means

---

723   HENRY BIENEN. POLITICAL CONFLICT AND ECONOMIC CHANGE IN NIGERIA 120 (Routledge, 1985).

724   Gboyega, *supra* note 719, at 164.

for social advancement in the South. This was promoted by the British colonial government and missionary schools. This produced an elite class of interpreters and civil servants.

According to Sunday Isong Obong,[725] in Nigeria religious diversity goes hand in hand with cultural diversity. He pointed out that in the North, which is predominantly Muslim, Muslim institutions have turned toward religious and political activism. The Muslim religion was practiced like a jihad. The jihad was a form of religious war which was animated by both religious and political interests. The South, which is predominantly Christian also tend to play politics with religious lineage. Thus, it is not uncommon to see favoritism in jobs according to religious membership. Thus, if a Catholic is a director of a bureau, he is likely to favor Catholics for employment rather than others outside that sect.

Makau Mutua has declared that religion permeates every sphere of African life and that any attempt to eradicate or force the African religion into oblivion will lead to the collapse of African norms and cultural identities.[726] He further argued that conversion to colonist religions was made a precondition for enjoyment of education and health care services and the Africans have no option than to succumb to the dictates of the new religion.[727]

Mutua was of the view that the colonialist religion, with the backing of the state, sought to eradicate and discredit the African religion or other forms of competing faith.[728] He also felt, and the author agrees with him that religion has the correlative duty to respect the human rights of adherents of other religions or beliefs.[729] Christianity and Islam ought to accommodate other religions, instead of trying to convert their followers to their faith. The religious crusade and holy jihads waged by both Christians and Muslims were cited by Mutua as one of the repercussions of the foreign religions in Africa.[730] This assertion tallies with the situation in Nigeria where bloody religious face-offs have become regular occurrences leading to wanton

725   Sunday Isong Obong, Aspects of the Structure of Selected Tribal Groups in Nigeria (January 1972) (unpublished thesis, College of Arts and Sciences, Chicago, IL).

726   Makau Mutua, *Limitation on Religious Rights: Problematizing Religious Freedom in the African Context*, 5 BUFF. HUM. RTS. L. REV. 75 (1999).

727   *Id.* at 76.

728   *Id.* at 79.

729   *Id.* at 81.

730   *Id.* at 83.

destruction of lives and properties.[731] It is a common practice to see Christians and Muslims castigating adherents of other religions as unbelievers and also to see them as inferior.[732] Additionally, Mutua strongly pointed out that the forces of Christianity and Islam, with the assistance or connivance of the state, ensured the relegation of indigenous religions and the imposition of foreign religions.[733] This author submits that discrimination on the basis of religion runs contrary to the provisions of International Covenant on Civil and Political Rights (ICCPR) which expressly states that:

> All persons are equal before the law and are entitled without any discrimination to the equal protection of the law. In this respect, the law shall prohibit any discrimination and guarantee to all persons equal and effective protection against discrimination on any ground such as race, colour, sex, language, religion, political or other opinion, national or social origin, property, birth or other status.[734]

4.7.3 Indigenous Beliefs

A minority of the Nigeria populace still practices its traditional religions,[735] that is, its indigenous beliefs. Indigenous practices continue to thrive in Nigeria because the faithful see both Islam and Christianity as imported religions which have come to pollute and extinguish their ancient traditional religions.[736] Some of Nigeria's native religious beliefs tie genealogical descent to a particular site where they worship the spirit of their ancestors. They so much believe in this practice that they feel empty without it. This attachment to the land is another proof of evidence that substantiates and legitimizes their claims to the land and its resources. According to religious scholars, the theology combines ancestor worship with the worship of spirits, or the supernatural entities in which they believe, in a particular group or territory.

---

731   TERENCE RANGER, EVANGELICAL CHRISTIANITY AND DEMOCRACY IN AFRICA 61 (Oxford Univ. Press, 2008); *see also* Rosaland Hackett, *Exploring Theories of Religion Violence: Nigeria's "Maitatsine" Phenomenon,* in RELIGION AS A HUMAN CAPACITY: A FESTSCHRIFT IN HONOR OF E. THOMAS LAWSON 194 (Brian Wilson & Timothy Light, eds., Brill Academic Pub., 2004).

732   Mutua, *supra* note 726, at 84.

733   *Id.* at 92.

734   International Covenant, *supra* note 149, at Art. 26.

735   PHILIP PEEK & KWESI YANKAH, AFRICAN FOLKLORD: AN ENCYCLOPEDIA 292 (Routledge, 2004).

736   Bah, *supra* note 590, at 39.

In most parts of Nigeria, traditional beliefs have fused with imported religious tradition. It is not uncommon to find Muslims and Christians carrying out ancient religious rites, such as wearing amulets which they believe will serve as protection against some unseen forces as evil attack or bad luck. Some even believe that it will protect them from an accident. The younger generations, however, do not believe in mixing the ancient traditional religions with the new faith. They believe that this amalgamation will amount to renunciation of the new faith.

The Ibo of South-eastern Nigeria also believe in long juju of Arochukwu. This long juju of Arochukwu, otherwise called "Aro oracle" of nineteenth century, was the Ibo institution that governs people's daily affairs because of the non-availability of a centralized government.

The Aro, a sub-section of the Ibo people, set up an oracle or mouthpiece of chukwu, the supreme deity which the Ibo ethnic group held in high esteem. They skillfully worked upon the deep-seated religious sentiment and fear of chukwu throughout Iboland and the delta. The oracle of Long Juju was popularly believed by the peoples of the delta to possess the ability as well as the power of bestowing fertility.[737] Thus, there is the general belief that the oracle can make people that are barren fertile. The oracle was also believed to have power to confer material gains of all sorts upon the consultants. The Ibo invaders used this oracle to boost their influence over the people of the area.

The Aro oracle was both feared and respected almost universally because of its efficacy.[738] This fact was used to promote their trading activities and their economic position in general. They operated almost like a modern syndicate. They organized Aro settlements in all important centres in Iboland and the Delta, especially along the main trade routes. Long Juju of Arochukwu was instrumental during the period of slave trade, as the practice was used to lure and sell as slaves unwary persons that came to consult the oracle. Those that managed the Aro practice usually would create situations which necessitated consultation of the oracle and suspects who were hurried to the oracle to have their innocence or guilt established would mysteriously disappear. The Aro also used the oracle as a means of

---

737   T. A. OSAW, S. N. NWABARA & A. T. O. ODUNSI, A SHORT HISTORY OF WEST AFRICA, A.D. 1000 TO THE PRESENT 138 (NY: Hill and Wang, 1975, 1968).

738   Cookey, ETHNOHISTORICAL, supra note 611, at 8-9.

blackmailing wealthy persons and dispossessing them of their wealth. This was made possible because of the fear and efficacy associated with the practice and this makes Long Juju become the most dreaded institution in both Iboland and the Niger Delta.

In Nigeria there are real religious edifices, otherwise called shrines, built by the people faithful to this traditional religion. For instance, what characterized the traditional religious life of the Urhobo people of eastern Nigeria are the various shrines they have in their towns and villages.[739] These edifices which they believe represented their ancestors are regularly worshipped and people often come with requests and wishes.[740] The religion is divided up into many sectors, some are exclusive while some complement each other. Only the followers initiated into all of these can enter into the entire particular shrine. The fact that a shrine belongs to a particular group does not necessarily mean that other groups with the same cultural background have access to it since their beliefs differ.

The Igbo ethnic groups are also into divination practices, whereby it is seen as a universal phenomenon and a standardized process of deriving hidden or secret knowledge from a learned cultural tradition based on an extensive body of knowledge.[741] Divination is of different types in African societies.[742] It ranges from simple beliefs about, and the interpretation of, omens and dreams to complicated methods such as horoscopes. It is believed that this is the means through which the human and spiritual world communicate and are reconciled.

Worship and practice of these traditional religions are necessitated by the enormous daily problems[743] confronting individuals that include, but is not limited to, mistakes in naming a child, determining causes of afflictions, the need to improve one's situation, barrenness problems or other medical and social problems. Divination practitioners are, therefore, consulted to

---

739   HISTORY OF THE URHOBO PEOPLE OF NIGER DELTA 385 (Peter Ekeh, ed., Urhobo Historical Society, 2007); see also Charles Gore, *Ritual, Performance and Media in Urban Contemporary Shrine Configuration in Benin City, Nigeria,* in RITUAL, PERFORMANCE, MEDIA 68-9 (Felicia Hughes-Freeland, ed., Routledge, 1998).

740   JACOB K. OLUPONA, AFRICAN SPIRITUALITY: FORMS, MEANINGS, AND EXPRESSIONS 15 (NY: Crossroad, 2000).

741   PHILIP M. PEEK, AFRICAN DIVINATION SYSTEMS WAYS OF KNOWING 1 (Indiana Univ. Press, 1991).

742   Olupona, *supra* note 740, at 87.

743   *Id.* at 44.

sort out, advise and explain solutions to the above stated complex problems. The ethnic groups patronize these various traditional religions to ensure continued favors from the spiritual forces. People maintain good relations through paying homage and offering sacrifices, in properly timed and performed rituals with the supervision of the priest.

One of the mostly worshipped gods among the Yoruba of the Southern Nigeria is Ogun,[744] otherwise called "the god of iron," war and hunting. Ogun shrines are usually simple altars located outdoors in the open air at the foot of a sacred tree, by the side of a wall, or in a blacksmith's workshop. Iron is the essential element in an Ogun's shrine.[745] An Ogun shrine is made up of a living tree, sacred to Ogun, whose branches are trimmed to about four feet and this provides a platform for the sacrifices. During the course of the worship ceremonies, each of these symbolic elements such as fluids from snails, the woven skirt and gin drink is placed upon the shrine. The intention of the rituals is to get protection against accidents involving iron, such as machetes, industrial machinery, automobiles, and accidents from weapons, such as knives and guns. Animals used for Ogun sacrifice are snails, tortoises and dogs, while the food and drink used are yams and palm wine respectively. A sacred day is usually set apart for the divination and the worship is fairly elaborate.[746]

In conclusion, it could be deduced from the above facts, especially the history of the Ogoni, the Koma people and the Igbo/Ibo that they have been in existence since time immemorial and could, therefore, be regarded as first or original inhabitants of their territory. It could also be deduced from the history of these groups that they have a subsistence economy which, amongst others, included farming, fishing and hunting. The history causes us to understand that these are age-old occupations passed from generation to generation before the advent of modern civilization. Their economy is land-based because of these occupations which evidences their strong ties to their land.

The history of the groups of various indigenous religions helps one to understand that the groups have their various gods or deities which they

---

744   *Id.* at 33.

745   Henry John Drewal, *Art or Accident: Yoruba Body Artists and their Deity Ogun*, in SANDRA BARNES, AFRICA'S OGUN OLD WORLD AND NEW 240-41 (Indiana Univ. Press, 1989).

746   S. O. OSO, AN INTRODUCTION TO WEST AFRICAN TRADITIONAL RELIGION 60 (Ado Ekiti, Nigeria: Omolayo Standard Press & Bookshops, 1978).

worship and believe in religiously. The Long Juju of Arochuckwu was one of such gods and its worshippers believe in its efficacy. One major point that these various traditional religions established is that the majority of these deities or gods that the people worshipped are land-based. Therefore, dislocation of these people from their land and degradation of such land by the nation states and their cohorts in the name of civilization and development were highly inhuman and unfair.

4.8 RELATIONS AMONG THE ETHNIC GROUPS AND THE NIGERIAN STATES

In the past, conflicts often occurred between Nigerian ethnic groups. Whenever conflicts arose, however, there were always amicable ways to address misunderstandings arising between individuals in the market place or farmland.[747]

Despite the diversities in their culture, language and size, the African ethnic groups came together and related very well among themselves. Chaotic situations can, however, not be ruled out as each of these peoples desperately tries to retain its identity.[748] This is because the Federal System of Government in Nigeria, which is the center, appears to concentrate too much power in the federal or central government, while other levels of government are mere appendages with little or no power or influence.[749] This gave rise to feeling of insecurity among the various ethnic groups who felt that their future existence and well being is not guaranteed. The relationship among these groups, therefore, gave rise to their ethnicity.

The way and manner the central government operates is that it garners resources from all areas in the Nigerian geographical area, and disburses, using criteria devised by it, to other tiers of government. Over the years, these resources distributions have been permeated by inequality and corruption and the increment in government units has not helped matters. This has resulted in less and less resources going to some states and local

747 Masajuwa Florence & Osagiator Ojo, *Sexism, Ethnicity and Discrimination in Contemporary Nigeria*, in P. E. IGBINOVIA, K. U. OMOYIBO, & E. O. UGIAGBE, SOCIAL PSY-CHOLOGY OF CHANGE AND DIVERSITY IN CONTEMPORARY NIGERIA 280 (Lagos: Ababa Press, 2004).

748 *Id.* at 279.

749 ROTIMI SUBERU, FEDERALISM AND ETHNIC CONFLICT IN NIGERIA 10 (US Institute of Peace Press, 2001) *see also* KALU NDUKWE KALU, STATE POWER, AUTARCHY AND POLITICAL CONQUEST IN NIGERIAN FEDERALISM 189 (Rowman & Littlefield, 2008).

governments which made it very difficult to meet the yearnings of the ethnic groups. There is, therefore, a deafening cry of marginalization by each of the ethnic groups as they hustle to have better access to the dwindling resources. Overall, the entire concept of Nigeria is based on ethnic survivalism. This means the survival of the fittest and most ambitious, but this has not in anyway helped the relationship among the ethnic groups because the competition among them has resulted in a bitter rivalry.[750]

Ethnic groups in Nigeria are social formations distinguished by the communal character of their boundaries[751] and the relevant communal factor may be language, culture, or both. In Africa and particularly in Nigeria, language has clearly been the most crucial variable.

---

750   Palph Uwazuruike, *Leader, Movement for the Actualization of Sovereign State of Biafra* (MASSOB), in NEWSWATCH, June 30, 2003, at 15.

751   OKWUDIBA, *supra* note 702, at 5.

CHAPTER FIVE

NIGERIAN RULES FOR SOCIAL ORDERING

5.1 NIGERIAN LAWS

One of the characteristics of the Nigerian legal system is the overwhelming influence of English law upon its growth. English law forms a substantial part of Nigerian law.[752] As good as the intentions of the international human rights instruments are, they are more or less worthless without the cooperation of the nation states. The Nigerian Constitution of 1999 is the supreme law of the land and its provisions have binding force on authorities and persons throughout the Federal Republic of Nigeria.[753]

Nigeria, being an independent country, must incorporate any international law into its domestic law before such law could have any effect. The provision of the relevant section of the Constitution[754] states that "No treaty between the federation and any other country shall have the force of law to the extent to which any such treaty has been enacted into law by the National Assembly."

This automatically means international instruments are not self-executing in Nigeria.[755] Any international instrument needs to be ratified by the country before it could be operational on the international plane. In addition to this, such ratified instruments need to be domesticated according to the provisions of the enabling legislation. The highest court in Nigeria, the Supreme Court in a popular case,[756] has established that international

---

752   O. A. OBILADE, THE NIGERIAN LEGAL SYSTEM 4 (London. Sweet & Maxwell 1979).

753   Constitution of the Federal Republic of Nigeria, *supra* note 713, at Section 1(1).

754   *Id.* at Section 12.

755   KEIR STARMER & THEODORA A. CHRISTOU, HUMAN RIGHTS MANUA AND SOURCEBOOK FOR AFRICA 827 (British Inst. of Int'l & Comp. Law, 2005).

756   Fawehinmi v. Abacha, 9 NWLR (Pt. 475) 710, 747 (1996).

instruments are not self-executing in Nigeria. The Court further emphasized that international treaties are in a legal class of their own and do not easily have a place in the Nigerian hierarchy of laws.

It is only when a treaty is enacted into law by the National Assembly that it could become operative in the country, as was the case with the African Charter on Human and Peoples Rights which was incorporated into Nigeria municipal/domestic law. This becomes binding on the Nigerian courts and must be seen and treated like all other laws of Nigeria and like all other laws the court must uphold it. The Supreme Court further held in the *Abacha* case[757] that international law cannot prevent the National Assembly from removing any treaty from the Nigerian body of municipal laws.

Nigeria had to ratify and implement several instruments before they became operational in the country, which instruments include, amongst others, the African Charter of Human and Peoples' Rights (ACHPR), the International Covenant on Civil and Political Rights (ICCPR), the Convention Against Torture, and the Convention on the Rights of the Child.

The Organization of African Unity, to which Nigeria is a member, on January 1981, adopted the African Charter on Human and Peoples' Rights providing for rights and obligations between member states[758] and between citizens and member states.[759] The said treaty was adopted by Nigeria in 1983 when the National Assembly enacted the African Charter on Human and Peoples' Rights (Cap10 Laws of the Federation of Nigeria 1990).

5.1.2 The Sources of Nigerian Law

T.O. Elias in his book[760] pointed out the sources of Nigerian law. The learned scholar listed the main sources of Nigerian law and they are as follows:

(a) Local laws and customs.
(b) English common law
(c) Local legislation which includes Federal Acts of Parliament and

---

757   *Id.*

758   African Charter, *supra* note 459, at Art. 23.

759   *Id.* at Art.19.

760   OLAWALE ELIAS, NIGERIA: THE DEVELOPMENT OF ITS LAWS AND CONSTITUTION, 311 (LONDON: Stevens, 1967).

Regional Laws of the Regional legislatures
(d) Judicial precedents
(e) Constitution
(f) Law reports, and
(g) Textbooks and monographs on Nigerian law

(a). Local laws and customs. These are a very important source of Nigerian law because it is the law that the British administration used to administer the country. These laws and customs are still in existence and they have not been varied or suspended by statutes or ordinances affecting Nigeria. Nigerian custom was held in high esteem then, but before it could be enforced by the court, the following three conditions had to be satisfied:

(1) The customary law will only be applied on the condition that it has not been altered by validly enacted laws;
(2) The said custom must not be barbarous, in other words, it must not be repugnant to natural justice, equity and good conscience; and
(3) Both parties to a dispute must be Nigerians.

A custom is a rule of conduct and when such a rule of conduct attains a binding or obligatory character it becomes a customary law.[761] According to Remigius Nwabueze[762] customary law is the starting-point of Nigerian legal history. He indicated that before the emergence of colonialism, customary law enjoyed monopolistic application in Nigeria, which is composed of politically and legally independent nationalities.[763] The body of Nigerian jurisprudence, as earlier pointed out, consists of customary law, received English law, and the law made by the Nigerian legislature or any other law making authority in Nigeria. A fact that must be noted is that the different regions of Nigeria were and still are under different customary law systems. For instance, the Ibo customary law applies to the Ibo people in Eastern Nigeria, the Yoruba customary law to the Yorubas in Western Nigeria and Islamic or Muslim law is regarded as customary law by the Hausas of Northern Nigeria.

One of the major features of customary law is that it is unwritten. This was buttressed by Justice Dan Ibekwe when he said:

---

761   (1931) A.C. 662 at 673.
762   Remigius Nwabueze, *The Dynamics and Genius of Nigeria's Indigenous Legal Order*, 1 Indigenous L. J. 153 (2002).
763   *Id.* at 155.

Regrettably enough, our own customary law is unwritten. It was handed down the ages, from generation to generation. Like a creed, it seems to live in the minds of people. This explains why little was really known at the beginning about the vast body of laws which had always govern our ancestors from time immemorial.[764]

Thus, to qualify as customary law, a norm must be generally accepted by the people subject to it. This position was affirmed by the privy council in the case of *Eshugbayi Eleko v. Government of Nigeria,* where Lord Atkin stated:

> their lordships entertain no doubt that the more barbarous custom of earlier days may under the influences of civilization become milder without losing their essential character as custom…It is the assent of the native community that gives a custom its validity, and therefore whether barbarous or mild, it must be shown to be recognized by the Native community whose conduct it is supposed to regulate.[765]

A rule of customary law is normally ascertained through the use of assessors who are regarded as having expert knowledge of the particular local law and custom. The opinions of the experts are, however, not binding on the presiding judge as such opinions are seen and treated as persuasive authority. The evidence of experts can be dispensed with where such rule of customary law has been so frequent before the courts that its judicial notice has been taken.[766]

While the indigenous peoples have the right to practice their customs, the exercise of such rights should be on the condition that such customs shall not be repugnant to natural justice. There are some archaic customs in Nigeria in the olden days. For instance in Calabar, there used to be the practice of killing twins because of the traditional belief that twins always

---

764   Sir Carleton Kemp Allen, Law in the Making 67-70 (Oxford: Clarendon Press, 1964).

765   D. O. Ibekwe, *Conflict of Cultures and Our Customary Law,* in African Indigenous Law: Proceedings of Workshop, 7-9 August, 1974, 297 (Enugu: Government Printer, 1974).

766   *Id.* at 311.

bring bad luck. It was Mary Slessor that stopped this barbaric practice.[767] There is no way this type of cultural practice can be allowed to exist because it is against natural justice. Also the custom of inhuman treatment to widows for the purpose of finding out whether they were responsible for their husband's death is against natural justice. The discrimination against a girl-child, whereby it is the cultural belief that educating a girl-child is a waste, is also a cultural practice that should not be allowed to continue. Thus any agitation for those cultural rights that violate human rights or that are inhuman should be disregarded.

(b). English common law, equity and statutes of general application. These three branches of English law apply as they stood in England on January 1, 1900. The English common law will apply in Nigeria only in situations where it has not been modified by local legislation and also where the subject matter does not fall within certain reserved matters of local customary law such as land tenure, succession as inheritance, marriage and the family, and chieftaincy disputes.

Section 45(2) of the Interpretation Act of Nigeria,[768] however, provides that "such imperial laws shall be in force so far as the limits of the local circumstances shall permit and subject to any federal law."

The above serves as a limitation on the application of the English statute. There are several situations where the application of the statute was limited. One such limitation is in the case of *Lawal v. Younan*[769] where the Federal Supreme Court held that children, not born in lawful wedlock under the Marriage Ordinance or where the parents were not married under the Native law and Custom, would still be legitimate as long as the children were acknowledged by the supposed father. The English statute was also

---

767   PHILLIS JESTICE, HOLY PEOPLE OF THE WORLD: A CROSS-CULTURAL ENCYCLOPEDIA 811 (ABC-CLIO, 2004); *see also* OLADIPO G. B. OGUNSEITAN, OPAQUE WALLS I: EPISTLES ON MAN, RELIGION, POLITICS & NUMEROLOGY 151 (Kraft Books, 1995). In the eighteenth century in Calabar, Nigeria, the birth of twins is thought to be an evil sign. Twin babies are cruelly murdered, and their mother is driven from her home to die in the jungle. Mary Slessor rescued from death hundreds of baby twins and other deserted babies thrown out in the forest to perish of hunger or to be eaten by ants or leopards. She was able to disuade the Calabar people from this barbaric act by preaching Christian doctrines to them.

768   Interpretation Act of Nigeria, Cap. 89 Laws of Nigeria (1958).

769   (1961) ALL NLR 245.

limited in the case of *Daniel v. Bamgbose*[770] where the court held that the children from nine marriages contracted by the deceased can succeed to the property of the deceased who died intestate. The court further elaborates that the term "children" under the English Statute of Distribution 1970 will also cover children of polygamous marriages. The most important test here is to establish that the children are legitimate.

(c) Local legislation. This includes all federal enactments referred to as "Acts" and the regional ones referred to as "laws." It must be noted that all British statutes not of "general application in England" as at January 1, 1900, do not apply unless expressly made applicable by local legislation.

(d) Judicial precedents. These are court decisions cited as an analogy to determine similar questions of law in similar cases. The English doctrine of judicial precedent applies in Nigeria. Examples of this are the decisions of the Supreme Court of Nigeria, which is the highest court in the country, which are binding upon all other Nigerian courts, and those of the Regional High Courts bind all lower courts within their jurisdiction.

(e) Law reports. These are a series of books containing judicial opinions from selected case laws. Examples of these include reports of certain judgments of the Supreme Court, Nigeria Law Reports covering the 1880 to 1947 and containing the selected judgments of the Divisions Courts and of the full court of both the Lagos Supreme Court and the Nigerian Supreme Court, Judgments of the Court of Appeal of Nigeria, Judgments of the High Courts of Nigeria and Judgments of the West Africa Court of Appeal (WACA).

(f) Textbook and monographs serves as persuasive authority as a court may decide to accord them weight depending on the standing of their authors.

5.2 OWNERSHIP OF LAND IN NIGERIA

Under the traditional system of ownership, people were guaranteed land for all purposes ranging from farming to fishing. The introduction of the legal instrument in the name of the Land Use Act of 1978 now vests land ownership in the federal government at the federal level while states and

---

770   (1955) A.C. 107.

local government hold land in their area in trust.[771]

History has shown that in Nigeria, as in practically all of the former British West African colonies, individual ownership of land in the accepted English sense is unknown, as land is held under community ownership, and not, as a rule, by individual as such.[772] There have been several claims that Nigeria has been ceded to the colonialists by the local rulers then and that the claim to communal, joint or family ownership of land no longer exist. On the claim that title to native land had been passed by the local Emirs, chiefs and other rulers in the protectorates to the Royal Niger Company, several writers have given their opinion as to what is the true position of the issue. One of such writers is Olawale Elias who pointed out that emirs and other native rulers were never lords and masters of the land. They were only political, religious and military rulers of their respective states and are seen as trustees of the land on behalf of the people to whom the land belonged.[773]

By virtue of the above facts, the trustee cannot give away by treaties any rights in land of a proprietary character. Olawale Elias has described communal lands as those which the individual members of the group have a recognized interest and those over which no claim of right is ever asserted whether by groups or by individuals. The communal term has also been stated to apply to lands like sacred groves and other fetish lands, market-sites, dumping grounds of the villages, churches and mosques and lands surrounding these. Individual rights to land, on the other hand, are applied to parcels of land ranging from those over which only limited inalienable rights of the user are claimed by individuals to those carrying absolute freehold titles.

5.2.1 The Land Use Act of 1978

The Nigeria Land Use Act of March 29, 1978 is one of the most innovative enactments in Nigerian law. It imposes for the first time in the whole of Nigeria, a common and uniform system of land titles and land control. The act represents a uniform system of land law that was imposed

---

771   SOFO C. A. ALI-AKPAJIAT & TONI PYKE, MEASURING POVERTY IN NIGERIA 44 (Oxford: Oxfam GM, 2003).

772   Elias, *supra* note 760, at 6.

773   *Id.* at 31.

throughout the country.[774] The Act provision expressly states that

> Subject to the provision of this Act, all land comprised in the territory of each state in the federation are hereby vested in the military governor of that state and such land shall be held in trust and administered for the use and common benefit of all Nigerians in accordance with the provision of this Act.[775]

The Act made a fundamental division between "urban" and other land. While land in the urban areas is under the control of state governor,[776] other lands will be under the control of the local government.[777] This Act vests all lands in the state through the office of the military governor of each state. The land is held in trust and administered through the government's authority to use and benefit of all Nigerians.

The operation of the Land Use Act is similar to the operations of the Public Land Ordinance of 1903. This was buttressed in the popular case of *Amodu Tijani v. The Secretary Southern Provinces*,[778] where the Public Land Ordinance of 1903 of the colony provides that the governor may take any land required for public purposes for an estate in fee simple or for a less estate, on paying compensation to be agreed on or determined by the supreme court of the colony. Where the land required is the property of a native community, the head chief of the community may sell and convey it in fee simple, any native law or custom to the contrary notwithstanding.[779] Where the compensation is paid to a head chief, in respect of any land which belongs to a native community, such compensation is to be distributed by him among the members of the community or applied or used for their benefit in such proportions and manners as the native council of the district in which the land is situated.

In the *Amodu Tijani* case the appellant claimed for the whole value of the land in question, as being land which he was empowered by the ordinance to sell. The Chief Justice of the Supreme Court held that although

---

774   A. N. Allott, Recent Reforms in Area and Customary Courts in Nigeria Legislation, 22 J. Afr. L. 133 (1978).

775   Land Use Act, Laws of the Federation of Nigeria 1990, Chapter 202, Section 1.

776   *Id.* at Chapter 202, Section 2(1)(a).

777   *Id.* at Chapter 202, Section 2(1)(b).

778   (1921) 2 AC 399, 403-4.

779   *Id.*

the appellant had a right which must be recognized and paid for, this right is a

> merely seigneurial right giving the holder ordinary right of control and management of the land in accordance with the well known principles of native law and custom, including the right to receive payment of the nominal rent or tribute payable by the occupier, and that compensation should be calculated on that basis, not on the basis of absolute ownership of the land.[780]

Their Lordships in the case made a preliminary observation and stated that, in interpreting the native title to land, much caution is required. There is a tendency to render the title concept in terms which are appropriate only to systems which have grown up under the English law. It was pointed out in the case, that as a rule, in the various systems of native jurisprudence throughout the Empire, there is no such full division between property and possession as English lawyers are familiar with.

As a result of the cession of Lagos to the British crown by former Rulers or Monarchs, the radical title became vested in the British Sovereign and that title was qualified as a usufruct since the property still belongs to the community. In the instance of Lagos, in the case of *Tijani v. Secretary of Southern Nigeria*,[781] Viscount Haldane in the report on land tenure in West Africa stated that "The next fact which is important to bear in mind in order to understand the native land law is that the notion of individual ownership is quite foreign to native ideas. Land belongs to the community, village, or family have an equal right to the land."

The chief or headman of the community or village, or headman of the community or village is to some extent in the position of a trustee, and as such holds the land for the use of the community or family. He has control of it, and any member who wants a piece of it to cultivate or build a house upon, goes to him for the land, but the land so given still remains the property of the community or family.

The headman cannot make any important disposition of the land without consulting the elders of the community or family and their consent must in all cases be given before a grant can be made to a stranger. In Lagos,

---

780   *Id.*
781   4 N.L.R. 18 (1923).

however, there are individual owners. This is due to the introduction of English ideas, but this does not, however, mean that the native idea has been discarded. As in most cases, land is still held by the family and this is evident in the cases of land purporting to be held under crown grants and English conveyances. Chief Rayner further pointed out that the original grantee may have held as an individual owner but upon his death all his family claim an interest which is always recognized and the land becomes family land again. He further states that from his experience in Lagos, except where land has been bought by the present owner, there are few very natives who are individual owners of land.[782]

Their Lordships in the case of *Attorney General of Southern Nigeria v. Holt*[783] in 1915 also asserted that where the cession passed any proprietary rights, they were rights which the ceding king possessed beneficially and free from the usufructuary[784] qualification of his title in favor of his subjects. Also in the case of *Oduntan Onisiwo v. The Attorney General of Southern Nigeria*,[785] it was held that the cession of 1861 does not impair the ownership rights of private landowners, including the families of Idejos. Their Lordships went further to state that a mere change in sovereignty is not to be presumed as meant to disturb rights of a private owner, and the general terms of a cession are prima-facie to be construed accordingly. They further noted that the introduction of the system of crown grants was made not with a view to altering substantive title already existing.

The above two cases buttress the fact that the monarchs or rulers were trustees and whatever land title they might have passed are mere usufructs. The fact is that the land still belongs to the community.

On the question of whether the headship has any right over or title to the land in question for which compensation is payable and if so, on what basis such compensation should be fixed, the Lordship states that a "seigneurial right gives the holder the ordinary rights of control and management of land in accordance with the well known principle of native law and custom, including the right to receive payment of the nominal rent or tribute payable by the occupiers, and that compensation should be

---

782   *Id.*

783   2. N.L.R. 1 (1915) AC, 599.

784   A legal right to use and derive profit from property belonging to someone else provided that the property itself is not injured in any way.

785   2. N.L.R. 77.

calculated in that basis and not on the basis of absolute ownership." Their Lordships, therefore, reiterate in the case of *Amodu Tijani* that title to land is prima facie based not on such individual ownership as English law has made familiar, but on a communal usufractuary occupation. The original native right was a communal right, and it must be presumed to have continued to exist unless the contrary is established by the context or circumstances.

The Land Tenure Law of 1962 and the Land Use Act of 1978 are two laws that concern the right to lands in Nigeria. These laws redefined the rights and obligations of the government and those of the cultivators and others with interests in land. The governments were vested with ownership of the land while the individuals were allowed only rights of occupancy, or use under two forms of title, a statutory right which is granted by the government and a customary right which is the title of the members of a community as guided by the local law and custom.[786] The Land Use Act is seen as mere adoption of the Land Tenure Law of 1962.

According to Famoriyo, the land in Nigeria makes up the basis for social, economic and political development.[787] The economic conception of the land is that it is considered as a source of human health, the natural source of the raw materials required by man for his daily requirement of food, fiber and energy.[788] Studies have shown that the objectives for which the Land Use Act was promulgated have largely remained unfulfilled, as the said Act has been abused and seriously undermined.[789]

The second stanza of the preamble raised the people's hope where it guaranteed the rights of all Nigerians to use and enjoy land in Nigeria and the natural fruits thereof in sufficient quantity to enable them to provide for

786   Alegwu Ega, *The Need to Redefine Rights under Customary Land Tenure in Northern Nigeria,* in Perspectives on Land Administration and Development in Northern Nigeria: Proceedings of the Workshop on Land Resources, Kano, September 25-28, 1986, 41 (Michael Mortimore, et al., eds., Kano: Dept. of Geography, Bayero University, 1987).

787   O. A. Famoriyo, *Acquisition of Land and Compensation in Nigeria,* in Perspectives on Land Administration and Development in Northern Nigeria: Proceedings of the Workshop on Land Resources, Kano, September 25-28, 1986, 102 (Michael Mortimore, et al., eds., Kano: Dept. of Geography, Bayero Univ., 1987).

788   *Id.*

789   Lasun Mykail Olayiwola & Olufemi Adeleye, 18.2 Land Reform- Experience from Nigeria (Promoting Land Administration and Good Governance, 5th FIG Regional Conference, Accra, Ghana, March 8-11, 2006).

the sustenance of themselves and their families. There is another promising section[790] which states that all land is to be held in trust and administered for the use and common benefit of all Nigerians. It is, however, the submission of this author that these guarantees are nothing but lip service which only raised hopes of the people with nothing forthcoming. Studies have indicated that as of today, the land is less available to the ordinary Nigerian than it was before the Land Use Act. There was favoritism in the allocation policies of various governments, especially during the civilian era where the Land Use and Allocation committees were tools in the hand of governors, who merely endorsed lists approved by governors. There is also a bad practice whereby new governments always revoke land allocated by its predecessors with the aim of favoring their loyalists. Allocations of land was hardly made to the low income earners. The state government zeal to generate internal revenue has also put land beyond the reach of ordinary Nigerians. The Land Use Act thus concentrates both economic and political powers in the hands of governor. The 1978 Decree was supposed to take care of community ownership of the land by making land open to development by individuals, corporations, institutions and government,[791] but the reverse is the case. In most cases, adequate alternatives compensation or accommodations were not provided for those that were displaced from their lands.

5.3 INDIGENOUS SYSTEMS OF TENURE

Due to Nigeria's diversity of tribes and cultural patterns, there are general permanent features of its indigenous systems of tenure because

(a) the local laws and customs with respect to land, in addition to being unwritten law, vary from place to place in certain particular details; and
(b) the number of specialized studies of them is not large.

To understand the native land law, it must be noted that the notion of individual ownership is quite foreign to native ideas. It is the general belief that the land belongs to the community, the village or the family, but never to an individual.[792] All the members of the community, the village or the

---

790   Land Use Act, *supra* note 775, at Section 1.
791   Samuel Egwu. Structural Adjustment, Agrarian Change and Rural Ethnicity in Nigeria 55-56 (Research Report no. 103, Nordiska Afrikainstitute, 1998).
792   Elias, *supra* note 760, at 93.

family, have an equal right to the land. However the family head,[793] the chief or headman of the community or village is the trustee and he holds the land for the use of the community or family. He has control of the land and any member who wants a piece of it to cultivate or build upon goes to him for it, but the land so given still remains the property of the community or family.[794] This trustee has to seek the consent of the community or family elders before the land is granted to any stranger. However, where the grantee's occupation is against the general family's interest such grantee can be evicted and the land revoked by the chief or headman.[795] Olawale Elias pointed out that individual members of a family may acquire an absolute property title in the land by

(a) Appropriation of unoccupied or uncultivated virgin land;
(b) An absolute interest in an allotted portion of the family land given with the family consent;
(c) It may be in form of gift from another land-owing family that has surplus land; and
(d) One may become a land owner due to the partitioning of family land into specific lots.[796]

Land, however, acquired by an individual in any of these ways becomes family land at the death of the first occupier. While an allottee cannot sell his allotment or mortgage it, he can pledge it or the crop on it for debt. He can temporarily give its use to a stranger without family approval, subject to performing his entire obligation under the customary law. The land right or interest of the individual will, however, cease on the following conditions:

(a) By express surrender or release
(b) By abandonment
(c) By failure of effectual occupation or user
(d) By alienation or attempted alienation
(e) By denial of the title of the land-owing family
(f) By refusal or failure to pay the customary dues or render the

---

793   The family head is the oldest male member of a family who happens to be the first-born, however, if the first-born is a female and happens to be strong and have an influential character or if there are no male members that are pushy in the family, such a senior female may be elected family head.

794   Elias, *supra* note 760, at 94.

795   Idewu Inasa & Ors v. Saka Oshodi (1934), A.C.99.

796   Elias, *supra* note 760, at 165.

customary services.

So many reasons had been proffered for the principle of inalienability of land. According to Olawale Elias, that notion of inalienability derives from a religious attitude towards the land regarded as a sacred trust of the living that is undertaken in the memory of the dead. Another reason is that alienation of such land will amount to the giving away of ancestral land to individuals or groups who are seen as strangers. The lands are also made inalienable out of a desire to preserve it for the future generations. There is the general belief that if the land was willed away, there will be nothing for their coming generations to inherit and thus agitation over land rights is an issue that is never treated with levity.

According to Erica Irene Daes, land is central to the lives of indigenous peoples, as it is the basis of their economic survival, spiritual well-being and cultural identity.[797] Charlene Yates has also pointed out that the concept of the land embraces the whole territory they use, including the forests, the rivers, the mountains, the seas, the surface and the natural resources.[798]

5.4 EFFORTS MADE TO RECOGNIZE THE IMPORTANCE OF LAND TO INDIGENOUS PEOPLES

It has been recognized in Abuja,[799] Nigeria, that the indigenous perspective is an integral part of the debate on the land and development, therefore the challenge for the commonwealth to respond has been set. Charlene Yates pointed out that indigenous land issues are a pan-commonwealth concern and that the issue of land rights has arisen in every inhabited territory colonized in the commonwealth. The problem was borne out of the colonial legacy. While there has been some progress made in dealing with this issue within the domestic sphere of individual countries,

---

797   Daes, *supra* note 340 [Final paper prepared for the UN Sub-commission on the Promotion and Protection of Human Rights (E/CN.4/sub.2/2001/21, 11 June 2001) para 24].

798   Charlene Yates, *Conceptualizing Indigenous land Rights in the Commonwealth Indigenous Land Rights and Resource Management in the Commonwealth Project*, Commonwealth Lawyers Association/ Commonwealth Policy Studies Unit, *available at* (http://www.cpsu.org.uk/fileadmin/Eco_Devt_and_Legal_Reform/Indig_land_rights_and_resources.pdf).

799   Abuja Commonwealth Head of State meeting (CHOGM), December 3rd, 2003, *available at* http://www.humanrightsinitiative.org/cwhr/decdoc/abuja_communique-dec03.pdf.

there is a problem that it will remain domestically contained despite the fact that the problems relating to the land and its resources are the direct result of colonialism.[800] This could be substantiated by the fact that the people of Nigeria have no land disputes among themselves nor with governments prior to the colonization by the British and if any existed it was at a minimal level which cannot be compared with the magnitude that accompanied colonial rule and which continued to exist decades after independence.

Yates made it clear that the emerging domestic case law on indigenous land rights reveals that legal precedents in one country can potentially act as precedents across the commonwealth at least where common law exists, which presents the opportunity to identify cases of best practice.[801] The civil society meeting statement issued in Abuja, Nigeria, on December 3rd included a paragraph on the rights of indigenous peoples and the right to self-determination as follows:

> In this, the penultimate year of the UN Decade for indigenous peoples, we ask the commonwealth to acknowledge that many indigenous peoples in the commonwealth continue to be significantly disadvantaged and that special measures should be encouraged to overcome the continuing effect of racism, colonialism or globalization, with their full participation and consent. Further, we urge the establishment of mechanisms to guarantee the rights to self-determination of people of the overseas territories of member countries.[802]

At Abuja, the commonwealth project prepared memoranda to the Commonwealth Heads of Government and meeting member states were urged to recognized indigenous peoples as "people" with the right to freely determine their own future, one free from discrimination and where all peoples are equal. They were, therefore, called upon to endorse the right of indigenous peoples to self determination. The Commonwealth Policy Studies Unit (CPSU) also urged member states to adopt Article 3 of the

---

800   Yates, supra note 798, at 4-5.

801   *Id.* at 6.

802   Helena Whall, *Indigenous People's Rights in the Commonwealth*, Minority Rights and Reconciliation in the Commonwealth, A Cumberland Lodge Conference, February 11th – 13th, 2004.

United Nations Declaration of the Indigenous Peoples' Rights.[803] Despite this clarion call, the Commonwealth Heads of State did not make a commitment to indigenous rights at the Abuja summit.

The research undertaken by the project on the status of indigenous peoples in twenty commonwealth countries highlights the similar experiences of indigenous peoples living in the commonwealth. The research states that all indigenous peoples routinely suffer from discrimination, social, economic and political marginalization and poverty. The CPSU worked closely with a Pan-commonwealth network of indigenous people called Commonwealth Association of Indigenous People (CAIP), established in 1999. CAIP actively lobbies the commonwealth and its member states at both commonwealth and UN fora to recognize the rights of indigenous peoples.[804]

The African Charter to which Nigeria is a state party containing the treaty stated in its preamble that nation states must pay respect to the economic, social and cultural rights and that these rights is a guarantee for the enjoyment of civil and political rights. It also pointed out that the promotion and protection of morals and traditional values recognized by the community shall be the duty of state.[805] Helena Whall pointed out that many of the problems facing indigenous peoples in the commonwealth today are the direct result of colonialism and that the recognition of the rights of indigenous peoples by the commonwealth is part of the unfinished business of decolonization and that the commonwealth has a responsibility to make amends for the poor treatment of the past.[806]

5.5 OIL PIPELINE ACT

This is an act that made provision for licenses to be granted for the establishment and maintenance of pipelines incidental and supplemental to oilfields and oil mining and for purposes ancillary to such pipelines. This act is relevant to this book because it made provision for compensation to be paid to the local community whose interest (land impliedly inclusive) may be injuriously affected.

---

803   *Id.* at 12.

804   *Id.* at 2.

805   African Charter, *supra* note 459, at Art. 17(3).

806   Helena Whall, *The Challenge of Indigenous Peoples, The Unfinished Business of Decolonization*, 92.372, THE ROUND TABLE: THE COMMONWEALTH JOURNAL OF INTERNATIONAL AFFAIRS 638 (2003).

The Oil Pipeline Act in Nigeria[807] has indirectly recognized the right of the local community to their land in its provisions where it states that:

> Where the interests injuriously affected are those of a local community, the court may order the compensation to be paid to any chief, headman or member of that community on behalf of such community or that it be paid in accordance with a scheme of distribution approved by the court or that it be paid into a fund to be administered by a person approved by the court on trust for application to the general, social or educational benefit and advancement of that community or any section thereof.[808]

The provisions of the African Charter which are enforceable in Nigeria are similar to the provisions of the Oil Pipeline Act. This is because the Charter made provisions for compensation in situations of dispossession and spoliation of peoples' property.[809] The provision in the African Charter and the Oil Pipeline Act of 1990 stated that the peoples shall have the right to a general satisfactory environment favorable to their development,[810] and that the oil pipeline shall prevent oil pollution of both land and water.[811]

5.6 NIGERIAN LAW AND CULTURAL POLICY

The Nigerian Constitution enjoined the state to protect, preserve and promote the Nigerian cultures which enhance human dignity,[812] and to encourage studies that enhance cultural values.[813] The states are also mandated to ensure adequate facilities for social, religious and cultural life.[814] In Nigeria, the English language was made the official language by the British colonialists during their reign and since they left in 1960 the English language has come to stay as it is still the only language that is used in all schools and for all official transactions or business. There was even a time

---

807 Oil Pipelines, Act Chapter 338, Laws of the Federation of Nigeria 1990, *available at* http://www.nigeria-law.org/Oil%20Pipelines%20Act.htm.

808 *Id.* at Section 12.

809 African Charter, *supra* note 459, at Art.21 (1) & (2).

810 *Id.* at Art. 24.

811 Oil Pipelines, *supra* note 807, at Section 17(4).

812 Constitution of the Federal Republic of Nigeria, *supra* note 713, at Art. 21(a).

813 *Id.* at Art. 21(b).

814 *Id.* at Art. 17(3) (b).

when a former Minister of Education in Nigeria, Professor Babs Fafunwa, suggested that schools should revert back to teaching in their mother tongue. This step would have been in line with the provision of the United Nations Declaration on Language[815] which granted indigenous peoples the right to be provided education in their own languages. There was a general outcry against the move, but it never saw the light of day. The motive for the teaching of the mother tongue language by the learned professor was to afford the school children the benefit of studying and being taught in their local or native languages and thus enhance their academic performance, but the argument canvassed by those against it was that the implementation will cause irredeemable confusion to the kids.

This point will be explained and highlighted by a story in one of the Nigerian dailies by Akeem Lasisi,[816] who pointed out that the homes of most members of the elite in Nigeria are "a study in dilemma and cultural contradictions," and this usually applies to the language of communication. The writer stated that the orientation that most children get is that the indigenous language is a dirty and traditional language from which they need to distance themselves. Most parents even went a step further to keep the traditional or indigenous language from their children, so that the English he or she is being "born" into will not in any way get diluted or polluted. The writer came to the conclusion that the syndrome presents one of the greatest threats to the indigenous languages that have already been described as being endangered. In his own words, Professor Oladipo Salami[817] confessed that the idea of relegating the indigenous language to basically non-existence makes him feel bad. He pointed out that most children are in a dilemma because they do not speak their mother tongues and also cannot speak good English. It is a case of double tragedy causing such children to be culturally alienated. The learned professor reiterated that what Prof. Babs Fafunwa proposed then would have by now have solved much of the dilemma if the government had allowed the implementation of the idea. The professor said it is his business as a socio-linguist to examine language in relation to the society and to discuss it in relation to politics, economy, identity and every other element around the soul of an individual, a community and the nation. He is thus able to appreciate the gravity of

---

815   U.N. Declaration, *supra* note 217, at Art. 14 (1).

816   Akeem Lasisi, *How My Family Resolved the Indigenous Language Dilemma*, PUNCH ON THE WEB, (Sunday, 13th January, 2008).

817   Head of English Department, Obafemi Awolowo University, Nigeria.

the cultural dilemma that the total subjugation of an indigenous language generates.

The professor relating his family experience said he and his wife, while bringing up their children, communicated with them in English because they felt it would be an embarrassment if the child of an accomplished linguist were not able to communicate in brilliant English. The father and mother communicated with each other using both English and the indigenous language, while they communicated with the children in the Queen's language. This led to confusion in the family and the professor came to the realization that the cultural identities of the children were under threat if they were not introduced to the indigenous or traditional language, too. The professor said this incident made him to realize that the orientation he was giving his children was not natural and the children were being denied the knowledge of themselves. This is just a sample of the cultural situation in most colonized countries, especially Nigeria.

The Nigerian Constitution declares that the states are obligated to ensure that there are adequate facilities for social, religious and cultural life.[818] States are also obligated to protect, preserve and promote Nigerian cultures which enhance human dignity.[819] The Nigerian Ministry of Culture and Social Welfare has two departments responsible for administering and implementing cultural policies. The Federal Department of Culture is responsible for the formulation and execution of the national cultural policies. The National Council of Arts and Culture encourages and develops all aspects of Nigerian cultures and interacts with private or public organizations. Also involved in cultural life and policies are the Ministry of Information and the Ministry of Education.[820]

The promotion and development of culture is the exclusive responsibility of each Nigerian state, and thus, state or provincial authorities have all established State Art Councils set up by law. It is, therefore, common to see the states with their own established state art council. A very good example is the Oyo state of Nigeria which has the Oyo State Council of Arts and Science. The Ondo state also has the Ondo State Council of Arts and Science. Additionally, the Lagos State, the former capital of Nigeria, has the

---

818   U.N. Declaration, *supra* note 217, at Art. 17(3)(b).

819   *Id.* at Art 21(a).

820   *Cultural Policy in Nigeria,* prepared by CultureLink (IRMO, 1996), *available at* http://www.wwcd.org/policy/clink/Nigeria.html.

Lagos State Council of Arts and Science. According to the materials produced by the Culture Link,[821] the functioning of the public and semi-public bodies dealing with culture, as well as, the main inputs in the cultural infrastructure such as the building of museums, theaters, and the establishment of libraries are mainly funded from the federal budget.[822]

The Nigerian Constitution has provisions regarding the rights of Nigerian people to develop and promote their cultures, but it is disappointing that these rights are inoperative. The legislative powers of the Nigerian Constitution defines the mandate of the federal government, as well as, of the state and provincial authorities in the field of culture. According to the list, each Nigerian state government has the obligation to promote and develop traditional cultures.

The UNESCO, the Universal Declaration on Cultural Diversity,[823] which aims to preserve cultural diversity states that culture is the common heritage of humanity and should be recognized and affirmed for the benefit of present and future generations.[824] It asserts that cultural diversity is inseparable from respect for human dignity. It implies a commitment to human rights and fundamental freedoms, in particular the rights and fundamental freedoms of persons belonging to minorities.[825] The provisions of the declaration further say that it is the existence of cultural rights that can create an enabling environment for cultural diversity.[826] This automatically means there cannot be cultural diversity in the absence of cultural rights. It states that all persons have the right to express themselves and to create and disseminate their work in the language of their choice, and particularly in their mother tongue. In addition, it expresses that all persons have the right to participate in the cultural life of their choice and conduct their own cultural practices, subject to respect for human rights and fundamental freedoms.

UNESCO Convention on the protection and promotion of the

---

821   *Id.*

822   *Id.*

823   Universal Declaration on Cultural Diversity, adopted by the 31st Session of the General Conference of UNESCO, Art. 1, Paris, 2 November, 2001, *available at* http://www2. ohchr.org/English/law/diversity.htm.

824   *Id.*

825   *Id.* at Art. 4.

826   *Id.* at Art. 5.

diversity of cultural expression also enjoin states to draw cultural policies.[827]

As good as the provisions of this declaration are, states do not usually comply with them. The author wishes to assert that most Commonwealth countries were burdened with the language of their colonial masters and Nigeria is not an exception.

The Vienna Declaration on Human Rights[828] pointed out that the right of self-determination is a prerequisite to cultural rights. The declaration stated that people could, by virtue of right of self-determination, freely determine their political status, and freely pursue their economic, social and cultural development.[829] The declaration further expounded that human rights are interrelated.[830] The declaration states that the human rights of women and of the girl-child are an inalienable, integral and indivisible part of universal human rights. It also advocated for the eradication of all forms of discrimination on grounds of sex as prioritized by the international community.[831] It supported the right of every human being, especially people belonging to minorities, to enjoy their culture, to practice their own religion and to use their own language without interference or any form of discrimination.[832] It is a fact that without access to rights over their lands, territories and natural resources, indigenous peoples cannot enjoy any cultural rights.[833]

5.7 THE NIGERIAN LAW ON RELIGION AND CULTURAL LIFE

The Nigerian Constitution expressly stated that there shall not be any state religion,[834] in other words, there is freedom of religion and citizens are free to choose whatever religion they desire. Also, there shall be no

---

827   Convention on the Protection and Promotion of the Diversity of Cultural Expression – Paris 20, October 2005, *available at* http://unesdoc.unesco.org/images/0014/001429/142919e.pdf.

828   Vienna Declaration, World Conference on Human Rights, Vienna, 14-25 June 1993, U.N. Doc. A/CONF.157/24 (part I) at 20.

829   *Id.* at Art. 2.

830   *Id.* at Art. 5.

831   *Id.* at Art. 18.

832   *Id.* at Art. 19.

833   According to the statement of M. Tauli-Corpuz, Chairperson of the permanent forum on Indigenous Issues at the Forum's Sixth Session.

834   Constitution of the Federal Republic of Nigeria, *supra* note 713, at Section 10.

discrimination on the ground of religion,[835] while everyone is free to change or propagate his religion or belief.[836] The Constitution frowns at coercing anybody to receive religious education that contravenes his religion or belief.[837] Nigeria citizens shall also not be deprived of this entitlement, or restricted or disadvantaged on the basis of religion.[838]

The Nigerian Supreme Court in the case of *Zaidan v. Mohssen*[839] established the fact that Islamic law of the deceased and not the customary law of the place of residence will govern the estate of a Lebanese Muslim who died intestate in Nigeria. This case is in alliance with the case of *Adesubokan v. Yinusa*[840] where the Supreme Court held that the devolution of a Muslim testator property under the Wills Act cannot be stopped or impeded by customary or religious injunction. This case supported the freedom of religion including the freedom to change one's religion or belief, and freedom[841] as provided for by the Nigerian Constitution.

Religion is part of the Nigerian people and cultural life. Anne Rosenberg has expressed that the religion plays an important part in the lives of most Nigerians. Fifty percent of the populations are Muslim, forty percent are Christian, while hundreds of traditional African religions are observed. Nigeria's earliest religious beliefs were based on animism, which is the belief that objects in nature have souls. Natural objects are also considered sacred or holy. For instance, if animists want to fish in a river, they must first make an offering to the spirit of the river.[842] Nigerians build shrines at places dedicated to a god, where they pray, bring offerings and seek the god's advice.

According to Rosa Uzoma, indigenous African societies rarely tolerated religious pluralism, but the coming of Islam and Christianity brought religious pluralism and social upheaval to Nigeria by bringing different cultures and ideas with them.[843] Thus, the indigenous African

835   *Id.* at Section 15(2).

836   *Id.* at Section 38(1).

837   *Id.* at Section 38(2).

838   *Id.* at Section 41(1) (a &b).

839   (1973) 11 SC 1.

840   (1971) ALL NLR 225.

841   Constitution of the Federal Republic of Nigeria, *supra* note 713, at Section 38(1).

842   Anne Rosenberg, Nigeria the Culture 6 (Crabtree Pub., 2001).

843   Rose Uzoma, *Religious Pluralism, Cultural Difference and Social Stability in Nigeria,* 2004 B.Y.U.L. Rev. 651.

beliefs, Islam and Christianity are the three main religions practiced in Nigeria. Rose Uzoma further pointed out that indigenous religions typically involve the worshipping of idols who serve as intermediaries to the main god.[844]

Worshipers of traditional religions believe that their families descended from the spirits of objects found in nature. The animal or plant that is a family's ancestor is called a totem. A family's totem is considered sacred, thus if a family's totem is a lion, the family members are forbidden to harm lions. In Nigeria most of those that practice traditional religions holds their ancestors in high esteem. Ancestor worship plays an important role in traditional religions in Nigeria. Worshipers believe that the souls of their ancestors remain on earth and influence their family's daily lives. It is the general belief of these worshippers that if the ancestors are happy then the worshipers will enjoy successful harvest and be blessed with healthy children, but if the ancestors are unhappy then the worshippers may be visited with calamities. To worship their ancestors, therefore, the people pray or make offerings at altars.

5.8 NIGERIA AND ITS RELATION WITH THE UNITED NATIONS

Nigeria has a cordial relationship with the United Nations. This could be substantiated by Nigeria's ratification of most of the United Nation's treaties. Nigeria was admitted into the United Nations on 7th October 1960, just six days after its independence.

Below are some of the Conventions that Nigeria signed, acceded to and or ratified.

---

844   *Id.*

RATIFICATION / ACCENSION		
CONVENTIONS	SIGNATURE DATE	DATE
International Covenant on the Economy, Social and Cultural Rights (ICESCR		29th July, 1993
Convention Eliminating Discrimination Against Women treaty (CEDAW)	23rd April, 1984	
The Optional Protocol to CEDAW	8th September, 2000	22nd November, 2004 respectively.
Convention Against Torture	28th July 1988	28th June, 2001
Convention on the Right of Children	26th January, 1990	19th April, 1991
The Optional Protocol for both Sale of Children and Armed Conflict	8th September, 2000	
Rome Statute of the ICC (International Criminal Court)	1st June, 2000	27th September, 2001
International Convention Against Apartheid in Sports	16th May 1986	20th May 1987
International Convention on the Elimination of All Forms of Racial Discrimination		16th October, 1967.
Non-applicability of statutory limitations to war crimes against humanity		1st December, 1970
International Convention on the suppression and punishment of the crime of Apartheid	26th June, 1974	31st March, 1977.
Convention on the Rights of persons with disabilities	30th March, 2007	
Slavery Convention	26th June, 1961	
Convention relating to the Status of Refugees		23rd October, 1967.
African Charter of Human and Peoples' Rights		Incorporated into Nigeria legislation in 1983
the International Civil and Political Rights (ICCPR)		29th July, 1993

Nigeria ratified the ICESCR in 1984. Part of the provisions of the covenant which applies to indigenous peoples is the right to self-determination. This is because the covenant expressly stated that: "All peoples have the right to self-determination.[845] The covenant also states that "All people may, for their own ends, freely dispose of their natural wealth and resources without prejudice"[846] and the people must not be deprived of their own means of subsistence.

Nigeria also ratified the Convention on the Rights of Children (CRC) in 1991 and the provision of the covenant states that nation states are obligated to ensure that the education of the child shall be directed to the preparation of the child for responsible life in a free society, in the spirit of understanding, peace, tolerance, equality of sexes, and friendship among.... persons of indigenous origin.[847]

Nigeria ratified the ICCPR in 1983 and some of its provisions allowed for the right of self-determination which permits them to freely determine their political status and freely pursue their economic, social and cultural development.[848] In addition, they are free to dispose of their natural wealth and resources without prejudice.[849] This position was also supported by the General Comment of Human Rights Committee.[850]

The African Charter of Human and Peoples' Rights, which is not a United Nations treaty, is another charter which Nigeria ratified. Nigeria incorporated it into its legislation in 1983 and some provisions of the charter confer some rights on indigenous peoples. The charter expressly stated that all people shall have right to self-determination and that they can determine their political status and social development according to the policy that suits them.[851] The charter grants all peoples the right to freely dispose of their wealth and natural resources,[852] and the right to their economic, social

---

845   ICESCR, *supra* note 155, at Art. 1(1).

846   *Id.* at Art. 1(2).

847   Convention on the Rights of the Child, *supra* note 157, at Art. 29(d).

848   ICCPR, *supra* note 149, at Art. 1(1).

849   *Id.* at Art. 1(2).

850   Human Rights Committee, General Comment 12, Article 1 (Twenty-first session, 1984), Compilation of General Comments and General Recommendations Adopted by Human Rights Treaty Bodies, U.N. Doc. HRI/GEN/1/Rev.1 at 12 (1994).

851   African Charter, *supra* note 459, at Art. 20(1).

852   *Id.* at Art. 21(1).

and cultural development.[853]

The term "indigenous peoples" might not have been expressly mentioned in these conventions, but it could be deduced from the term "all peoples" that the drafters of these conventions intended it to also cover the indigenous peoples. In addition, most of the contents of the conventions are related to the indigenous peoples' situation.

5.8.1 The Human Rights Situation in Nigeria

It is a fact that since its independence in 1960, Nigeria as a country has been ruled often by the military governments that do not believe in nor practice democracy. However, the country has signed and or ratified some of the above listed international human rights treaties, but such treaties cannot be enforced locally unless enacted into the law by the National Assembly by virtue of Section 12 of the 1999 Constitution. In addition to the Nigerian Constitution, the Human Right Commission was also established in November 1995 for the promotion and protection of human rights in Nigeria.

5.8.2 The National Human Rights Commission of Nigeria

This Commission was established by the National Human Rights Act of 1995 in compliance with a United Nations General Assembly resolution which enjoins member states to establish human rights institutions for the promotion and protection of human rights. The establishment of the Commission is to serve many purposes, among which are to create an environment conducive to extra-judicial recognition, to promotion and protection of human rights and to ensuring compliance with treaty obligations, amongst others.

The Human Rights Committee in its report denoted that Nigeria does not have legal protection for rights in the country.[854] This is evident by the large number of detainees in various prisons all over the country that have

---

853   *Id.* at Art. 22(1).

854   Human Right Committee Report of 24th July 1996.

not been charged or tried. It was also stated in the report[855] that the Special Rapporteur on extrajudicial, summary or arbitrary executions, Mr. Bacre Waly N'diaye, and the Special Rapporteur on the independence of judges and lawyers, Mr. Param Cumaraswamy's were denied access to Nigeria for a fact-finding mission by the Nigerian authorities on the ground that the Nigerian government is not comfortable with their standard terms of reference. All the above facts show that the attitude of the Nigerian government towards human rights protections and the treatment of indigenous peoples' issues is not an exception.

Nigerian law has not been favorable to protecting human rights, and the rights of indigenous peoples are not an exception. Okeke pointed out in his article [856] that various decrees and edicts effectively eliminated the jurisdiction of the Nigerian courts to adjudicate human rights violations. An example of government's lackadaisical attitude towards the promotion of human rights is the case of *SERAC and CESR v. Nigeria*,[857] where the African Commission on Human Rights found that the Federal Republic of Nigeria violated Article 2 which guaranteed that the individual is entitled to enjoy the rights and freedom stated in Article 4 of the African Charter which stated that nobody should be arbitrarily deprived of his rights. Article 14 guarantees the right to property and stipulated that that the right could only be encroached upon in accordance with the appropriate law. Article 16 mandates state parties to protect the health of their people. Article 18(1) mandates the state parties to protect the family because it is the basis of the society. Article 21 mandates state parties to ensure that nobody is deprived of their wealth and natural resources, and Article 24 guarantees the peoples' right to their economic, social and cultural development and mandates that the state parties ensure the actualization of these rights.

---

855   Report of the Special Rapporteur, Soli Jehangir Sorabjee, on the Question of the Violation of Human Rights and Fundemental Freedoms in any Part of the World, with Particular Reference to Colonial and Other Dependent Countries and Territories, Commission on Human Rights, pursuant to Commission Resolution 1997/53, E/CN.4/1998/62.para. 3, *available at* http://www.unhchr.ch/Huridocda/ Huridoca.nsf/0/a55c3d667425f3cfc125660f004afbcf?Opendocument.

856   Christian Okeke, *International Law in the Nigerian Legal System,* 27 Cal. W. Int'l L. J. 311 (1997).

857   African Commission on Human and Peoples' Rights, 15th Annual Activity Report, The Social and Economic Rights Action Center and the Center for Economic and Rights, Nigeria Communication 155/96, 2001-2002, *available at* http://www.cohre.org/store/attachments/SERAC%20and%20CESR%20v.%20Nigeria.doc.

While the Nigerian government has not officially agreed that indigenous peoples exist in Nigeria, it has in the past made efforts to ameliorate the suffering of the people in the Niger-Delta area of Nigeria. This it did by forming a permanent statutory agency named the "Oil Mineral-Producing Areas Development Commission (OMPADEC) which was established in 1992 to administer the three percent of mineral revenues in the federal account for the rehabilitation and development of mineral-producing areas.[825] This agency made little or no progress and the government replaced it with the Niger Delta Development Commission (NDDC)[858] in 1999, another centrally coordinated agency for alleviating the developmental and ecological problems of the oil-bearing communities.[859]

The current federal government has created another agency in 2008 named the Niger Delta Ministry to deal with the problems of the oil-rich Niger-Delta area. While the ministry is not yet fully underway, its creation has been received with mixed feelings. There is the belief that the Niger Delta Ministry will suffer the same fate as the OMPADEC and the NDDC, both of which neither achieved positive results nor lived up to expectations.

---

858   Niger Delta Development Commission Act No.2 1999 of the National Assembly.

859   ROBERT ROTBERG, CRAFTING THE NEW NIGERIA: CONFRONTING THE CHALLENGES 71 (Lynne Rienner Publishers, 2004).

CHAPTER SIX

THE RIGHTS OF INDIGENOUS PEOPLES: THEIR APPLICATION TO NIGERIA

Having gone through the previous chapters, the first question that comes to the readers mind is: Does any group in Nigeria qualify for indigenous peoples' status and its appurtenant rights?

It has been pointed out earlier in chapter one, which dealt with the definition, that the conditions or criteria stipulated by Western scholars will be very difficult to meet for peoples of developing countries, especially those in Nigeria. By way of reiteration, being regarded as first in time with strong ties or relationships with the land or territory, having an age-old economy of subsistence, being vulnerable to other dominant groups of the society and being culturally distinct are the only objective elements out of all the elements propounded in various working definitions and the report of the African Commissions Working Group on Indigenous Populations also corroborated this.

The condition that people claiming to be indigenous must "consider themselves distinct from other sectors of the society" is a subjective condition which should not be given much weight because such a condition could be influenced by sentiment. The condition that the peoples claiming to be indigenous must form at present non-dominant sectors of society is objective because it is this factor that makes them vulnerable to the other dominant groups of the society. This could be easily verified by available facts.

The condition for such people to be non-dominant sectors of society should only serve as a complementary factor and not relied on solely as it can be abused because the major reason for not being part of the dominant sectors of society can vary. The author will use the example of Nigeria to illustrate this point. Additionally, the criteria of "being vulnerable" as a vital factor in determining who is indigenous and who is not, cannot exclusively qualify any group as indigenous. Rather, it will only complement other factors such as "being regarded as first in time" and showing proof of subsistence.

In Nigeria, as stated earlier, there are over three hundred and fifty ethnic groups, and out of these ethnic groups we have the three major ethnic groups which are the Hausa, the Yoruba and the Ibo. Although the colonialists ruled Nigeria through indirect rule, it is a fact that Northern Nigeria was known to have the upper hand on the issue of political power over other groups which continued even after independence. Therefore, the discussion on the issue of dominance will depend on the angle from which one is arguing.

As previously mentioned, political power has been dominated by the Hausas of Northern Nigeria and the major reason for this was that they have a larger population than the rest of the country. Also, they concentrate on sending their children to military schools and the majority of them do not really believe in elaborate education. By this, the author means that only a little percentage of the Hausa children have a university education. They are usually content with a primary education and out of the few that attend school, the majority of them end up in military schools. The Hausas see this move as a smart way of positioning their children as future military leaders of the country.

It is, therefore, not a coincidence that the country has witnessed so many coups since its independence. Right from the time of the 1966 Biafra war, Yakubu Gowon took over as Head of State to 1975. Murtala Muhammed took over in 1975 and ruled till he was assassinated in 1976. In 1979 it was the turn of Shehu Shagari and he ruled till 1983. Muhammadu Buhari ruled from 1983 to 1985, and Ibrahim Babangida ruled from 1985 to 1993. Sanni Abacha was the Head of State from 1993 to 1998. Abdusalam took over in 1998 and ruled for a year. Umaru Yar'adua came to power in May, 2007, and ruled till 2010.

The above listed Head of States or Presidents are all from Northern Nigeria, the region that has had more bite at the presidency than any other region or tribe in Nigeria. Therefore, an argument could be made to establish the fact that the Hausa of Northern Nigeria has had more political power than other ethnic groups and thus they are politically dominant.

When it comes to entrepreneurship, the Ibo tribes are seen as the most industrious of all the ethnic groups in Nigeria. The reason for this is not so far fetched as the Ibo people see this way as the only way they can be relevant in Nigeria. Before now, the Ibo people of Nigeria did not believe in an elaborate education, but they fare better than the Hausas. Among the Ibo people of Nigeria, the girl-child is disadvantaged due to the cultural practice of male preference. Many families are unable to cope with the exorbitant costs of education and for that reason are forced to withdraw their girl-children from school. The Ibos believe that it is not a wise thing to invest so much money on a girl-child only for her to marry and start bearing her husband's name. The Ibos see girl-child education as a waste of resources. Hence, they prefer to invest in the male-child, but such education is not at advance levels as most of their children are made to learn a trade after their secondary education. Consequently, it is common to see most of the Ibo male children becoming apprentices immediately after their secondary education, learning one trade or the other. In the Nigeria of today, the Ibo ethnic group is the most industrious one. They have the technological knowledge to manufacture many things ranging from mechanical, electrical and electronic materials. They have a base in Abia, Abia state of Nigeria, where they manufacture all kinds of equipments and household materials. Hence, an argument could be made that the Ibo tribe dominates industry.

The Yoruba of the Western Nigeria strongly believe in education and have produced many academics. They usually encourage their children to go to school and have a qualitative education. As a result of this, there are so many Yoruba ethnics with several degrees that populate the country's higher institutions as professors employed in teaching jobs.

A careful examination of the above stated facts will show that the Hausas of Northern Nigeria dominate political power in Nigeria, while both the Ibos of Eastern Nigeria and Yorubas of Western Nigeria are non-dominant. It could equally be argued that the entrepreneurship or economy industry is dominated by the Ibo people, while the Yoruba and the Hausas are non-dominant in that sector.

The Yorubas could also be said to dominate the education sector, while both the Hausas and the Ibos are not dominant. Hence, it is a fact that many factors may be responsible for the dominance of a particular society at the expense of others.

Despite the fact that each of the tribes discussed above are dominant in one way or the other, it is still possible for any of the groups belonging to the tribes discussed to be non-dominant. This could be proved by availability of dependable evidence. An example is the Koma people of Taraba state who have no signs of modern development in their domain. They have nobody to represent them in government, they have no electricity, they have no tarred roads, they have no pipe borne water, and to crown it all, they still dress half-naked in the twenty-first century. They are non-dominant in the sense that they have no voice in government and consequently, cannot influence or make contributions to policies on how they are being governed.

The issue of dominance is one of the vital factors in determining who is indigenous and who is not. Still care must be taken to only attach complementary weight to it since it is open to abuse. The major element that should be given a greater weight is the vulnerability of the group claiming indigenous peoples status.

As formerly said in chapter one of this subject, the "pre-invasion and pre-colonial" condition can not be given much weight in Nigeria. While it could be argued that colonialism was responsible for the dislocation of many peoples from their ancestral place, it is also true that the invasion criterion has nothing to do with the fact that a group of people have been inhabitants of a place since time immemorial and have an age-long subsistence economy. The condition of pre-invasion and pre-colonial can at best be seen as an influential or contributory factor and not a major one.

In reiterating the point made in chapter one of this subject, proof of being regarded as the original or first inhabitant or descendant, evidence of means of subsistence since time immemorial, vulnerability of the group in question to other dominant groups in the society and being culturally distinct from the dominant groups in the society should be the four major conditions to be met. The condition of first inhabitant or descendant could be proved by self-identification as propounded by the World Bank. Thus, if a group is claiming to be part of a particular tribe or ethnic group, there must be people to corroborate such a claim. A vivid example to illustrate this point is that of a particular sub-ethnic group in Nigeria called "Igbomina." The tribe used to be in the Kwara state of Nigeria, but during the creation of more states in Nigeria in 1991,[860] a new state named Osun state was created. This caused the Igbomina people hitherto in Kwara state to be now split into northern Osun state and the eastern Kwara state. Hence, if a controversy arose in the Osun state as to where the Igbomina people in the Osun state originated, the Igbomina in the Kwara state will readily testify to the fact that the Igbomina sub-ethnic people of the Osun state were part and parcel of the Kwara state Igbomina before the state creation exercise. This illustration will show that self-identification can play a vital role in determining the first inhabitants or descendants of a certain place. Another factor that may establish first inhabitants or descendants is the proof of age-old religions which the said group had been practicing, as well as evidence of the burial sites of their forefathers or ancestors. These factors will add weight to the argument of the peoples claiming indigenity. These evidences will also serve to support the strong ties or relationships that the peoples have with their land or territory. Their occupation is land-based. Their religion or worship centers are also tied to their land, which is usually communally owned and they see it as their heritage passed to them by their forefathers.

Other factors or conditions, which will be a major criterion to determine if a group of people is indigenous or not is the proof that the said group of people has a subsistence economy. Here, subsistence economy will mean the occupation that had been sustaining the said group from time immemorial, so such an occupation will be in the league of occupations such as farming, cattle rearing or gathering, fishing and so forth. Modern day occupations such as engineering, mechanics, tailoring and others of this latter period will, therefore, not suffice.

The third major factor is the fact the group claiming indigenous peoples' status must be non-dominant in the society and this makes them vulnerable to the other dominant members of the society. This factor can, however, only complement the other two discussed factors. The reason for this is that the criterion of non-dominance of a group can be abused and thus care must be taken not to solely rely on this factor in order to qualify any group as indigenous.

The fourth factor is that the people claiming indigenous peoples' status should be culturally distinct from the dominant section of the society. This could be proved with the aid of dependable objective facts such as difference in cultures, languages and ways of life.

---

860   This was carried out by the federal government on Nigeria on August 27th, 1991.

Having laid the above foundation, the ethnic groups in Nigeria will be examined to see if any of them comply or conform to the above stated conditions.

A careful examination of the Nigerian ethnic groups shows that most of them satisfied the first or second criteria. For instance, the history of Fulani of Northern Nigeria revealed that they came to the Hausa states in the thirteenth century. This fact shows that they could not be regarded as first occupants or original settlers in the territory. Although they were able to dominate most of the Hausa states through conquests, the fact still remains that they came to join the Hausa ethnic group in Northern Nigeria and, therefore, do not meet the critical criteria to qualify as indigenous peoples.

The Hausa ethnic group of Northern Nigeria is said to have Arabic origin and hence its claim to being regarded as first settlers or original inhabitants is doubtful, so it cannot be qualified for the indigenous peoples' status. Besides, the Hausas do not meet the criteria of non-dominance and are not vulnerable to any group in Nigeria. The reason for this is because the Hausa have been in control of the country's political power more than any other group in the country's history. Accordingly, it will be an uphill task to argue that the Hausas are indigenous peoples because they did not meet the criteria stipulated in the definition.

The history of the Igbo ethnic group revealed early human habitation in the region which was established and supported by evidence of archaeological findings. These findings showed not only early human habitation, but that these people survived on farming and hunting. Excavations also revealed that some of the early inhabitants were blacksmiths who turned iron objects into machetes, hoes and other farming tools.

It could be deduced from the above characteristics of the Igbo ethnic group of Nigeria that they satisfied the condition of being regarded as the first settlers or original inhabitants of a place or territory. Their characteristics also showed that they have an ancient occupation in farming, hunting and blacksmithing which they survive on as their means of sustenance. Thus, it could be concluded that the Igbo of eastern Nigeria have a subsistence economy.

In respect of the third factor which deals with non-dominancy, the Igbo ethnic group is the least dominant of the three major ethnic groups in Nigeria. Although this group is industrious, they are always overlooked when it comes to the sharing of political power. It could be emphatically argued that the Ibos are a non-dominant group in Nigeria. However, among the Igbo groups, there are lesser groups who are more dominant than another. In other words, Igbo's non-dominance will make them vulnerable to the other dominant groups of the society at the national level. At this juncture, it must be pointed out that this author is not trying to identify all the indigenous peoples in Nigeria. The main essence of this subject is to prove that indigenous peoples exist in Nigeria. Therefore, a review of these major groups will show that indeed there are indigenous peoples in Nigeria.

Once a group is identified as indigenous, the government will have to perform the obligations they owe these people under customary international law as well as treaty law – at least on the level of international law. Consequently, if other indigenous peoples are identified as such, they can always benefit from the available rights for indigenous peoples.

The Yoruba ethnic group based in southwestern Nigeria comprise smaller communities of people who are said to have originated from ile-Ife in Osun State which is seen as and claimed to be the cradle of all Yoruba tribes. Therefore, the Yorubas could be regarded as the first or original inhabitants of their territory, and they would meet the first requirement. Additionally, some of them have an age-old means of sustenance provided by farming, hunting and fishing. This group will, therefore, meet the second criterion which requires any group claiming to be indigenous to have an age-old occupation which had been sustaining them. The Yoruba ethnic group has been taking active part in the governance of the country, although they are not as dominant as the Hausas of Northern Nigeria who have had the largest share of the political power in Nigeria. Hence, the group cannot complain of being non-dominant or to being vulnerable to the other dominant group of the society.

With the above stated facts, it could be concluded that the Yoruba ethnic groups are not indigenous as they do not satisfactorily meet the criteria that qualifies any group for indigenous peoples' status.

History shows that the people of Niger Delta have a long history of human existence which can be corroborated by the long list of the kings of

Bonny and Nembe. The people of the Niger Delta comprise several small ethnic groups, among which are the Ogoni people. The Ogoni people stand out because of their agitation for their rights which has received worldwide publicity. History also shows that communication with the kings in Niger Delta, as stated in chapter four, and trading by the people of this area have long existed before the coming of Europeans. Local traditions of the people of this area and the reports and comments from traders and merchants show that groups in Niger Delta already had an established industry and a great organization before the Europeans arrival.

The Ogoni people, being part of the Niger delta, would be deemed to have fulfilled the first criterion which stipulates that groups must be regarded as first settlers or the original inhabitants of a territory before such a group could lay claim to indigenous peoples' status.

The Ogoni people are predominantly farmers, hunters, and fishermen. These are the occupations they have been practicing since time immemorial and upon which their sustenance depends. It could be concluded that the Ogoni people satisfy the second criteria which requires any group claiming to be indigenous to have a means of sustenance which could be proved by an age-old subsistence economy.

The Ogoni people are non-dominant members of the society and this is evident in their non-representation at the federal or central level of government. It was the outcry against their treatment that led to the emergence of the Movement for Survival of Ogoni People (MOSOP), an organization championing the cause of the Ogoni people for them to be recognized as indigenous people and for attendant rights to be applied to them. It was also in the pursuit of these rights that the MOSOP leader, Ken Saro Wiwa, was executed by the Nigerian government.

The Ogoni people are not only dominated by the other ethnic groups as far as the sharing of political position is concerned, their land is also degraded by the activities of oil communities who extract oil from their land with the connivance of the government.

The Ogoni are also culturally distinct from other tribes as they have Khana, Gokana, Tai, Baan and Eleme[861] languages which are different from

---

861   RAYMOND G. GORDON, JR., ETHNOLOGUE: LANGUAGES OF THE WORLD (Dallas: SIL International, 2005).

that of other dominant groups of the society. They rely on their shamans to cure illnesses and their religion and everyday life revolves around their land which represents a bond to their ancestors buried there.

The above mentioned characteristics of the Ogoni people satisfy all the criteria stipulated in indigenous peoples' definition and thus will qualify them for the status.

The Koma people is another Nigeria ethnic tribe in the Northern Nigeria. History does not state when exactly this group of people became inhabitants of the territory, but evidence showed that this people had been living in the territory since time immemorial. This fact is supported by the evidence that in this twenty-first century, there is no form of modern civilization as these people do not wear clothes, but only use leaves to cover their private parts to shield their nakedness. Their ancient way of life is also reflected in the fact that they still make fire by the primitive way of striking two stones together, and they rely on their natural cooling system which is a clay pot of water buried in the ground.

The above facts show that the people fulfill the requirement of being regarded as first settlers or original inhabitants of a territory as stipulated by the first criterion. The available evidence also qualifies them for the fourth criterion which states that people desiring indigenous peoples' status must be culturally distinct. This could be proved by the ways of life of the Koma people who do not believe in anything now orthodox. They still practice their traditional culture of dressing half naked, using local medicine for treatment, and using a clay pot to cool their water instead of a modern refrigerator.

The Koma people are predominantly farmers and hunters. Their farming occupation was assisted by their fertile soil which supports drought-resistant crops. This goes to show that the people have a means of sustenance that they have depended on from time immemorial.

The Koma people are non-dominant both at the state and federal or central level of the government. Research shows that these people do not have any representation in government and this caused them to be neglected and at the same time become vulnerable to other dominant groups of the society. The various governments in Nigeria have neglected them so much that there is no sign of modern development in their territory. They do not have electricity, motorable roads or pipe borne water. Research also shows that the Koma people are being exploited by other groups in the society.[862] It was stated that the Koma have lost over 116 children to various missionaries and organizations that came under the pretense of helping and giving succor to the people. The whereabouts, however, of the children taken away and not having been located has caused fear that child-traffickers might have been taking advantage of this people.

It could be concluded from the above facts that the Koma people satisfy all the criteria in the indigenous peoples' definition and thus would be qualified for the status and the attending rights.

The indigenous peoples have brought to the attention of the United Nations their request for their right to self-determination. This claim is aimed to eradicate the states' arbitrary laws and practices which tend to discriminate against indigenous peoples. Nation states have equally argued that giving such rights would amount to using double standards in its treatment of its populace[863] and that this can lead to a breakdown of law and order. The argument of the African states is not tenable because their major reason for refusing the actualization of self-determination can be attributed to two factors. The first reason is the fact that the nation states do not want their authority to be challenged and the second reason is that the states do not want to lose their hold on the valuable natural resources which they get from the indigenous peoples' land. Nigeria's Niger Delta area is a good example of where the government encouraged corporate entities to exploit the natural resources on indigenous peoples' lands to the detriment of the inhabitants, which causes the indigenous peoples to be endangered.

The activities of the Nigeria government clearly contravene the provisions of the ILO Convention (No. 169) which expressly stated that the rights of indigenous peoples to the natural resources on their land shall be protected, which includes their right to use, manage and conserve the resources[864] as minerals on the land. Permission should also be sought from the people before their land is explored or exploited and the people should not only be allowed to participate in the process, but the people should be

862   David Molomo, *116 Children Vanish from Koma Without Trace,* Daily Sun, Aug. 2, 2008.

863   Andrew Huff, *Indigenous Land Rights and the New Self-Determination,* 16 Colo. J. Int'l Envtl. L. & Pol'y 295 (2005).

864   Convention Concerning Indigenous and Tribal Peoples in Independent Countries, *supra* note 118, at Art. 15(1).

fairly compensated for any damage that might occur on the land.[865] Now, Nigeria has not ratified this convention; thus, it is not bound by it.

The United Nations affirmed that the right of self-determination is an international principle which all people in the world are entitled. It is one of the conditions for achieving lasting and comprehensive peace.[866] This is because without peace nothing meaningful could be achieved and wherever peace is lacking, violence will be inevitable.

The Human Rights Commission in its report of 2003 also argued that the right to self-determination is a crucial part of indigenous peoples' rights because it is the foundation on which other rights will be laid. In other words, the actualization of other indigenous peoples' rights largely depends on the self-determination right. One other reason for the refusal of nation states to allow the actualization of the right of self-determination for indigenous peoples is the fear of the states that the right might lead to secession.

It could be submitted that this fear has been addressed in the UN Declaration of Indigenous Peoples' Rights which states that indigenous peoples have rights of self-government in matters relating to their internal and local affairs and finance of their functions.[867] The declaration further stated that the rights of indigenous peoples does not in any way authorize or encourage any action that may impair totally or in part the territorial integrity or political unity of sovereign and independent states.[868] It could also be declared that the enjoyment of self-determination is internal and it can be called internal self-determination or self-government as discussed in chapter two of this book.

---

865   *Id.* Art. 15(2).

866   Commission on Human Rights, Report (Fiftieth-ninth Session, 17 March - 24 April 2003), Economic and Social Council Official Records, 2003, Supplement no.3 E/2003/23, E/CN.4/2003/135 at 33.

867   United Nations Declaration on the Rights of Indigenous Peoples, *supra* note 223, at Art. 4.

868   *Id.* at Art. 46(1).

Customary International law recognizes autonomy rights of indigenous peoples; this is evidenced by findings from global review of state practice. [869]

In addition, indigenous people depend so much on their land that it is has become a sort of security for them and without it, the continued existence of the people's culture may be jeopardized or adversely affected. There is, therefore, the need to protect the indigenous peoples' right for the self-determination right to be meaningful. The nation-states should always bargain or negotiate with the indigenous peoples in respect of their land and its attendant resources. This is for both parties to benefit from the land resources without any rancor.

The case of *Mayagna (sumo) Awas Tingni Community v. The Republic of Nicaragua* facts are very similar to the situation in the Ogoni land of Niger Delta of Nigeria. The Inter-American Court of Human Rights concluded in the case that Nicaragua violated the right to judicial protection to property of the Mayagna community. The court acknowledged the property rights of the indigenous peoples, and this property right was held to originate from the indigenous tradition which barred the nation states from granting concessions to third parties on such land. Nigeria should tow this line and come up with customary international law that will protect the land rights of its indigenous peoples.

The Inter-American Court stated that the Nicaraguan government must adopt legislative and administrative measures to create a mechanism which will ensure effective and official recognition of traditional indigenous community land and this must conform with the peoples' customary law, values, usage and customs.

The *Mayagna* case became a landmark development in international law, as it established the state's domestic laws and administration of the said law. The case was also significant because it was one of the very few decisions that recognized indigenous right to their ancestral land. This will serve as a precedent for defending the indigenous peoples quest for their right to their

---

869   Wiessner, Rights and Status, *supra* note 42, at 127; Marc Weller, *Settling Self-Determination Conflicts: Recent Developments*, 20 Eur. J. Int'l. 111, 116 (2009); Federico Lenzerini, *Sovereignty Revisited: International Law and Parallel Sovereignty of Indigenous Peoples.* 42 Tex. Int'l. L. J. 155, 186 (2006); NICOLA WENZEL, DAS SPANNUNGSVERHÄLTNIS ZWISCHEN GRUPPENSCHUTZ UND INDIVIDUALSCHUTZ IMVÖLKERRECHT 508 (2008).

land and its attendant resources.

The activities of the Transnational Corporations (TNC) have not helped the situation of indigenous peoples. Indigenous people reside in lands whose resources have not been explored. Since these resources were discovered, there has been incursions into indigenous peoples' lands and the people have been worse off as a result. For instance, most of the TNCs are oil companies that had taken over the indigenous peoples' land for their activities,[870] with the people receiving nothing.

Most times, it is believed that the government always makes concessions without the consent of the indigenous peoples and the TNC never bothers to ascertain whether there are traditional owners or not. This has always led to confrontations between the indigenous peoples and the TNCs. For example, the Niger delta area of Nigeria has been an area of tension for the oil companies because of the indigenous peoples' hostility. The indigenous peoples' lands are also taken over by the government for developmental purposes. Most times, the TNCs are indirectly responsible for the financial and economic support for this development and this is due to the TNCs expertise and control of the world markets.[871]

Indigenous peoples' struggles against the TNCs have received worldwide attention and support from the international civil society, trade unions and various non-governmental organizations. For instance, in Nigeria the unrest generated by the people of the Niger delta area and the TNC is now in the international news.

The government of Nigeria is always swayed by the proceeds from the operations of the multinational corporations which subscribe to the principle of "profit-first, and environmental concerns last." The Nigerian government should take steps to control the transnational corporations by enforcing the relevant environmental regulations. According to Sonarajah, foreign corporations have the obligation to abide by the laws and regulations of the host state.[872] Based on this fact, the Nigerian government is in a position to call the transnational corporations to account whenever the corporations are seen to be contravening the environmental standards. Human safety

---

870   Independent Commission, *supra* note 51, at 101.

871   *Id.* at 103.

872   M. Sornarajah, The International Law on Foreign Investment 64 (Cambridge University Press, 2004).

must always supersede any economic interest, and this author strongly believes that this should be the attitude of the Nigerian government in its dealings with foreign corporations.

Only when the Nigerian government enforces the relevant environmental regulations will the locals no longer be hostile, thereby allowing the corporations to have the confidence to carry out their trade without fear of any molestation or reprisals.

The demand of indigenous people for self-determination was been halted by secession fears on the part of nation states. They think that the political self-determination right might embolden the indigenous peoples to a demand for secession and it is a fact that the nation states do not want their national integrity to be infringed. This is a major basis for rejecting the right of indigenous peoples to political self-determination.

The true position is that most indigenous peoples are primarily striving for self-determination in a cultural sense, not secession and national independence. This was necessitated by the threat posed by the hostile activities of the government towards the indigenous peoples which tend to lead to their dissolution and extinction unless they have a guarantee of legal rights, political authority and sufficient financial means to maintain their identity in their homelands.

The above facts could be linked to the Civil War in Nigeria, otherwise called the Biafra war, which lasted from 1967 to 1970. The major reason for the war, as stated earlier, was the resolve of Ibo/Igbo people of Eastern Nigeria to agitate for their independence from Nigeria. The complaint of the Ibo/Igbo was that they were marginalized and discriminated against by the remaining section of the country which monopolized the administrative and political positions to the detriment of the Ibo/Igbo.

A careful examination of the essence of self-determination rights showed that the main essence of the right of self-determination is to empower the indigenous people to regulate their internal or traditional activities. In other words, it is more of an internal self-government. Areas such as foreign policy, security, citizenship, and so forth that could bring conflict with the nation states were exclusively reserved for the national authority with a proviso that the exercise of that right will not infringe the indigenous peoples' self-determination rights. Areas of common interest such as natural resources should be discussed between both the local communities and the national authority to reach an amicable compromise that will be acceptable to both parties. It also stated that title to the land should be established whenever issues of the loss of a religious site or a traditional area arose. Autonomy may be granted to indigenous peoples, especially in their decision-making process,[873] but archaic ancient practices may be prohibited. A very good example was the practice of killing newly born twins in Calabar, Eastern Nigeria, just because the community believes that twins always bring bad luck. It took the intervention of a missionary, Mary Slessor to stop this barbaric practice. This type of practice may be an ancient practice, but it should be prohibited because of its infringement on human rights, particularly the right to life.

By way of reiteration, the right of self-determination for indigenous peoples must be embodied and shaped according to local conditions, and both the indigenous community and national authority must cooperate and accede in good faith to each other for the self-determination rights to materialize and be workable.

The most conspicuous group of Eastern Nigeria that is non-dominant is the Ogoni people of Niger Delta area of Nigeria. In the course of this struggle for power, political dominance passed to the major groups in the region at the expense of smaller groups like the Ogoni, who were more or less treated like second class citizens by the dominant groups.[874] The Nigerian government controls the indigenous peoples' land and the natural resources therein through the promulgation of Petroleum Decree and Land Use Act and this enabled them to receive royalties and petroleum taxes with little or no returns to the producing communities. The activities of oil exploration has had a negative effect on the traditional farming and fishing economy of the indigenous peoples on which they relied as means of livelihood.[875]

The Petroleum Act[876] is one of the laws promulgated by the government to explore petroleum from the territorial waters and the continental shelf of Nigeria and vests ownership of all on-shore and off-shore revenue from the

---

873   Wiessner, supra note 7, at 353.

874   Ben Naamen, *The Ogoni: An Endangered Indigenous People*, 2 INDIGENOUS AFFAIRS 19 (1995).

875   *Id.* at 20.

876   Petroleum Act, Chapter P10 (Chapter 350 LFN 1990) Laws of the Federation of Nigeria, *available at* http://www.nigeria-law.org/Petroleum%20Act.htm.

petroleum resources in the federal government. It would have been justified if the revenue generated from indigenous peoples' land were equitably distributed among the various groups, but the reverse is the case, as the indigenous people from whose domain the wealth was gotten was heavily marginalized in the distribution of the wealth and the people were worse off now than before oil was discovered in their domain.

In the absence of judicial precedents in Africa on the issue of property rights of indigenous peoples, decided cases from other continents such could be relied on to adjudicate on indigenous peoples' matter. Accepted state practices on law has also been proven to constitute customary international law rights of indigenous peoples to their lands, their cultures and self-government. The general customary international law is as follows:

> First, indigenous peoples are entitled to maintain and develop their distinct cultural identity, their spirituality, their language, and their traditional ways of life. Second, they hold the right to political, economic and social self-determination, including a wide range of autonomy and the maintenance and strengthening of their own system of justice. Third, indigenous peoples have a right to demarcation, ownership, development, control and use of the lands they have traditionally owned or otherwise occupied and used. Fourth, governments are to honor and faithfully observe their treaty commitments to indigenous nations.[877]

Inequality of access to formal education could be said to be responsible for the underdevelopment of some tribes as Obi Ikpo Marizu had pointed out that education is highly political in Nigeria and the reason for this was due to the colonial background and the country's ethnic divisions. The British colonial administration used a "divide and rule" policy, thus creating unequal distribution of formal education in the country. The northern Muslim, however, perceived a Western type of education as an embodiment of a foreign culture which threatened their Islamic system,

---

877   Wiessner, Rights and Status, *supra* note 42, at 128; *see also* S. James Anaya and Robert A. Williams, Jr., *The Protection of Indigenous Peoples' Rights over Lands and Natural Resources under the Inter-American Human Rights System*, 14 HARVARD HUM.. RTS. J. 33 (2001); S. JAMES ANAYA, INDIGENOUS PEOPLES IN INTERNATIONAL LAW 49-72 (2nd ed., 2004); Chidi Oguamanam, *Indigenous Peoples and International Law: The Making of a Regime*, 30 QUEEN's L. J. 348 (2004); Sarah M.Stevenson, *Indigenous Land Rights and the Declaration on the Rights of Indigenous Peoples: Implications for Maori Land Claims in New Zealand*, 32 FORDHAM INT'L L. J. 298-343 (2008).

while the Southern traditionalists regarded western education as a gateway to modern civilization.[878]

Both the Ogoni people of Niger Delta area of Nigeria and the Koma people of Taraba state of Nigeria are qualified for the indigenous peoples' status based on their meeting of all the laid down criteria. The condition of self-identification was also fulfilled by these groups; the only problem they have is with the various governments and not with the people of their society. The governments shy away from their responsibilities to these groups by their habitual practice of claiming that there are no indigenous peoples in Africa.

It is also apparent that these groups have always been oppressed and have no voice in the government. These groups have their own culture, language, food and ways of living which is totally different from that of dominant groups. The history of some of the ethnic groups also establishes that some of them are non-dominant and are at the mercy of dominant groups of the society. This factor, therefore, makes these non-dominant groups vulnerable, and in need of protection.

It could be claimed that some of these ethnic groups satisfied the conditions needed to attain indigenous peoples' status, while the majority of them could not fulfill the criteria because they fall short of one or two conditions.

Once again, it would exceed the bounds of this book to review all ethnic groups and identify all the indigenous peoples in Nigeria. The review of the major groups have shown that there are indigenous peoples in Nigeria.

---

878   Obi Ikpo Marizu, *Social Evaluation Survey on Ethnic Relations in Nigeria*, 7.2 NORDIC J. AFR. STUDIES 39, 47 (1998).

CHAPTER SEVEN

CONCLUSION

The working definition proffered by the Special Rapporteur of the Sub-commission on Prevention of Discrimination and Protection of Minorities, Mr. Jose Martinez Cobo, will not help Africa's indigenous peoples' cause because of the "pre-invasion and pre-colonial" condition, as stated in chapter one. In Africa and particularly in Nigeria, indigenous peoples' status would be better determined by the following criteria: being traditionally regarded as the first inhabitant of a territory with proof of a special relationship with the land, having an age-old subsistence economy, and being vulnerable and culturally distinct from the dominant society.

The rights of self-determination, land rights, and cultural rights are the principal ones claimed by the indigenous peoples. This need has arisen because their lands were taken from them, the conqueror's way of life was imposed upon them, their political freedom was limited, and they were thrust into poverty and despair from these limitations.

African nation states tend to claim that they do not have indigenous peoples within their domain, but the facts in chapters two and three prove otherwise. Indigenous peoples' rights have been recognized in Africa. The Richtersveld community of South Africa, the indigenous peoples of the Kalahari Desert in Botswana, and the Batwa of Rwanda, Burundi and Uganda serve as excellent examples.

The facts in chapter four reveal that some ethnic groups in Nigeria, such as the Ogoni and the Koma qualify for the "indigenous peoples status" based on the available information; they have met the conditions stated in chapter one of this thesis. On the other hand, other ethnic groups examined such as Efik/Ibibio, Fulani, Hausa, Igbo/Ibo, Nupe, Tiv and Yoruba do not qualify for indigenous peoples status.

Nigerian law does not make provision for the indigenous peoples separately; however, the indigenous peoples of Nigeria are still entitled to some rights under the various international conventions signed, ratified or acceded to by the Nigerian government – as well as under customary international law.

Having discussed the various attempts at giving "indigenous peoples" a standard definition, the rights of indigenous peoples, the African nation states' attitudes towards the indigenous peoples' question, Nigerian ethnic groups, Nigerian laws and the applicability of the working definition set forth in this study to the characteristics of Nigerian ethnic groups, this author submits that indigenous peoples exist in Nigeria and that the Nigerian government should endorse and take steps to incorporate the United Nations declaration on indigenous peoples' rights wholly or in part into their domestic law. The need to incorporate the United Nations Declaration on the Rights of Indigenous Peoples has arisen because the indigenous peoples of Nigeria should start enjoying all of the rights to which they are entitled, just as their counterparts in other parts of the world.

The time has come for the Nigerian government to enact legislation in accordance with customary international law that will grant the indigenous peoples the right to their lands, territories and resources which they traditionally owned, the right to celebrate their culture, and the right to govern their internal affairs. This is also reflected in the provisions of the United Nations Declaration.

Commendably, a number of countries such as Denmark, the United States, Canada, Nicaragua and Panama have granted to the indigenous peoples rights of autonomy, and the outcome has been positive. The Nigerian situation should not be an exception. For instance, autonomy was granted to the Greenlandic indigenous peoples of Denmark in November 2008 after seventy-five percent of the referendum votes were in favor of Greenland having partial control over their administration of justice and legal affairs. Also in 1987, the Nicaraguan government granted autonomy to the indigenous peoples of Miskitos, Sumos and Ramas which means that these peoples shall have their inherent right to self-determination observed, but the right shall be exercised within the framework of the Nicaraguan state.

The Nigerian government should also grant autonomy to identified indigenous peoples or groups in Nigeria. This is to allow these peoples to have their self-government, customary law, and traditional structure of governance.

In light of the overwhelming evidence mustered that some groups in Nigeria meet the indigenous peoples' criteria, the government should ratify, and adopt all of the necessary declarations and conventions conferring rights upon indigenous peoples and abide by already established customary international law. This is to give the indigenous peoples a sense of belonging in their domain.

The Ogoni people are not the only indigenous peoples in Nigeria, but the government seems to concentrate on befriending only the Niger-Delta area. This author is persuaded that if the government recognizes the status of indigenous peoples in their domain, the Koma people of Adamawa can come into the light to claim their rights, especially the major ones of self-determination, land rights and cultural rights. Furthermore, this policy should lead to peace.

Professor Daes has opined and this author agrees, that the knowledge of the indigenous peoples will be beneficial to the study of science, particularly medicine. This is because much can be learned from the indigenous peoples' traditional ways of survival, reproduction and well-being under the harsh and difficult conditions that they have found themselves. This is in contrast to the modern global system which is gradually disintegrating with little or no stability in sight. The scourge of deadly diseases, especially HIV/AIDS, are part of the problems with which the modern society has had to contend, their advanced medical knowledge notwithstanding. A great deal can be learned from the indigenous peoples' social and cultural life to benefit Nigeria, unless things remain unchanged and indigenous peoples are driven into oblivion. Justice requires that this should not happen because "indigenous peoples" truly exist in Nigeria and they are entitled to all of the rights enjoyed by their counterparts all over the world.

BIBLIOGRAPHY

Abuja Commonwealth Heads of State Meeting (CHOGM), Abuja Communiqué (December 3, 2003), *available at* http://www. humanrightsinitiative.org/cwhr/decdoc/abuja_communique-dec03.pdf.

Adamu, Fatima L. *A Double-edged Sword: Challenging Women's Oppression within Muslim Society in Northern Nigeria,* in Gender, Religion and Spirituality. Edited by Caroline Sweetman. Oxfam Publishers, 1999.

Adamu, M. The Hausa Factor in West African History. Oxford University Press, 1978.

Adeleye, R. A. *Hausaland and Borno, 1600-1800,* in History of West Africa. Edited by J.F.A. Ajayi and Michael Crowder. NY: Columbia University Press, 1972.

Adelson, Glenn, James Engell, Brent Ranalli and Kevin Van Anglen. Environment: An Interdisciplinary Anthology. Yale University Press, 2008.

African [Banjul] Charter on Human and Peoples' Rights. OAU Doc. CAB/LEG/67/3 rev. 5, 21 I.L.M.58 (1982), *available at* http://www1.umn. edu/humanrts/ instree/z1afchar.htm.

African Commission on Human and Peoples Rights, Report of the African Commission's Working Group on Indigenous Populations/Communities, 92-93. IWGIA: Bilingual edition, 2005.

African Commission on Human and Peoples' Rights History, *available at* http://www.achpr.org/english/_info/history_en.html.

African Commission to the Assembly of Heads of State and Government of the OAU, Fourteenth Annual Activity Report (2000-2001) of the 37th Ordinary session/Fifth ordinary session of the AEC, 9-11 July 2001, Lusaka, Zambia, AHG/229, XXXVIII.

Africa's Indigenous Peoples: "First Peoples" or " Marginalized Minorities?" Edited by Alan Barnard and Justin Kenrick. Center of African Studies, University of Edinburgh, 2001.

Aguolu, C. C. *The Role of Ethnicity in Nigerian Education.* 48.4 The Journal of Negro Education 517 (1979).

Agyeman, Julian, Robert Doyle Bullard, and Bob Evans. Just Sustainabilities: Development in an Unequal World. MIT Press, 2003.

Ajala, Mabel Olufunmilayo. Nigerian Proverbs and Wisdom: Explained. Seaburn, 2007.

Alexkor Ltd. and Another v. Richtersveld Community and Others, 2003 SACLR LEXIS 79.

Alfredsson, Gudmundur. *The Right to Self-Determination and Its Many Manifestations in* The Right of Indigenous Peoples in International Law: Selected Essays on Self-Determination. Edited by Ruth Thompson. Native Law Centre, University of Saskatchewan, 1987.

Ali-Akpajiat, Sofo C. A. and Toni Pyke. Measuring Poverty in Nigeria. Oxford: Oxfam GM, 2003.

Allen, Sir Carleton Kemp. Law in the Making. Oxford: Clarendon Press, 1964.

Allott, A. N. *Recent Reforms in Area and Customary Courts in Nigeria Legislation.* 22 Journal of African Law 133 (1978).

American Convention on Human Rights, O.A.S.Treaty Series No. 36, 1144 U.N.T.S. 123, entered into force July 18, 1978. *Reprinted in* Basic Documents Pertaining to Human Rights in the Inter-American System, OEA/Ser.L.V/II.82 doc.6 rev.1 (1992) Art 21.

Amodu Tijani v. the Secretary, Southern Nigeria, (1921) 2 AC 399, 403-4.

Anaya, Special Rapporteur, S. James. Report on the Situation of Human Rights and Fundamental Freedoms of Indigenous People, Human Rights Council, 9th sess., agenda item 3, A/HRC/9/9 (August 11, 2008), *available at* http://www2.ohchr.org/english/bodies/hrcouncil/docs/9session/A-HRC-9-9AEV.doc.

Anaya, James. Indigenous Peoples in International Law, 2nd ed. Oxford University Press, 2004.

_____ *The Right of All Peoples to Self-Determination in International Law* in Operationalizing the Rights of Indigenous Peoples to Self-Determination. Edited by Pekka Aikdo and Martin Scheinin. Institute for Human Rights, ABO Akedemi University, 2000.

Anaya, James, and Claudio Crossman. *The Case of Awas Tingni v. Nicaragua: A New Step in the International Law of Indigenous Peoples.* 19 Arizona Journal of International and Comparative Law 13 (2002).

Anaya, James, and Siegfried Wiessner. *The UN Declaration on the Rights of Indigenous Peoples: Towards Re-empowerment.* JURIST, October 3, 2007, *available at* http://jurist.law.pitt.edu/forumy/2007/10/un-declaration-on-rights-of-indigenous.php.

Anaya, James & Robert A. Williams, *The Protection of Indigenous People's Right Over Lands and Natural Resources under the Inter-American Human Rights System.* 14 Harvard Human Rights Journal 33 (2001).

Asch, Michael. *Aboriginal Self-Government and Canada Constitutional Identity, in* Michael Levin, Ethnicity and Aboriginality: Case Studies in Ethnonathionalism University of Toronto Press, 1993.

Attorney General of Southern Nigeria v. Holt, 2. N.L.R. 1 (1915) AC, 599.

Australia Government Endorses UN Declaration on the Rights of Indigenous Peoples, available at http://www.indigenousportal.com/World/Australia-Government-endorses-UN-Declaration-on-the-Rights-of-Indigenous-Peoples.html (accessed on November 15th, 2010).

Australian Census Analytic Program: Australians' Ancestries: 2001. Australian Bureau of Statistics, Cat. No 2054.0.

Bah, Abu Bakarr. Breakdown and Reconstitution: Democracy, the Nation-State, and Ethnicity in Nigeria. Lexington Books, 2005.

Bakwuye, C. *Ogonis Protest over Oil Revenue.* Daily Sunray, January 6, 1993.

Bamgbose, Ayo. *Issues in the Analysis of Serial Verbal Constructions.* 12.2 Journal of West African Languages 3-21 (October 1982).

Barkan, Elazar. The Guilt of Nations: Restitution and Negotiating Historical Injustices. The Johns Hopkins University Press, 2001.

Bascom, William Russel. The Yoruba of Southwestern Nigeria. Holt, Rinehart & Winston, 1969.

Berge, Gunnvor. *Reflections on the Concept of Indigenous Peoples in Africa,* in Hanne Veber, Jens Dahl, Fiona Wilson, Espen Waehle: "... Never drink from the same cup." Proceedings of the conference on Indigenous Peoples in Africa. Tune, Denmark, 1993. IWGIA Doc. No.74, Copenhagen, 1993.

Bienen. Henry. Political Conflict and Economic Change in Nigeria. Routledge, 1985.

Bishop, Kristyna. *Squatters on Their Own Land: San Territoriality in Western Botswana.* 31 Comparative and International Law Journal of Southern Africa 92 (1998).

Bohannan, Paul. *The Impact of Money on an African Subsistence Economy,* in Johnneta B. Cole, Anthropology for the Nineties: Introductory Readings. Simon and Schuster, 1988.

Brierly, J. L. The Law of Nations. Oxford University Press, 1960.

Brysk, Alison. From Tribal Village to Global Village: Indian Rights and International Relations in Latin America. Stanford University Press, 2000.

Building the Future: Yukon First Nation Self-Government, Minister of Indian Affairs and Northern Development and Federal Interlocutor for Métis and Non-Status Indians. Ottawa, Canada, 2008, *available at* http://www.ayc.yk.ca/ user/image/ building_the_future_yukon_first_nation_self-government.pdf.

Burt, Ben. The Yoruba and their Gods. London: British Museum Publishers, 1977.

Byers, Michael. Custom, Power and the Power of Rules: International Relations and Customary International Law. Cambridge University Press, 1988.

Cairo Resolution of 1964, Organization of African Unity, OAU doc, AHG/Res. 17(1) Section 4-6, The Restitution of Land Rights Act 22 of 1994, *available at* http://www.info.gov.za/acts /1994/a22-94.pdf.

Canada Endorses the United Nations Declaration on the Rights of Indigenous Peoples. World News Report, a*vailable at* http://www.einnews.com/pr-news/227062-canada-endorses-the-united-nations-declaration-on-the-rights-of-indigenous-peoples.

Canadian Charter of Rights and Freedoms, Part I of the Constitution Act, 1982, being Schedule B tothe Canada Act 1982 (U.K.).

Canada Constitution Act, 1982.

The Case of the Mayagna (Sumo) Awas Tingni Community v. Nicaragua, Judgment of August 31, 2001, *available at* http://www.indianlaw.org/sites/indianlaw.org/files/AT%202001-08-31%20InterAmerican%20Court%20Judgment%20Official%20English.pdf.

Case of the Moiwana Community v. Suriname, Inter-American Court of Human Rights (IACrtHR), 15 June 2005, *available at*: http://www.unhcr.org/refworld/docid/4721bb292.htm.

CBA's 2002 Aboriginal Self-government. What does it mean in practice?, CBA's 2002 Aboriginal Law Conference.

Centre for Minority Rights Development (Kenya) and Minority Rights Group International on behalf of Endorois Welfare Council v. Kenya, 276/2003, *available at* http://www.escr-net.org/caselaw/caselaw_show. htm?doc_id=1216218.

Chigere, Nkem Hyginus M. V. Foreign Missionary Background and Indigenous Evangelization in Igboland (Lit. Verlag, 2002).

Clinton, Robert. *The Rights of Indigenous Peoples as Collective Group Rights.* 32 Arizona Law Review 739, 742 (1990).

Cobo, Special Rapporteur José R. Martínez. "Study of the Problem of Discrimination Against Indigenous Populations," Final E/CN.4/ Sub.2/1983/21/Add.8, 30th September, 1983, *available at* http:// www.un.org/esa/socdev/unpfii/documents/MCS_xxi_xxii_e.pdf.

Cohan, John Alan. *Environmental Rights of Indigenous Peoples Under the Alien Tort Claims Act, the Public Trust Doctrine and Corporate Ethics, and Environmental Dispute* Resolution, 20 UCLA Journal of Environmental Law and Policy 133, 137 (2001-2002).

Coles, Catherine, and Beverly Mack. Hausa Women in the Twentieth Century. University of Wisconsin Press, 1991.

Colombia Constitution, Article 9 & 63 (1991), *available at* http://confinder.richmond.edu/admin/docs/colombia_const2.pdf.

Committee on the Elimination of Racial Discrimination, General Recommendation XXIII on Indigenous Peoples, 18 August 1997, CERD/C51/Misc.13/Rev., para.3 (1977).

Constitution of the Bolivarian Republic of Venezuela.

Constitution of the Federal Republic of Nigeria, 1999.

Constitution of the Republic of South Africa Act 108 of 1996 Section 25(7), *available at* http://www.info.gov.za/documents/constitution/1996/ a108-96.pdf.

Constitutive Act of the African Union, *available at* http://www.africa-union.org/root/au/AboutAu/Constitutive_Act_en.htm.

Continents of the World: Africa, Mbendi Information Services, *available at* http://www.mbendi.com/land/p0007.htm.

Convention Concerning Indigenous and Tribal Peoples in Independent Countries, 169 I.L.O. 1989, Art. 1(a), 28 I.L.M. 1382 (entered into force Sept. 5, 1991), *available at* http://www.unhchr.ch/html/menu3/b/62.htm.

Convention Concerning the Protection and Integration of Indigenous and Other Tribal and Semi-Tribal Populations in Independent Countries, June 26, 1957, International Labour Organisation Convention No. 107, Art. 2(1), 328U.N.T.S. 247.

Convention on the Elimination of All Forms of Racial Discrimination, Convention on the Prevention and Punishment of the Crime of Genocide, and Universal Declaration of Human Rights, *available at* http://www.unhchr.ch/html/menu3/b/d_icerd.htm.

Convention on the Prevention and Punishment of the Crime of Genocide, 78 U.N.T.S. 277 (Jan. 12, 1951).

Convention on the Rights of the Child, 1990.

Convention 169 Indigenous and Tribal Peoples Convention. 1989: A Manual. International Labour Organisation, June 7, 1989.

Cookey, S. J. S. *An Ethnohistorical Reconstruction of Traditional Igbo Society,* in West African Culture Dynamics: Archeological and Historical Perspectives. Edited by B. K. Swartz, Jr., and Raymond E. Dumett. The Hague: Mouton Publishers, 1980.

_____ King Jaja of the Niger Delta: His Life and Times, 1821-1891. NY: NOK, 1974.

Cooper, Joshua. *The Ogoni Struggle for Human Rights and a Civil Society in Nigeria, in* Stephen Zunes, Lester R. Kurtz and Sarah Beth Asher, Nonviolent Social Movements: A Geographical Perspective. Wiley-Blackwell, 1999.

Cote et al. v. The Queen, (1996) 3 S.C.R. 139.

Coughlin, Kathryn M. *Nigeria in* Muslim Cultures Today: A Reference Guide. Edited by Kathryn M. Coughlin. Greenwood Press, 2006.

Coulter v. Brazil (Yanonami), Case 7615, Inter-Am. C.H.R.

Crowder, Michael. The Story of Nigeria. London: Faber and Faber, 1962.

Crowder, Michael, and Guda Adbullahi. Nigeria: Introduction to its History. Longman, 1979.

Cultural Policy in Nigeria, prepared by CultureLink (IRMO, 1996), *available at* http://www.wwed.org/policy/clink/Nigeria.html.

Curtin, Philip D. The Atlantic Slave Trade, University of Wisconsin Press, 1969.

Daes, Chairperson-Rapporteur Mrs. Erica-Irene A. "Indigenous Peoples and Their Relationship to Land," (working paper for Working Group on Indigenous Populations) U.N.ESCO, Commission on Human Rights, Sub-Commission on Prevention of Discrimination and Protection of Minorities, 53rd session, E/CN.4/Sub.2/2001/21 (11 June 2001).

_____ Indigenous Peoples: Keepers of Our Past-Custodians of Our Future. Copenhagen, 2008.

_____ "On the Concept of "Indigenous People," (working paper for Working Group on Indigenous Populations) U.N.ESCO, Commission on Human Rights, Sub-Commission on Prevention of Discrimination and Protection of Minorities, 14th session, U.N. Doc. E/CN.4/sub.2/ AC.4/Sub.2AC.4/1996/2 (1996).

Dalton, Jennifer E. *Aboriginal Self-determination in Canada: Protection Afforded by the Judiciary and Government*, 21.1 Canadian Journal of Law and Society 11, 12 (2006).

Daniel v. Bamgbose, (1955) A.C. 107.

Davidson, Basil, and F. K. Buah. A History of West Africa to the Nineteenth Century: With F. K. Buah and the Advice of J. F. Ade Ajayi. Anchor Books, 1966.

Davis, Megan. *Indigenous Struggles in Standard-Setting: The United Nations Declaration on the Rights of Indigenous Peoples*, 9 Melbourne Journal of International Law 439, 465 (2008).

Davis, Michael. *Establishing a Workable Autonomy in Tibet*, 30.2 Human Rights Quarterly 227-58 (2008).

Delgamuukw v. British Columbia, (1997) 153 DLR (4th) 193.

Delgamuukw v. The Queen, (1997) 153 DLR (4th) 193.

Deng, Francis Mading, and William Zartman. Conflict Resolution in Africa. Brookings Institution Press, 1991.

Dibua, Jeremiah. Modernization and the Crisi of Development in Africa: The Nigerian Experience. Ashgate Publishers, Ltd., 2006.

Dioka, L. C. *Inter-Group Relations Among Nigerian Communities, in* Nigerian Peoples and Cultures. Edited by Akinjide Osuntokun and Avodeji Olukoju. Nigeria: Davidson, 1997.

Dorsett, Shaunnagh, and Lee Godden. A Guide to Overseas Precedents of Relevance to Native Title. Aboriginal Studies Press, 1998.

Drewal, Henry John. *Art or Accident: Yoruba Body Artists and their Deity Ogun, in* Sandra Barnes, Africa's Ogun Old World and New. Indiana University Press, 1989.

Durning, Alan Thein. *Guarding of the Land: Indigenous Peoples and the Health of the Earth*. 112 World Watch Paper 21-22 (December, 1992).

Eboreime, Joe, and Joe Ekpere. *The Koma of Gongola State, Nigeria: A Preliminary Ethnographic Report*, 53 The Nigerian Field 89, 91 (1988).

Ega, Alegwu. *The Need to Redefine Rights under Customary Land Tenure in Northern Nigeria, in* Perspectives on Land Administration and Development in Northern Nigeria: Proceedings of the Workshop on Land Resources, Kano, September 25-28, 1986. Edited by Michael Mortimore, et al. Kano: Department of Geography, Bayero University, 1987.

Egwu, Samuel. Structural Adjustment, Agrarian Change and Rural Ethnicity in Nigeria. Research Report no. 103, Nordiska Afrikainstitute, 1998.

Ekstedt, John W. *Aboriginal Self-Government: Implications of the Australian Experience, in* John H. Hylton, Aboriginal Self-Government in Canada: Current Trends and Issues. Canada: Purich Publishers, 1994.

Elias, Olawale. Nigeria: The Development of Its Laws and Constitution. London: Stevens, 1967.

Encyclopedia Britannica. 2001, *available at* http://media-2.web.britannica.com/eb-media/23/61723-004-4EDF3E92.gif.

Encyclopedia of Educational Psychology. Edited by Neil J. Salkind and Kristin Rasmussen. Sage, 2008).

Ethnic Map of Nigeria - OnlineNigeria.Com, *available at* http://www.onlinenigeria.com/mapethnic.asp.

Etuk, Emma S. *Efik/Ibibio, in* Ethnic and Cultural Diversity in Nigeria. Edited by Marcellina U. Okehie-Offoha and Matthew N. O. Sadiku, 2004.

Evans, Malcolm, and Rachel Murray. The African Charter on Human and Peoples' Rights: The System in Practice, 1986-2006. Cambridge University Press, 2008.

Ewen, Alexander. *Africa and Eurasia, in* Voice of Indigenous Peoples. Edited by Alexander Ewen. Clear Light Publishers, 1994.

Ezeomah, Chimah. The Education of Nomadic People: The Fulani of Northern Nigeria. Nafferton Books, 1983.

Ezetah, Chinedu. *International Law of Self-Determination and the Ogoni Question: Mirroring Africa's Post-Colonial Dilemma.* 19 Loyola of Los Angeles International and Comparative Law Review 815 (1996-1997).

Fajana, A.J. Nigeria and Her Neighbours. African University Press, 1964.

Falola, Toyin. The History of Nigeria (Greenwood Press, 1999).

Falola, Toyin, and Akanmu Gafari Adebayo. Culture, Politics and Money among the Yoruba. Transaction Publishers, 2000.

Famoriyo, O. A. *Acquisition of Land and Compensation in Nigeria, in* Perspectives on Land Administration and Development in Northern Nigeria: Proceedings of the Workshop on Land Resources, Kano, September 25-28, 1986, Edited by Michael Mortimore, et al. Kano: Department of Geography, Bayero University, 1987.

Fawehinmi v. Abacha, 9 NWLR (Pt. 475) 710, 747 (1996).

Ferguson, John. The Yorubas of Nigeria. Open University Press, 1970.

Florence, Masajuwa, and Osagiator Ojo. *Sexism, Ethnicity and Discrimination in Contemporary Nigeria, in* P. E. Igbinovia, K. U. Omoyibo, and E. O. Ugiagbe, Social Psychology of Change and Diversity in Contemporary Nigeria. Lagos: Ababa Press, 2004.

Forest and Indigenous Peoples of Asia. Edited by Minority Rights Group International, 98/4, 1999.

Fox, James R. Dictionary of International and Comparative Law. Oceana, 2003.

Franks, C. E. S. *Rights and Self-Government for Canada's Aboriginal Peoples*, *in* Aboriginal rights and Self-Government. Edited by Juan D. Lindau and Curtis Cook, 2002.

Gboyega, Alex. *Nigeria: Conflict Unresolved, in* Governance as Conflict Management: Politics and Violence in West Africa. Edited by William Zartman. Brookings Institution Press, 1997.

Gearey, Adam. Globalization and Law: Trade, Rights, War. Rowman and Littlefield, 2005.

General Assembly. GA/10612, Sixty-first General Assembly Plenary 107th & 108th Meetings.

G., Willem van Genugten. *Protection of Indigenous Peoples on the African Continent: Concepts, Position Seeking, and the Interaction of Legal Systems.* 104 American Journal of International Law 64 (2010).

Ghanea-Hercock, Nazila, Alexandra Xanthaki and Patrick Thornberry. Minorities, Peoples and Self-Determination: Essays in Honour of Patrick Thornberry. Martinus Nijhoff Publishers, 2004.

Gibson, Joel. *Australia Will Sign UN Charter on Indigenous Rights: Dodson.* The Sydney Morning Herald, March 12, 2009, *available at* http://www.smh.com.au/national/australia-will-sign-un-charter-on-indigenous-rights-dodson-20090311-8vak.html.

Gordon, April. Nigeria's Diverse Peoples: A Reference Sourcebook. ABC-CLIO, 2003.

Gordon, Jr., Raymond G. Ethnologue: Languages of the World. Dallas: SIL International, 2005.

Gore, Charles. *Ritual, Performance and Media in Urban Contemporary Shrine Configuration in Benin City, Nigeria, in* Ritual, Performance, Media. Edited by Felicia Hughes-Freeland. Routledge, 1998.

Gorenstein, Ethan and Ronald Comer. Scientific American Reader to Accompany Abnormal Psychology. Macmillan, 2001.

Graham, Lorie. *Reparations, Self-Determination, and the Seventh Generation.* 21 Harvard Human Rights Journal 47 (2008).

Greenberg, J. *Studies in African Linguistic Classification: The Niger-Congo Family.* 2 Southwestern Journal Anthropology 79-100 (1949).

Gwich'in Compreensive Land Claim Agreement, Annual Report of the Implementation Committee (April 11, 1999 – March 31, 2000). Minister of Public Works and Government Services, Canada. Catalogue no. R31/9/2000, *available at* http://www.ainc-inac.gc.ca/al/ldc/ccl/fagr/gwich/gwi/gwi-eng.pdf.

Hackett, Rosaland. *Exploring Theories of Religion Violence: Nigeria's "Maitatsine" Phenomenon,* in Religion as a Human Capacity: A Festschrift in Honor of E. Thomas Lawson. Edited by Brian Wilson and Timothy Light. Brill Academic Publishers, 2004.

Harhoff, Frederik. *Self-Determination, Ethics and Law, in* The Living Law of Nations, Essays on Refugees, Minorities, Indigenous Peoples and the Human Rights of other Vulnerable Groups in the Memory of Atle Grahl-Madsen. Edited by Gudmundur Alfredsson and Peter Macalister-Smith. N.P. Engel, 1996.

Harmon, Daniel E., and Richard E. Leakey. Nigeria: 1880 To the Present : The Struggle, the Tragedy, the Promise (Exploration of Africa: the Emerging Nations). Chelsea House, 2000.

Hartle, Donald D. *Archaelogy East of the Niger: A Review of Cultural-Historical Developments, in* West African Culture Dynamics: Archaeological and Historical Perspectives. Edited by B. K. Swartz, Jr. and Raymond E. Dumett. The Hague: Mouton Pub. 1980.

Harvan, Mary. *The Gods of the Delta: Ken Saro-Wiwa and the Literature of the Ogoni Struggle, in* Mapping the Sacred: Religion, Geography and Post Colonial Literature. Edited by Jamie S. Scott and Paul Simpson-Housley. Rodopi Publishers, 2001.

Haveman, Paul. Indigenous Peoples' Rights in Australia, Canada & New Zealand. Auckland: Oxford University Press, 1999.

Henriksen, John. *Implementation of the Right of Self-Determination of Indigenous Peoples.* Indigenous Affairs 7, 3/01, International Work Group for Indigenous Affairs (IWGIA). Edited by Marianne Jensen. Copenhagen, 2001.

Higgins, Rosalyn and Maurice Flory. Terrorism and International Law. Routledge, 1997.

History of the Urhobo People of Niger Delta. Edited by Peter Ekeh. Urhobo Historical Society, 2007.

Hitchcock, Robert K. *Human Rights and Indigenous Peoples in Africa and Asia, in* Human Rights and Diversity: Area Studies Revisited. Edited by David P. Forsythe and Patrice C. McMahon. University of Nebraska Press, 2003.

Hitchcock, Robert K., and John D. Holm. *Bureaucratic Domination of Hunter-Gatherer Societies: A Study of the San in Botswana.* 24.2 Development and Change 305-38 (1993).

Hitchcock, Robert K., and Diana Vinding. Indigenous Peoples' Rights in Southern Africa: An Introduction. IWGIA, 2004.

Hodgson, Dorothy L. *Becoming Indigenous in Africa.* 52.3African Studies Review 9 (Dec. 2009).

Horn, Rebecca. Postconquest Coyoacan. Stanford University Press, 1997.

Howard, Bradley Reed. Indigenous Peoples and the State: The Struggle for Native Rights. Northern Illinois Press, 2003.

Huff, Andrew. *Indigenous Land Rights and the New Self-Determination,* 16 Colorado Journal of International Environmental Law and Policy 295 (2005).

Human Rights Committee, General Comment 23, Article 27 (Fiftieth session, 1994), Compilation of General Comments and General Recommendations. Adopted by Human Rights Treaty Bodies, U.N. Doc. HRI/GEN/1/Rev.1.

Hurley, Mary C. *Aboriginal Title: The Supreme Court of Canada Decision in Delgamuukw v. British Columbia* (Parliamentary Research Branch, 1998, rev. February 2000).

Hunter, John. *Judicial Recognition of Aboriginal Self-Government: Where Do We Stand? in* Aboriginal Self-Government. What Does It Mean in Practice? CBA's 2002 Aboriginal Law Conference.

Hylton, John H. *The Case for Aboriginal Self-Government: A Social Policy Perspective, in* John H. Hylton, Aboriginal Self-Government in Canada: Current Trends and Issues. Canada: Purich Publisher, 1994.

Idewu Inasa & Ors v. Saka Oshodi (1934), A.C.99.

The ILO and Indigenous and Tribal Peoples. U.N., International Labour Organization, Leaflet no. 8, *available at* http://www.unhchr.ch/html/racism/indileaflet8.doc.

Ibekwe, D. O. *Conflict of Cultures and Our Customary Law, in* African Indigenous Law: Proceedings of Workshop, 7-9 August, 1974. Enugu: Government Printer, 1974.

ILOLEX Database of International Labour Standards *available at* www.ilo.org/ilolex/english/newratframeE.htm.

Indigenous Peoples: A Global Quest for Justice: A Report for the Independent Commission on International Humanitarian Issues. London: Zed Press, 1987.

Indian Self-Determination Act Amendments of 1988, P.L. 100-472, *available at* http://64.58.34.34/osg/Default.aspx?Info=BackGroundInformation.

Indigenous Peoples in Africa: The Forgotten Peoples? The African Commission's Work on Indigenous Peoples in Africa. Transaction Publishers, 2006.

Indigenous Peoples of Africa Co-ordinating Committee IPACC Press Release. Indigenous Peoples Caucus, 5 December 2006, *available at* http://www.ipcaucus.net/HRday/IPACC.html.

"*Indigenous Peoples.*" Operational Policies OP 4.10. The World Bank Operational Manual (July 2005), *available at* http://wbln0018.worldbank.org/Institutional/Manuals/OpManual.nsf/B52929624EB2A3538525672E00775F66/0F7D6F3F04DD70398525672C007D08ED?OpenDocument.

"*Indigenous Peoples.*" Operational Directive OD 4.20. The World Bank Operational Manual, September 1991, *available at* http://www.worldbank.org/html/fpd/em/power/wbpolicy/420OD.stm.

The Indigenous Peoples Rights Act of 1997. Republic Act No. 8371. Sec. 56.

International Covenant on Civil and Political Rights. Art. 27, General Assembly Resolution 2200A(XXI) of 16 December 1996.

International Covenant on Economic, Social and Cultural Rights. G.A. res. 2200A (XXI), 21 U.N.GAOR Supp. (No. 16), U.N. Doc. A/6316 (1966), 993 U.N.T.S. 3, Art. 1, Jan. 3, 1976, *available at* http://www1.umn.edu/humanrts/instree/b2esc.htm or http://www.unhchr.ch/html/menu3/b/a_cescr.htm.

International Law: An Overview. Wex, Legal Information Institute, Cornell University Law School, *available at* http://topics.law.cornell.edu/wex/international_law.

International Law Association. "Rights of Indigenous Peoples." The Hague Conference, Interim Report (2010): 7.

International Security and the United States: An Encyclopedia (Karl R. DeRouen & Paul Bellamy, eds., Praeger Security International, 2008).

International Work Group for Indigenous Affairs, The Indigenous World, 2000-2001.

Interpretation Act of Nigeria, Cap. 89. Laws of Nigeria, 1958.

Inuit Circumpolar Council and Saami Council (Arctic Caucus) Press Statement. *Africans Deny Inuit and Saami Human Rights.* Indigenous Peoples Caucus, *available at* http://www.ipcaucus.net/HRday/Saami.html.

Jaggar, Philip J. Hausa. John Benjamins Publishing Company, 2001.

Janis, Mark. An Introduction to International Law. Aspen Publishers, 2003.

Jestice, Phillis. Holy People of the World: A Cross-Cultural Encyclopedia. ABC-CLIO, 2004.

Johnson, Samuel. The History of the Yorubas: From the Earliest Times to the Beginning of the British Protectorate. Routledge, 1921.

Johnson v. M'Intosh, 21 U.S. 543 (1823).

Jones, Peter. Rights. St. Martin's Press, 1994.

Kalu, Kalu Ndukwe. State Power, Autarchy and Political Conquest in Nigerian Federalism. Rowman and Littlefield, 2008.

Karade, Ifa. The Handbook of Yoruba Religious Concepts. Weiser, 1994.

Karan, Pradyumna Prasa. The Non-Western World: Environment, Development, and Human Rights. Routledge, 2004.

Khaleel, Ibraheem. *Hausa, in* Ethnic and Cultural Diversity in Nigeria. Edited by Marcellina U. Okehie-Offoha and Matthew N. O. Sadiku. Africa World Press, 2004.

Kingsbury, Benedict. *"Indigenous Peoples" in International Law: A Constructivist Approach to the Asian Controversy.* American Journal of International Law 420, 420-21 (1998).

Kiyawa, Adamu. Language and the Politics of Ethnicity in Nigeria: A Sociolinguistic Perspective (1983) (unpublished dissertation, University of Wisconsin-Madison) (on file with Univ. of Wisconsin-Madison Library).

Krenak, Ailton. World Commission on Environment and Development (WCED) public hearing, Sao Paulo (Oct. 28-29, 1985), *quoted in* Our Common Future: Report of the World Commission on Environment and Development. U.N. Documents, 1985.

Kunnie, Julian, and Maqhudeni Ivy Goduka. Wisdom and Power: Affirming our Knowledge through Narratives. Ashgate Publishers, 2006.

Kymlicka, Will. Multicultural Citizenship: A Liberal Theory of Minority Rights. Oxford: Clarendon Press, 1995.

_____ *The Internalization of Minority Rights*, 6 International Journal of Constitutional Law 1, 5 (2008).

Lake, Edward John. The Church Missionary Atlas: Containing an Account of the Various Countries in which the Church Missionary Labours and of its Missionary Operations. Church Missionary House, 1879.

Land Use Act, Laws of the Federation of Nigeria 1990, Chapter 202.

Lasisi, Akeem. *How My Family Resolved the Indigenous Language Dilemma.* Punch on the Web (Sunday, 13th January, 2008).

Lawal v. Younan, (1961) ALL NLR 245.

Lazarus, Sule. *20 Years After: Koma People Still Naked.* Daily Independent Online, Saturday, May 13, 2006.

Lenzerini, Federico. *Sovereignty Revisited: International Law and Parallel Sovereignty of Indigenous Peoples.* 42 Texas International Law Journal 155, 186 (2006).

Leonard, Thomas. Encyclopedia of the Developing World. Routledge, 2006.

Lindau, Juan D., and Curtis Cook. *One Continent, Contrasting Styles: The Canadian Experience in North American Perspective, in* Aboriginal rights and Self-Government. Edited by Juan D. Lindau and Curtis Cook. McGill-Queen's University Press, 2000.

Mabo v. Queensland, 107 ALR 1 (1992).

Mabo v. Queensland II (1992) 175 C.L.R. 1 (Austl.).

Maya Indigenous Community of the Toledo District v. Belize, Case 12.053, Report No. 40/04, Inter-Am. C.H.R., OEA/Ser.L/V/II.122 Doc. 5 rev. 1 at 727 (2004), *available at* http://www1.umn.edu/humanrts/cases/40-04.html.

Maletsky, Christof. *Namibia Slammed for "Killing" UN Rights Resolution.* Indigenous Peoples Caucus, 1 December 2006, *available at* http://www.ipcaucus.net/HRday/Namibia.html.

Manwarring, Melissa. *A Small Step or a Giant Leap? The Implications of Australia's First Judicial Recognition of Indigenous Land Rights: Mabo and Others v. State of Queensland,* 107 A.L.R.177, 187 (1992).

Marizu, Obi Ikpo. *Social Evaluation Survey on Ethnic Relations in Nigeria,* 7.2 Nordic Journal of African Studies 39, 47 (1998).

Maslove, Allan. *The Financing of Aboriginal Self-Government, in* John H. Hylton, Aboriginal Self-Government in Canada: Current Trends and Issues. Canada: Purich Publishers, 1994.

Mason v. Tritton and Anor, 1994 NSW LEXIS 13901; BC 9404979.

Mathews, Martin P. Nigeria: Current Issues and Historical Background. Nova Publishers, 2002.

Maybury-Lewis, David. Indigenous Peoples, Ethnic Groups, and the State. Allyn and Bacon, 1997.

Mbaatyo, Akpe. *The Tiv, in* Ethnic and Cultural Diversity in Nigeria. Edited by Marcellina U. Okehie-Offoha and Matthew N. O. Sadiku. Africa World Press, 1995.

Mbagwu, T. C. Oil Palm Economy in Ngwaland (Eastern Nigeria) (1970) (unpublished Ph.D dissertation, Univ. of Ibadan).

Members of the Yorta Yorta Aboriginal Community v. Victorial & Ors, 194 A.L.R. 538, [2002] HCA 58, (12 December 2002).

Meijknecht, Anna. Towards International Personality: The Position of Minorities and Indigenous Peoples in International Law. Intersentia/ Hart, 2001.

Mgbeafulu, Mathias Chinonyere. Migration and the Economy1900 to 1975. IUniverse, 2003.

Mills, John A. *Legal Constructions of Cultural Identity In Latin America: An Argument Against Defining "Indigenous Peoples."* 8 Texas Hispanic Journal of Law of Policy 49 (2002).

Mitee, Ledum. *The Centrality of Self-Identity in Indigenous Peoples' Struggles: the Struggle of the Ogoni People.* (Paper submitted at Indigenous Rights in the Commonwealth Project Africa Regional Expert Meeting, Cape Town, South Africa, October 16-18, 2002).

Moddibo, Mohammed Ahmed and Alkasum Abba. *Education and National Integration Problems and Prospects, in* Okello Oculi, Nigerian Alternatives. Nigeria: Ahmadu Bello University, 1987.

Moiwana Village v. Suriname, Judgment of June 15, 2005, Inter-Am Ct. H.R., (Ser. C) No. 145 (2005), *available at* http://www1.umn.edu/ humanrts/iachr/C/145-ing.html.

Molomo, David. *116 Children Vanish from Koma Without Trace.* Daily Sun, Aug. 2, 2008.

Montejo, Victor. *Convention 169 and the Implementation of the Peace Accord in Guatemala.* 10.4 The Journal of the South and Meso American Indian Rights Center (SAIIC) (Fall, 1997), *available at* http://www. saiic.nativeweb.org/ayn/guatilo.html.

Moses, George. *Fulani, in* Ethnic and Cultural Diversity in Nigeria. Edited by Marcellina U. Okehie-Offoha and Matthew N. O. Sadiku. Africa World Press, 2004.

Murithi, Timothy. The African Union: Pan-Africanism, Peacebuilding and Development. Ashgate Publishers, Ltd., 2005.

Mutua, Makau. *Limitation on Religious Rights: Problematizing Religious Freedom in the African Context.* 5 Buffalo Human Rights Law Review 75 (1999).

Mutume, Gumisai. *'Indigenous' People Fight for Inclusion,* 21.1 Africa Renewal 2 (January 2007). United Nations Department of Public Information, *available at* http://www.unep.org/indigenous/pdfs/Newsletter-Africa-indigenous-struggle-Eng.pdf.

Naamen, Ben. *The Ogoni: An Endangered Indigenous People,* 2 Indigenous Affairs 19 (1995).

Nadel, Siegfried F. A Black Byzantium: The Kingdom of Nupe in Nigeria. NY: Oxford University Press, 1942.

Nass, Francis Jauro. Missionary Enterprise among the Koma People of Adamawa State ANET Productions, 1996.

National Geographic Society. Peoples of the World. U.S. National Geographic Society, 2001.

Newton, Nell Jessup. *At the Whim of the Sovereign: Aboriginal Title Reconsidered.* 31 Hastings Law Journal 1215 (1980).

Niger Delta Development Commission Act No.2 1999 of the National Assembly.

Nigerian Peoples and Cultures. Edited by Akinjide Osuntokun and Avodeji Olukoju. Davidson, 1997.

North Sea Continental Shelf (F.R.G. V Den./Neth.).

Nwabueze, Remigius. *The Dynamics and Genius of Nigeria's Indigenous Legal Order.* 1 Indigenous Law Journal 153 (2002).

Nzongola-Ntalaja, Georges. The Congo from Leopold to Kabila: A People's History. Zed Books, 2002.

OAU Charter, Art. 2(d), *available at* http://www.iag-agi.org/bdf/docs/oau_charter.pdf.

Obilade, O. A. The Nigerian Legal System. London: Sweet and Maxwell, 1979.

Obong, Sunday Isong. Aspects of the Structure of Selected Tribal Groups in Nigeria (January 1972) (unpublished thesis, College of Arts and Sciences, Chicago, IL).

Oduntan Onisiwo v. The Attorney General of Southern Nigeria, 2. N.L.R. 77.

Ogbaa, Kalu. The Nigerian Americans. Greenwood Press, 2003.

Ogoni, Trials, and Travails. Lagos: Civil Liberties Organisation, 1996.

Oguamanam, Chidei. *Indigenous Peoples and International Law: The Making of a Regime,* 30 Queen's Law Journal 348 (2004).

_____ International Law and Indigenous Knowledge: Intellectual Property, Plant Biodiversity and Traditional Medicine. University of Toronto Press, 2006.

Ohadike, Don. *Igbo Culture and History, in* Chinua Achebe, Things Fall Apart. Heinemann, 1996.

Ogunseitan, Oladipo G. B. Opaque Walls I: Epistles on Man, Religion, Politics & Numerology. Kraft Books, 1995.

Oil Pipelines Act Chapter 338, Laws of the Federation of Nigeria 1990, *available at* http://www.nigeria-law.org/Oil%20Pipelines%20Act.htm.

Okehie-Offoha, Marcellina U. *Igbo, in* Ethnic and Cultural Diversity in Nigeria. Edited by Marcellina U. Okehie-Offoha and Matthew N. O. Sadiku. Africa World Press, 1995.

Okeke, Christian. *International Law in the Nigerian Legal System.* 27 California Western International Law Journal 311 (1997).

Okolo, Jerry. *Nupe, in* Ethnic and Cultural Diversity in Nigeria. Edited by Marcellina U. Okehie-Offoha and Matthew N. O. Sadiku. Africa World Press, 1995.

Okonto, Ike and Oronto Douglas. Where Vultures Feast: Shell, Human Rights, and Oil. Verso, 2003.

Okpoko, A. Ikechukwu and A. Maduabuchi Ibeanu. *Igbo Civilization: An Archaeological and Historical Ethnographic Profile, in* Toyin Falola, Precolonial Nigeria: Essays in Honour of Toyin Falola. Edited by Akinwumi Ogundiran. Africa World, 2005.

Okwudiba, Nnoli. Ethnic Politics in Nigeria. Enugu: Fourth Dimension Publishers, 1978.

Okwu-Okafor, Obiora. *Self-Determination and the Struggle for Ethno-Cultural Anatomy in Nigeria: The Zangon Kataf and Ogoni Problems.* 6 ASICL PROC. 114 (1994).

Olayiwola, Lasun Mykail and Olufemi Adeleye. 18.2 Land Reform-Experience from Nigeria. Promoting Land Administration and Good Governance, 5th FIG Regional Conference, Accra, Ghana, March 8-11, 2006.

Oliver, Roland. The African Experience. Westview Press, 2000.

Olupona, Jacob K. African Spirituality: Forms, Meanings, and Expressions. NY: Crossroad, 2000.

Omojola, Kola. At the Crossroads: Challenges and Options for Nigeria. Pulsemedia, 1992).

On the Way to Statehood: Secession and Globalization. Edited by Aleksandar Pavkovic and Peter Radan. Ashgate Publishers, 2008.

Osaw, T. A., S. N. Nwabara and A. T. O. Odunsi. A Short History of West Africa, A.D. 1000 to the Present. NY: Hill and Wang, 1975, 1968.

Osmańczyk, Edmund Jan and Anthony Mango. Encyclopedia of the United Nations and International Agreements. 3d ed. Routledge, 2004.

Oso, S. O. An Introduction to West African Traditional Religion, Ado Ekiti, Nigeria: Omolayo Standard Press and Bookshops, 1978.

The Oxford English Dictionary. 2d. ed. 1989.

Oyejide, T. Ademola. The Effects of Trade and Exchange Rate Policies on Agriculture in Nigeria. International Food Policy Research Instution, IFPRI, 1986.

Oyewole, Anthony and John Lucas. Historical Dictionary of Nigeria. 2d ed. African Historical Dictionaries, No. 40. The Scarecrow Press, 2000.

Palmer-Fernandez, Gabriel. Encyclopedia of Religion and War. Routledge, 2004.

Pareroultja and Others v. Tickner and Others, (1993) 117 A.L.R. 206, 213 (Austl.).

Parkipuny, Moringe L. *Native Leaders Address at the United Nations in 1992 in* Voice of Indigenous Peoples. Edited by Alexander Ewen. Clear Light Publisher, 1994.

Parry and Grant Encyclopaedic Dictionary of International Law. 2d ed. 2003.

Peek, Philip M. African Divination Systems Ways of Knowing. Indiana University Press, 1991.

Peek, Philip and Kwesi Yankah. African Folklord: An Encyclopedia. Routledge, 2004.

Peluso, Nancy, and Michael Watts. Violent Environments. Cornell University Press, 2001.

Perry, Richard J. From Time Immemorial: Indigenous peoples and State Systems. Austin: University of Texas, 1942.

Petroleum Act. Chapter P10 (Chapter 350 LFN 1990) Laws of the Federation of Nigeria, *available at* http://www.nigeria-law.org/Petroleum%20 Act.htm.

Polanco, Hector Diaz. Indigenous Peoples in Latin America: The Quest for Self-Determination. Westview, 1977.

Political Constitution of the Republic of Ecuador.

'Race,' Ethnicity and Nation: International Perspectives on Social Conflict, Edited by Peter Ratcliffe. University College London Press, 1996.

Ranger, Terence. Evangelical Christianity and Democracy in Africa. Oxford University Press, 2008.

Recommendation of Sub-Commission on Human Rights. Resolution 4B (XXIII) of 26 August 1970.

Reference *Re Secession of Quebec,* [1998] 2 S.C.R. 217 reprinted in 23 Vt. L. Rev. 721, 760 (1998-1999).

Reisman, Michael, Mahnoush Arsanjani, Siegfried Wiessner, and Gayl Westerman. International law in Contemporary Perspective. NY: Foundation Press, 2004.

Report of African Commission on Human and Peoples' Rights (ACHPR) Working Group of Experts on Indigenous Populations/Communities, adopted by the African Commission on Human and Peoples' Rights at its 28th Ordinary session, 20 (IWGIA, 2005).

Report of the Meeting of experts, Para, 46 reprinted in: Partial Revision of the Indigenous and Tribal Population Convention, 1957 (No. 107); Report 6(1), International Labour Conference, 75th Sess.1988.

Report on the Seminar on "Multiculturalism in Africa: Peaceful and Constructive Group Accommodation in Situations Involving Minorities and Indigenous Peoples" held in Arusha, United Republic of Tanzania, 13-15 May 2000. Commission on Human Rights, Sub-Commission on the Promotion and Protection of Human Rights Working Group on Minorities, Sixth Session, Para.

28. E/CN.4/Sub.2/ AC.5/2000/WP.3, *available at* http://www.unhchr.
ch/huridocda/huridoca.nsf/(Symbol)/E.CN.4.Sub.2.AC.5.2000.
WP.3.En?Opendocument.

Report of the World Conference Against Racism, Racial Discrimination,
Xenophobia and Related Intolerance, General Assembly, Programme
of Action,September 8, 2001 in Durban, South Africa, U.N.Doc. A/
CONF.189/5 (2001), *available at* http://www.unhchr.ch/huridocda/
huridoca.nsf/(Symbol)/A.Conf.189.12.En?Opendocument.

Research, Indigenous Knowledge and Development Monitor, November
2000, *available at* http://www.iss.nl/ikdm/IKDM/IKDM/8-3/res-
macdonald.html.

Restatement of the Law Third, The Foreign Relations Law of the United
States (1987).

Reynold, Jerry. *Africa's Indigenous San in Court, Now Face Regulations,*
Knight Ridder/Tribune Business News (Washington, Jan 3, 2007).

Ring, Trudy, and Robert M. Salkin. International Dictionary of Historic
Places. Chicago: Fitzroy Dearborn Publisher, 1994.

Ritter, D. L. *An Overview of the Recognition of Native Title in the
Commonwealth of Australia.* 5 Legal Issues on Burma Journal (April
2000), *available at* http://www.burmalibrary.org/docs/LIOB05-
Ritter.htm.

Robertson, Charles. International Politics since World War II: A Short
History. M.E. Sharpe, 1997.

Robinson, Charles Henry. Nigeria, Our Latest Protectorate. H. Marshall
and Son, 1900.

Rosenberg, Anne. Nigeria the Culture. Crabtree Publishers, 2001.

Rosenthal, Ricky. The Splendor That Was Africa. Oceana Publications,
1967.

Rome Statute of the International Criminal Court, U.N. Doc. A/CONF.183/9, Preamble, para. 2, *available at* http://untreaty.un.org/cod/icc/statute/romefra.htm.

Rotberg, Robert. Crafting the New Nigeria: Confronting the Challenges. Lynne Rienner Publishers, 2004.

Samoa's UN Move Congratulated, Sunday Samoan, *availability at* http://www.samoaobserver.ws/ index.php?option=com_content&view=article&id=14481:samoas-un-move&catid=1:latest-news&Itemid=50.

Sanders, Douglas. *The Formation of the World Council of Indigenous Peoples.* IWGIA Document, 1977.

_____ *Indigenous Peoples: Issues of Definition,* 8.1 Journal of Cultural Property 4, 7 (1999).

_____ *The Legacy of Deskaheh: Indigenous Peoples as International Actors.* Cynthia Price-Cohen, Human Rights of Indigenous Peoples. NY: Transnational Publishers, 1998.

Sargeson, Sally. Collective Goods, Collective Futures in Asia. Routledge, 2002.

Saro-Wiwa, Ken. A *Deadly Ecological War in Which No Blood is Spilled But People Die All the Time, in* Speaking of Earth: Environmental Speeches that Moved the World. Edited by Alon Tal. Rutgers University Press, 2006.

Saugestad, Sidsel. *Contested Images: Indigenous Peoples in Africa,* 2 Indigenous Affairs 6-9 (1999).

_____ The Inconvenient Indigenous: Remote Area Development in Botswana, Donor Assistance, and the First People of the Kalahari. Uppsala, Sweden: Nordic Africa Institute, 2001.

Scheinin, Martin. *What are Indigenous Peoples? in* Ghanea-Hercock, Nazila, Alexandra Xanthaki and Patrick Thornberry. Minorities, Peoples and Self-Determination: Essays in Honour of Patrick Thornberry. Martinus Nijhoff Publishers, 2004.

Schinke, Robert, and Stephanie Hanrahan. Cultural Sport Psychology. Human Kinetics, 2009.

Scupin, Raymond, and Christopher Decorse. Anthropology: A Global Perspective. Prentice Hall, 1991.

Shaw, T., and S.G.H. Daniells. *Excavations at Iwo-Eleru, Ondo State, Nigeria.* 14 West African Journal of Archaeology ix-xiv (1984).

Sheleff, Leon. The Future of Tradition: Customary Law, Common Law and Legal Pluralism. Frank Cass Publishers, 1999.

Shillington, Kelvin Encyclopedia of African History. 2005.

Sieder, Rachel. Multiculturalism in Latin America Indigenous Rights, Diversity and Democracy. NY: Palgrave Macmillan, 2002.

Siderman de Blake v. Republic of Argentina, 965 F. 2d. 699. (9th Cir. 1992).

Simmons, Mary Kate. Unrepresented Nations and Peoples Organization Yearbook. Martinus Nijhoff Publishers, 1996.

Social and Economic Rights Action Center and the Center for Economic and Social Rights v. Nigeria (known as the Ogoni case), Decision Regarding Communication 155/96 (2001) Case No. ACHPR/COMM/A044/1, *available at* http://www.umn.edu/humanrts/africa/comcases/allcases.html.

Sorabjee, Special Rapporteur, Soli Jehangir. Report on the Question of the Violation of Human Rights and Fundemental Freedoms in any Part of the World, with Particular Reference to Colonial and Other Dependent Countries and Territories, Commission on Human Rights, pursuant to Commission Resolution 1997/53. E/CN.4/1998/62.para. 3, *available at* http://www.unhchr.ch/Huridocda/Huridoca.nsf/0/a5 5c3d667425f3cfc125660f004afbcf?Opendocument.

Sornarajah, M. The International Law on Foreign Investment. Cambridge University Press, 2004.

Special Committee on European Affairs of the New York City Bar. *Executive Summary: Thawing a Frozen Conflict: Legal Aspects of the Separatist Crisis in Moldovia.* 14 ILSA Journal of International and Comparative Law 379, 382.

Standard-Setting Activities: Evolution of Standards Concerning the Rights of Indigenous People. U.N. ESCOR, Commission on Human Rights, Sub-Commission on Prevention of Discrimination and Protection of Minorities, 13th sess., U.N. Doc. E/CN.$/Sub.2/AC.4/1995/3 (June 21, 1995).

Starmer, Keir, and Theodora A. Christou. Human Rights Manua and Sourcebook for Africa. British Institution of International and Comparative Law, 2005.

Statement by Indigenous Peoples Caucus. *UN's Human Rights Record Challenged by Indigenous Peoples.* Indigenous Peoples Caucus, 9 December 2006, *available at* http://www.ipcaucus.net/HRday/HRday.html.

Statement by Mr. José Antonio Ocampo Under-Secretary-General for Economic and Social Affairs and Coordinator of the Second Decade of the World's Indigenous People to the Sixth Session of the United Nations Permanent Forum on Indigenous Issues, New York, May 14, 2007.

Statute of the International Court of Justice art. 38(1), June 26, 1945, 59 Stat. 1031, 33 U.N.T.S. 993.

Stavenhagen, Rodolfo. *Oral Statement on the Situation of Human Rights and Fundamental Freedoms of Indigenous People.* UN Permanent Forum on Indigenous Issues, 6th Session, May 14-25 2007.

Stevenson, Sarah M. *Indigenous Land Rights and the Declaration on the Rights of Indigenous Peoples: Implications for Maori Land Claims in New Zealand,* 32 Fordham International Law Journal 298-343 (2008).

Stoller, Paul. Embodying Colonial Memories: Spirit Possession, Power and the Hauka in West Africa. Routledge, 1995.

Study of the Problem of Discrimination Against Indigenous Populations, U.N. Doc.E/CN.4/Sub.2/1986/7/Add.4, U.N. SalesNo. E.86.XIV.3 (1986).

Suberu, Rotimi. Federalism and Ethnic Conflict in Nigeria. US Institute of Peace Press, 2001.

Swift, Jeremy. *The Future of African Hunter-Gatherer and Pastoral Peoples.* 13.2 Development and Change 159, 159-181 (April 1982).

Symonides, Janusz. *Cultural Rights: A Neglected Category of Human Rights.* 50 International. Social Science Journal 559 (1998).

Tessitore, John, and Diana Ayton-Shenker. A Global Agenda: Issues Before the 56th Assembly of the United Nations. Rowman and Littlefield, 1991.

Thomas, Alan, Susan Carr and David Humphreys. Environmental Policies and NGO Influence: Land Degradation and Sustainale Resources Management in Sub-Saharan Africa. Routledge, 2001.

Tijani v. Secretary of Southern Nigeria, 4 N.L.R. 18 (1923).

Trine, Lunde. Escaping Poverty: Perceptions from Twelve Indigenous Communities in Southern Mexico. John Hopkins University Press, 2009.

Trzcinski, Krzysztof. *The Significance of Geographic Location for the Success of Territorial Secession: African Example.* 11 Miscellanea Geographica 213-14 (Warszawa, 2004).

Tsosie, Rebecca. *The New Challenge to Native Identity: An Essay to "Indigeneity" and "Whiteness.* 18 Washington University Journal of Law and Policy 55 (2005).

Tunde, Oduwobi, and Iwuagwu Obi. *Nigeria: An Ethno-Historical Survey, in* Nigerian Peoples and Cultures. Edited by Akinjide Osuntokun and Avodeji Olukoju. Davidson, 1997.

Udogu, Ike E. *The Issue of Ethnicity and Democratization in Africa, Towards the Millennium,* 29.6 Journal of Black Studies, 794 (July 1991).

Umozurike, U. O. The African Charter on Human and Peoples' Rights. Martinus Nijhoff Pub., 1997).

UN Declaration on the Rights of Indigenous Peoples: Canadian Parliament Calls for Implementation, News Release (April 11, 2008) *available at* http://www.indigenousportal.com/index2.php?option=com_conten t&task=view&id=3490&pop=1&page=0&Itemid=454.

UNESCO, Convention on the Protection and Promotion of the Diversity of Cultural Expression, Paris 20, Oct. 20, 2005, 45 I.L.M. 269, *available at* http://portal.unesco.org/en/ev.php-URL_ ID=31038&URL_DO=DO_PRINTPAGE&URL_SECTION=201. html.

United Nations Declaration on the Rights of Indigenous Peoples, 13 September 2007, no. 61/295 Art.33 (1) & (2), *available at* http:// www.un.org/esa/socdev/unpfii/documents/DRIPS_en.pdf.

United Nations Declaration on the Rights of Indigenous Peoples, U.N. Doc. E/CN.4/Sub.2/1994/2/Add.1 (1994).

United Nations General Assembly Resolution 1514 (XV) of 14 December 1960 on the Declaration on the Granting of Independence to Colonial Countries and Peoples, 947th Plenary Meeting, 14 December 1960, Art. 7.

United Nations Permanent Forum on Indigenous Issues, Report on the Sixth Session, U.N. Doc. E/C.19/2007/12 (May 14-25, 2007).

Universal Declaration on Cultural Diversity, 31st Session of the General Conference of UNESCO, Art. 1, Paris, 2 November, 2001, *available at* http://www2.ohchr.org/English/law/diversity.htm.

Universal Declaration of Human Rights (UDHR). General Assembly Resolution 217 A (III) of 10 December 1948.

USUN Press Release. Robert Hagen, *Declaration on the Rights of Indigenous Peoples,* United States Mission to the United Nations, No. 204 (07) (September 13, 2007) *available at* http://www.shunpiking. com/ ol0406/0406-IP-positionofUS.htm.

U.S. v. Dann, 873. F. 2d 1189 (9th Cir. 1989), Mary and Carrie Dann, Case 11. 140 (United States), Inter-Am. C.H.R. Report No. 75/02.

Uwazuruike, Palph. *Leader, Movement for the Actualization of Sovereign State of Biafra* (MASSOB). Newswatch, June 30, 2003.

Uzoma, Rose. *Religious Pluralism, Cultural Difference and Social Stability in Nigeria.* 2004 Brigham Young University Law Review 651.

Vaughan, Olufemi. Nigerian Chiefs: Traditional Power in Modern Politics, 1890s-1990s. Boydell and Brewer, 2006.

Veber, Hanne, Jens Dahl, Fiona Wilson, Espen Waehle: "... Never drink from the same cup." Proceedings of the conference on Indigenous Peoples in Africa. Tune, Denmark (1993) IWGIA, Doc. No.74, Copenhagen, 1993.

Venne, Sharon Helen. Our Elders Understand Our Rights: Evolving International Law Regarding Indigenous Rights. Penticton, British Columbia: Theytus, 1998.

Vess, Deborah. AP World History (REA) - The Best Test Prep For the AP World History. Research and Education Association, 2006.

Vienna Convention on the Law of Treaties, May 23, 1969, 1155 U.N.T.S. 331.

Vienna Declaration and Program of Action. World Conference on Human Rights in Vienna on 25 June 1993.

Villiger, Mark. Customary international law and Treaties. Boston, 1985.

Vinding, Diana. The Indigenous World. IWGIA, 2005.

Vogel, Howard. *Reframing Rights from the Ground Up: The Contribution of the New UN Law of Self-Determination to Recovering the Principle of Sociability on the way to a Relational Theory of International Human Rights for the 21st Century.* 20 Temple International and Comparative Law Journal 463 (2006).

Watson, Alan. *An Approach to Customary Law.* University of Illinois Law Review 561, 576 (1984).

Wax, Murray Lionel. Indian Americans: Unity and Diversity. Prentice-Hall, 1971.

Weller, Marc. *Settling Self-Determination Conflicts: Recent Developments.* 20 European Journal of International Law 111, 116 (2009).

Wenzel, Nicola. Das Spannungsverhältnis Zwischen Gruppenschutz und Indivisualschutz Imvölkerrecht (2008).

Westerlund, David, and Ingvar Svanberg. Islam outisde the Arab World. Palgrave Macmillan, 1999.

Western Sahara, Advisory Opinion, 1975 I.C.J. 12.

Westra, Laura, and Bill Lawson. Faces of Environmental Racism: Confronting Issues of Global Justice. Rowman and Littlefield Publishers, Inc, 2001.

Whall, Helena. *The Challenge of Indigenous Peoples, The Unfinished Business of Decolonization.* 92.372 The Round Table: The Commonwealth Journal of International Affairs (2003).

_____ *Indigenous People's Rights in the Commonwealth*, Minority Rights and Reconciliation in the Commonwealth. A Cumberland Lodge Conference, February 11 – 13, 2004.

Wheeler, J., and Peter Newell. Rights, Resources and the Politics of Accountability. Zed Books, 2006.

White, C. M. N. *African Customary Law: The Problem of Concept and Definition*. 9 Journal of African Law 86 (1965).

Wick, Raidza Torres. *Revisiting the Emergency International Norm on Indigenous Rights: Autonomy as an Option*. 25 Yale Journal of International Law 291, 296 (2000).

Wiessner, Siegfried. *Cultural Rights of Indigenous People: Achievements and Continuing Challenges*, European Journal of International Law 124 (2011).

_____ *Dedication*, 1 Intercultural Human Rights Law Review 1 (2006).

_____ *Demographic Change and the Protection of Minorities in* Globaler Demographischer Wandel Und Schutz Der Menschenrechte 155-85. Edited by Eckart Klein. Berliner Wissenschafts-Verlag, 2005.

_____ *Ethnic Groups in* I Encyclopedia of Genocide and Crimes Against Humanity. Edited by Dinah Shelton. Macmillan Reference, 1999.

_____ *Rights and Status of Indigenous Peoples: A Global Comprehensive and International Legal Analysis*. 12 Harvard Human Rights Journal 57, 111 (1999).

_____ *The United Nations Declaration on the Rights of Indigenous Peoples: Essays in Honor of Professor Koufa, in* The Diversity of International Law: Essays in Honour of Professor Kalliopi K. Koufa. Martinus Nijhoff Publishers, 2010.

Wilson-Haffenden, J. R. The Red Men of Nigeria. Routledge, 1967.

Xanthaki, Alexandra. Indigenous Rights and United Nations Standards: Self-Determination, Culture and Land. Cambridge University Press, 2007.

Yakye Axa Indigenous Community of the Enxet-Lengua People v. Paraguau, Case 12.313, Report No.2/02, Inter-Am. C.H.R., Doc. 5 rev. 1 (2002), Inter-American Court of Human Rights, June 17, 2005.

Yates, Charlene. *Conceptualizing Indigenous land Rights in the Commonwealth Indigenous Land Rights and Resource Management in the Commonwealth Project.* Commonwealth LawyersAssociation/ Commonwealth Policy Studies Unit, *available at* http://www.cpsu. org.uk/fileadmin/Eco_Devt_and_Legal_Reform/Indig_land_ rights_and_resources.pdf.

Zewde, Bahru. Society, State and Identity in African History (Ethiopia: Forum for Social Studies,2008).